Gift of

The John W. Bowman Family

in memory of

Timothy Dillon Bowman

the
PRESS
and the world of
MONEY

the
PRESS
and the world of
MONEY

How the News Media Cover Business and Finance, Panic and Prosperity and the Pursuit of the American Dream

John Quirt

Anton / California-Courier

Library of Congress Cataloging-in-Publication Data

Quirt, John

The press and the world of money: how the news media cover business and finance, panic and prosperity and the pursuit of the American dream / 1st Anton ed.

p. cm.

Includes bibliological references and index.
ISBN 0-9635504-0-3

1. Journalism, Commercial — United States.
2. Finance, United States. I. Title.
PN4888.C59Q57 1993
070.4'49650'0973 — dc20   93-22766

10 9 8 7 6 5 4 3 2 1

Acknowledgment is made to the following publications for permission to reprint portions of previously published articles:

Pages 193, 318, 338, 340 © BARRON'S, 1987, 1988, 1991, 1992. Reprinted by permission.

Page 346 — Excerpted by permission of FORBES magazine, 1992 © Forbes, Inc., 1992.

Pages 324, 330 — Reprinted by permission from FORTUNE magazine; © 1933, 1944 Time Inc. All rights reserved.

Pages 320, 322 — Reprinted from THE SATURDAY EVENING POST © 1930, 1932.

To
Marge and Harold,
journalists from
a time not long past.

Contents

Preface and Acknowledgments

The story that unfolds on these pages is written for those who follow the news from day to day, especially news about what's happening in the economy. The book offers a relaxed look at a topic that is often dealt with in a more sedate manner. All, including students, are invited to treat it as the equivalent of a finger exercise on the piano — useful and, one hopes, more endurable than sitting down at the keyboard and attempting a cold turkey start on the Warsaw Concerto.

Such forbearance seems appropriate in that the task at hand is formidable. As we shall see, the subject of the media and the money world — like the topic of money itself — is surrounded by a fair amount of abracadabra and piffle. It is approached here, following the introductory material, from a historical perspective in Part II. In Parts III and IV there is additional history and I have told

some of the story in the form of a personal account, drawing on the experience of having chronicled developments
in business and the economy for two television networks,
for *Time, Fortune* and the *Institutional Investor,* and for a
newspaper that has long since gone to glory, the *New York
Herald Tribune.*

To round out the tale, the observations of others are
presented in Part V. There, readers will find a variety of
opinions, laid out in a manner intended to be consistent
with the venerable tradition of op-ed page journalism.

Many of the chapters in the book provide an overview.
The Notes at the end of each chapter and the Appendix
are included for those who want more detail.

Throughout, the terms "business news" and "financial
news" are used interchangeably. While this may be intel-
lectually indecent, it is in keeping with another journalistic
tradition, or principle, the time-honored one of responsible oversimplification. Taking further liberties with the
language, I have granted equal status as a synonym to
"economic news" and "money news." The latter is a term
that has gained favor among television folk and in more
contemporary publications such as *USA Today.* It is a modern label with deep historical roots. James Gordon Bennett
offered readers of the *New York Herald* a "Money Page"
more than a century and a half ago.

This project has many debts. Those who gave useful
counsel during my research in the latter half of the 1980s
and early '90s include Barry Bosworth, Andrew Brimmer,
Charles Schultze, Michael Evans, Milton Friedman, John
Kenneth Galbraith, Lawrence Kudlow, Paul McCracken,
William Niskanen, Robert Ortner, Richard Rahn, Paul
Craig Roberts, Herbert Stein, Lester Thurow and the late
Arthur Burns.

Another economist who was helpful, during what proved to be the final year of his life, was Walter W. Heller. My relationship with Heller goes back some years. Shortly before he joined the Kennedy Administration, he tried to teach me something about economics when I was a student at the University of Minnesota. Later, in Washington, D.C., he tried again, when I was a reporter writing about the Kennedy program, which, as it turned out, was partly the Heller program. Two and a half decades after that, back in Minnesota, he went over it all with me once more, in the hope that I would finally get it straight.

Sylvia Porter, who excelled in this area of journalism in a way most of her male counterparts can only dream of, graciously made time for me during a period of failing health. Newspapermen, active and retired, to whom I am indebted include John M. Berry, Lindley H. Clark, Jr., Edwin Dale, Clyde Farnsworth, James Flanigan, William German, Will Hearst, John M. Lee, Joe Livingston, Hobart Rowen, Vermont Royster, Leonard Silk, Joe Slevin, William Thomas and Donald K. White. Magazine editors and columnists who offered useful guidance include Alan Abelson, Louis Banks, Dan Cordtz, Michael Johnson, Peter Landau, Marshall Loeb, Robert Samuelson, William Wolman and Sheldon Zalaznick.

My thanks, too, to William Adams, John Austin, Holmes Brown, Lawrence Chickering, Joseph Coyne, Michael Creedman, Paul Erdman, George J.W. Goodman ("Adam Smith"), Myron Kandel, Steve Hess, Art Garcia, Harry Gossett, Leonard Grossman, Patrick Mainz, Robert Nichols, William O'Neil, Robert Swingen, Jocelyn Quirt, George Reidy, Dean Rotbart, Eileen Rice, Charls Walker, Paul Weaver and Chris Welles.

J.Q.

I
INTRODUCTION

1 *Insights and Immodesty*

This is a book about media coverage of money — yours, mine, the millions and billions being made and lost on Wall Street and the hundreds of billions being spent in Washington. It's a lot to keep track of, to report on. Trillions, if you throw in the national debt and everyone's credit card bills and bank loans. It all adds up. A trillion here, a trillion there. A few trillion for all of the shares in the world's stock and bond markets, and more trillions for the value of the tractors and toasters and other goods and services produced around the globe.

There is much more coverage of this money today than in the past. The newspaper that serves as the bible of the money world, *The Wall Street Journal*, has grown to three sections and become considerably more imposing. So have the business sections of *The New York Times*, *The Boston Globe*, *The Washington Post*, *Philadelphia Inquirer*, *Chicago*

Tribune, Los Angeles Times, San Francisco Chronicle and many other daily papers. Not only are the sections fatter, most of them are no longer buried behind the sports news, so we can locate them faster as we fumble through breakfast. Increasingly, some of the more readable stories are finding their way out of the business section and onto the front page, where they attract a broader audience. Meanwhile, radio and television are trying to offer more coverage of money matters. And there are more articles on the subject in magazines, as well as more magazines that cover the subject. Noteworthy start-ups in the final third of this century have included *Inc., Money, SmartMoney* and the *Institutional Investor.*

In an era when business has been treated like a spectator sport, we have been regaled for well over a decade with tales of the games and the players. Whiz kids, barely old enough to vote, who started high tech firms and succeeded or failed, often in spectacular fashion. Swashbuckling tycoons who took over each other's companies when that was all the rage. We are told of Wall Street buckoes who are still trying to play smash-and-grab finance, of economic warriors from across the sea who are conquering world markets, and of workaday people cast aside by companies in this country that can no longer compete.

The press goes to great lengths in an attempt to cover all this, especially when the numbers are staggering or when some of the players operate near the edge of the law or outside of it. Like political leaders and movie stars, those who can manipulate money and subvert the system on a truly grand scale become candidates for cover stories in magazines and guests on talk shows. They write their biographies and find themselves in demand as luncheon speakers. In what must rank as one of the defining characteristics of our culture, the rascality in which they engage elevates them to the status of celebrity crooks.

Fascination with financial frolics is nothing new, of course. A century ago the maneuverings of robber barons like Jay Gould and Jim Fisk captured the attention of reporters.[1] So did the downfall of Richard Whitney, onetime president of the New York Stock Exchange, who was written up and photographed looking his patrician best in a three-piece suit as he entered Sing Sing Prison in 1938 after being convicted of embezzlement. Other buccaneers who have achieved celebrity status include Bernie Cornfeld, the mutual fund impresario, and Billie Sol Estes, who performed some amazing tricks in the grain business in the 1950s. One difference in recent times is that the rascality, the unprincipled pursuit of riches, is seen more readily as symptomatic of a deeper malaise. And it has commanded attention in more places — on TV and radio as well as in newspapers, and in many more magazines. When his insider stock trading caper collapsed in 1986, Ivan Boesky, the Wall Streeter who proclaimed that greed is good, made the cover of *Time, Fortune, Business Week* and several other magazines and quickly became one of the most famous names in America. Boesky's contemporary, junk bond czar Michael Milken, achieved similar notoriety. His credentials as a celebrity were affirmed by, among other periodicals, *Forbes*, which questioned him at length in prison and ran a 15-page article based on the interview.[2]

The ministrations of government may not be quite as alluring as the activities of a Whitney or a Boesky or a Milken, but they too have attracted greater notice, and they continue to do so as the press takes the full measure of the Clinton Administration's programs. The 1992 election offered fresh evidence that the public is interested in economic policy. In coming years we can expect to see a continuation of the trend — which began long before Clintonomics, and before Reaganomics[3] — toward more reporting of White House decisions affecting the economy as well as the deliberations of the Federal Reserve and Congressional debate over matters such as taxes and trade.

We read and hear more about the actions of government agencies and a lack of action in industries such as airlines where a hands-off approach has led to turmoil — and about disenchantment with Washington as a brothel where the privileged princes of perk and pork enjoy themselves while ordinary folks pay the bill and get to elect a new piano player every four years. Especially in the better publications, coverage of this sometimes disputatious interface between the political and the money world is no longer handled routinely by reporters who prefer politics and look down their noses at economics; it is now frequently left in the hands of people who have a serious interest in the subject.[4]

Meanwhile, the media have greatly expanded their coverage of personal finance. In newspapers and magazines and on radio and TV, we are advised how to cut our insurance bills, budget for college expenses and plan for our golden years. Some of the advice comes packaged in formula stories like "Ten Tips For Investment Success" or "Smart $$ Moves You Should Make Now," but we also are hearing about substantive issues like why so many people are working harder and earning less. We are kept appraised of the best and worst performing mutual funds, the cheapest credit cards, and the pros and cons of commodity options, certificates of deposit, Ginnie Maes, collateralized mortgages, reverse repos, zero-coupon bonds and an array of other financial products. The choices are multiplying and the decisions aren't getting any easier. Growing awareness of this has enlarged the market for suggestions about how to manage money.

Our appetite for information extends beyond financial advice and news about what's happening in the money world today. With some regularity the press reports on the spending plans of business and the mood of shoppers roaming the malls, our temples of consumption. It records the latest predictions for interest rates, economic growth, the price of gold and the value of the dollar. Curiosity and concern about the future have made forecasting a mainstay in this area of journalism. We are supplied with enough prophecies to keep the mind thoroughly occupied, including assurances that an era of boundless prosperity lies ahead as well as warnings that we may be destined for another 1930s-style Depression, with millions of unemployed workers marching in the streets and zillions in bad loans tumbling into default.

None of this media coverage comes guaranteed to prevent calamities or produce great riches. The more worthwhile reports, columns and commentaries can provide perspective, spark ideas, and help us make better judgments and economic progress, both as individuals and as a people. Now and then they may even manage to entertain a little, without detracting from their main mission, which is to inform. But that's about all that can safely be claimed, notwithstanding the hype employed by some of the more relentless purveyors of money news in their promotional campaigns. An example that comes to mind readily is a solicitation for a newsletter which arrived in the mail not long ago carrying a sales pitch that sounded practically irresistible — "How to do everything right!"

Like the brazen headlines on supermarket tabloids that promise to tell us how we can lose 50 pounds a week or communicate with dead movie stars, such immodesty breeds disbelief and ought to be avoided whenever possible. I was once asked by the late Sylvia Porter, at a time when this book was being planned, if I intended to give it a how-to spin. In other words, she wondered, was I inclined to call it something like How To Get Rich Reading The Business News? A responsible practitioner of her craft, Sylvia was not advocating such a course, only raising the question out of curiosity.[5] My response was that I would feel uncomfortable stepping out that far. If anything, I told her, I would be inclined to spin it around the other way and remind readers that they may be able to avoid getting poor by not accepting as gospel all of the business news they read and hear.

What can be said with confidence is that the ensuing chapters offer some insights into an area of journalism that has grown dramatically and deserves a closer look. There are a number of reasons behind its growth. In some cases, newspaper publishers pushed for bigger and better business sections after discovering they could sell more ads by sprucing up the old gray agate ghetto. It took them a while to figure that out, but once they did they took action. More fundamentally, however, the growth reflects a greater awareness that people have a vital stake in what happens in the money world. This realization has influenced the expansion of coverage in magazines as well as newspapers. In so far as the decision-makers in television stop to think about such matters, it probably helps explain what has been going on there as well.

There have been many headline-making events and developments over the past few decades that have helped foster this awareness: in the 1960s, Kennedy's fabled confrontration with U.S. Steel and, later, the emergence of a red hot stock market; in the '70s, higher inflation, Nixon's wage-price controls, an end to the gold standard, grain sales to Russia, and the oil embargo and gas shortage; in the '80s, high interest rates and a bad recession followed by a long recovery and another bull market, together with diminishing industrial competitiveness, financial scandals and the wrecking of perfectly good companies by paper entrepreneurs.

These and other events have aroused our curiosity (and in some cases our ire) and intensified our interest in business news. Thus far in the '90s the headlines continue to inspire awareness of the money world, partly by telling a story of reaction to the '80s. The balance of this decade undoubtedly will produce many more newsworthy economic developments as we keep working our way through the lengthy sobering up process that invariably follows a long period of financial excess.

However, our intensified interest cannot be explained solely in terms of headline-making events or the pressing issues of the day. Its origins run deeper than that, dating back to a time when American firms were making products that people all over the world wanted to buy, a time when living standards in this country were beginning to rise and young couples could afford single-family houses. Marshall Loeb has suggested that an appropriate starting point for the trend is the mid-1940s. Here is his view of what has been happening since then:

"I believe the explosion of interest goes back to the end of World War II. Keep in mind that during the war and thereafter, millions of middle-income people got into the habit of buying securities. At first they were exposed to the idea that they could buy Defense Bonds, which were later called War Bonds and, after the war, Savings Bonds. At the same time, lots of GIs got their mustering out pay and veterans' benefits and came back from the war with a certain amount of walking-around money. They along with many other Americans, including people who had worked in the defense industry, were relatively affluent all of a sudden, at least compared to the '30s.

"This continued through the stock market advance in the 1950s, which was interrupted by periodic busts and recessions, but nothing comparable to 1929 or the Depression. Throughout these years, the steady rise in prosperity was being chronicled by the media. In 1955 *Time's* Press section wrote that the biggest running story of the previous ten years had been the expansion of the U.S. economy.

"Along the way there have been shifts in emphasis. In the '50s, much interest was focused on big business and corporate leaders. With some regularity, *Time* put on its cover the CEOs (chief executive officers) of major corporations. Interest in those kinds of stories waned starting in the '60s, with the rise in skepticism about heroic individuals from all institutions, including business and government. However, all through this time interest in the economy continued to grow and real income (income after adjusting for inflation) kept going up.

"Another factor that came into play was the rise of the working woman and the increase in two-income families. Women as well as men began looking at their paychecks and saying, 'My God, look how much is being taken out for taxes.' Even two-earner families found that they were being walloped. This created a greater appetite for information about how to legitimately hold down the tax bill and how to save more prudently and invest more profitably.

"*Money* magazine was introduced in 1972, and while it had a good following and solid advertising, it was not an immediate smash success. However, interest in the magazine continued to build. In 1980, after seven and a half years on the market, it began to make a modest profit, and thereafter its growth was explosive. Probably due in part to its success, the '80s saw a further expansion of news and information about personal finance.

"All during this time, *The Wall Street Journal*'s circulation was growing along with the circulations of most business magazines. And specialization was taking place, with the launching of successful publications such as *Inc.*, which is aimed at the small entrepreneur.

"So we have had a whole concatenation of factors, and all along the way we can point to various dates and events that captured our attention. However, the simple fact is this: In the 1930s most people in this country did not have two red cents to rub together. They were poor. In most of the post-war period, a growing share of the population has become more affluent, more sophisticated and more interested in business because they realize it impacts on their lives."[6]

NOTES

1. A lively account of the attention paid to Jay Gould and Jim Fisk can be found in *The Gold Ring* by Martin Ackerman (New York: Dodd, Mead & Co., 1988). Ackerman's book described an attempt by Gould and Fisk to corner the nation's gold market in 1869 and the attention the scheme received in the press. Their shenanigans also formed the basis of a

novel, *Jubilee Jim & the Wizard of Wall Street* (New York: Dutton, 1990), written by Donald Porter, an investment professional.

2. *Forbes*, March 16, 1992. The article, entitled "My Story — Michael Milken," was illustrated with a sketch of Milken in prison looking rather forlorn. The piece was less critical than other press reports of his junk bond operation. It suggested that his transgressions were mainly technical in nature, and that the media may have incorrectly made Milken a symbol of greed and manipulation.

3. Columnist William Safire has pointed out that over the past couple of decades only presidents with a last name ending in the letter *n* have had their economic programs honored with the suffix *omics* — Nixonomics, Reaganomics, and Clintonomics. In *The New York Times Magazine* on November 1, 1992, Safire noted that "because of the lack of the concluding n," the terms Fordomics, Carteromics and Bushomics never caught on.

4. In a survey conducted in the late 1970s, Stephen Hess of the Brookings Institution found that covering economics as a beat was unpopular among members of the Washington press corps. It ranked 11th out of 13 beats or assignments in terms of prestige, according to his survey, lagging far behind politics and foreign affairs. The results of that study appeared in Hess's 1981 book, *The Washington Reporters*. Since then, he has said that "the picture has changed substantially. Among many members of the press corps, economics has gained ground in terms of prestige." A careful observer of the Washington journalism scene, Hess also is the author of *Live From Capitol Hill* (published by Brookings) which examines the relationship between the media and Congress.

5. The reader will find a number of Sylvia Porter's views on business reporting in chapter 22.

6. Loeb's observations about changes that have taken place over the years at *Fortune*, where he became managing editor in 1984, are summarized in chapter 19.

$

2   *The Image and the Mystique*

Happenings in the money world and the numbers used to document them bear some similarity to abstract art. They do not always mean the same thing to everyone who tries to interpret them. Consider, for example, the headlines and opening paragraphs of two stories which appeared the morning after the U.S. Treasury disclosed the Federal deficit for the month of May 1986. Here is how that news was reported in *The Wall Street Journal*:

Federal Deficit
Narrowed in May
To $39.4 Billion

WASHINGTON—The federal government's budget deficit narrowed to $39.4 billion in May from a record $41.99 billion deficit a year earlier, the Treasury said.

Last month's budget deficit, second only to the one a

year earlier, compared with a surplus of $9.93 billion in April, when income taxes were due.

And here is how the same news was reported in an Associated Press dispatch that appeared in *The New York Times* and numerous other papers:

U.S. Deficit
Soared in May

WASHINGTON, June 25 (AP)—The Federal budget deficit soared to $39.4 billion in May, the largest imbalance in a year, the Treasury Department said today.

The flood of red ink in May left the Government's deficit for the first eight months of the fiscal year at $165.8 billion, 3.2 percent ahead of the pace set last year.

It requires no great expertise in finance to sense that something is amiss here. These two news dispatches are both pegged to the same figure.[1] They dwell on the short term, explain very little and plainly are at odds with each other. Depending on which account you happened to read that day, you might have been either a) disappointed, or b) pleased to learn that the amount of red ink for the month in question a) increased, or b) decreased to $39.4 billion. You could have inferred that the government's finances, therefore, were either a) deteriorating or b) getting better.

In point of fact, one month is too short a time to infer much of anything about such matters, and the difference in interpretation stems largely from whether the comparison is made with prior months or with the same month a year earlier. Another way of handling this would have been to give the reader both comparisons, along with an explanation of the difference between them. However, that approach might seem too ponderous or a trifle messy to a journalist camped out on the sofa in the U.S. Treasury press office, waiting for the number to be released and under pressure to bat out a story quickly.[2] In any case, the contrast in these two pieces has to be a little disquieting. It's almost enough to make you wonder if reporters know the difference between up and down.

Here is another illustration of dissimilar interpretations. This time the disparity is closer to what we encounter on a day-to-day basis. The occasion was an appearance on Capitol Hill by Alan Greenspan. It was one of those command performances by a Federal Reserve chairman whose delphic utterances are monitored closely for clues to credit policy and the future course of interest rates. The morning after his testimony before a Congressional committee, the headline over David Rosenbaum's story in *The New York Times* read:

**Greenspan
Sees No Cut
In Rates Soon**

In this instance *The Wall Street Journal* agreed with the *Times*. The headline on David Wessel's article conveyed essentially the same thought:

**Greenspan Says
Credit Policy
To Stay Stable**

However, the *Los Angeles Times* concluded that the big news was something Greenspan said about interest rates coming down if the Federal budget deficit could be reduced. Tom Redburn's page-one article was headlined:

15

**Fed Chairman
Prepared to Cut
Interest Rates**

USA Today made a similar judgment. Its story, by Mark Memmott, carried the following headline:

**Fed: Reduce
deficit, get
lower rates**

All four of these newspapers accurately reported remarks that were made during the testimony, but differed over which ones should be played up.[3] As a result, two of the papers left readers with the impression that cheaper credit might be in the offing, while the other two left the opposite impression.

Interestingly, these are not the only two ways this story could have been treated. Consider the circumstances at the time. When Greenspan testified, in the summer of 1990, the U.S. economy showed signs of slipping while the Fed showed signs of being slow on the draw. That's not unusual. The Fed often hears the footsteps of inflation okay but seems slightly deaf when the thunder of recession rumbles in the distance. On this occasion, moreover, interest rates and credit policy were about the only means left for fixing the economy. Since the deficit had been allowed to balloon when times were good, fiscal policy was like a tool that had been disabled. Greenspan's appearance on Capitol Hill represented one more attempt to trigger action which might have remedied that situation — and a story focused on that idea would have been just as appropriate as the articles suggesting that interest rates were or were not about to go down. (A footnote to this episode is that, in the end, the Fed did what it had to do;

it cut rates further, but only after the economy had become weaker; then it lowered them sharply without waiting for Congress to act.)

Now let's look at two more sets of headlines, this time from the same publication. On April 6, 1992, *The Wall Street Journal* declared:

False Alarm?

Fall in Japanese Stocks Isn't Likely to Depress U.S. Issues, Experts Say

They Note That Earlier Fears Didn't Prove Justified, See No Big Outflow of Funds

But a Hint of Danger Lingers

Quoting numerous experts, the article reassured readers that while the Japanese market was sinking, there was little reason to worry that stock prices in the U.S. were about to follow suit. The last line, mentioning the hint of danger, enabled the *Journal* to hedge against the possibility that it might be wrong.

Three days later on its front page the paper quoted other oracles and offered a different view:

Tokyo Tremors

Japan's Market Plunge Is Causing Concern In U.S. Institutions

Treasury and Fed Keep Watch As Jitters Spread to Banks, Real Estate, Stock Market.

So far, No Reason for Alarm

This time, the *Journal* conveyed the impression that the American market might indeed be headed lower, though the last line hedged against the possibility that things could instead turn out the way it had suggested three days earlier. Readers may be forgiven if they felt slightly puzzled after seeing these two headlines. The truth is that neither the financial press nor the savants who are interviewed and quoted can be relied upon to tell us consistently what the market will do in the short run. Any claims to the contrary should be treated with skepticism.

A measure of skepticism is in order, too, for those who rely on the air waves for their economic news. On radio and TV newscasts there is little time to explain things, including economic figures that are reported on the air with decimal-point precision, giving an impression of accuracy that is unwarranted.[4] The numbers are unreliable, and at times there is a question of judgment. A network radio newscast I happened to catch on my car radio in October 1992 reported the latest monthly inflation figures, which were favorable, citing them as evidence that "the economy is still stuck." Listening to that report, one could not help but wonder if poorer figures on inflation might have been hailed as encouraging news. Of this, more later.

One of the most memorable examples of questionable judgment in the history of financial journalism occurred some years ago when *Business Week* ran a cover story entitled "The Death of Equities." Accompanied by six charts along with numerous statistics and quotes from various Wall Street soothsayers, the piece claimed that as a place to put your money the stock market was practically kaput, the preserve mainly of elderly folks who had bought into it during livelier times. The real action, said *Business Week*, was in other, more exciting investments. The article was an attempt to reach out and find a new trend — only the reach was too far. The piece probably should have carried a label warning that it could be injurious to the financial health of those who read it. It ran in the summer of 1979, and anyone who had sworn off stocks after reading it would have missed out on the greatest bull market ever, which began not long after it appeared.[5]

While it is not my intention to do so, I could probably fill another chapter or two with similar tales, including a few from my own files. Shortly after graduating from journalism school at the University of Minnesota, during my first year as a reporter on the *New York Herald Tribune*, I interviewed the head of Studebaker and wrote afterwards that he had a bold new strategy for mastering the car company's problems. Boy, was I wrong. Years later the head of Studebaker's public relations department ran into me at the National Press Club in Washington and admitted that the dominant strategy at the company the day of my visit was one he had devised to obfuscate and dissuade me of all skepticism during my questioning. It worked, thanks to my lack of experience. (The outcome of this episode is well known: Studebaker subsequently failed.)

If you are among those who suspect that when it comes to business and economics the press doesn't always get it right, the examples mentioned here should strengthen your suspicion. Instead of enlightening, they mislead or mystify, and in this regard they're not all that unusual. You can probably attest to this yourself if you've ever noticed that news reports of the activities or financial condition of companies you're familiar with are often inaccurate or inadequate. Business news has a disconcerting tendency to be this way at times, to fumble or muddle the issues and confuse or spook not only its audience but also those who do the reporting. John Kenneth Galbraith took note of this during the course of a long conversation we had some time ago. The subject of business and money, he observed, "is presumed to have a mystery of its own, a deeper mystery than the layman can understand." The press, he said, "often becomes infected with this notion and accepts the mystique instead of making an effort to understand and to explain."

As Galbraith sees it, economists help perpetuate the mystique and even regard themselves as its custodian. They have a habit, he says, of "reflecting on their peculiar insights much as a priest reflects on his peculiar capacity for getting people into heaven." Galbraith says others also participate in the mystique:

"There is a perception that anybody associated with large sums of money has special intelligence. Thus corporate executives who make poor decisions and international bankers who make unwise loans frequently are given gentle treatment by the press, and an individual who may be only barely competent to balance his own checkbook can be appointed to the Federal Reserve and regarded from that moment on as having almost magical knowledge of the American economy."

Galbraith's assessment of the prevailing state of business and financial reporting: "This is an area of journalism which was impossibly lousy some years ago and has improved, but it still has some very great flaws."

I, for one, would not quibble with that notion. Press coverage of the money world is available in quantity and has gotten better, but a certain amount of it still succumbs to the mystique. It reflects a shortage of lucid analysis or strains in an effort to sound a positive note. It places too much emphasis on the near term or comes infested with unfathomable numbers and statements that can be misinterpreted as well as with jargon that causes the eyes to glaze over — gibberish about "factor conditioning," "optimal strategizing" and "refocusing resources." Locutions such as these are the crabgrass of business journalism, creeping into stories incessantly and hindering the task of unmasking reality.

A term like "organization transition plan," for instance, surfaces recurrently in articles about company personnel announcements. It has a fine ring to it, suggestive of some benign and orderly procedure. However, it also can serve as camouflage for savage corporate bloodlettings and other dark deeds. As a case in point, Hughes Aircraft once saw fit to announce an "organization transition plan" that turned out to be a scheme for eliminating 6,000 jobs. Announcement of the plan slid by without much critical analysis. An exception was the *Los Angeles Times*, which wisely buried the term in the sixth paragraph of a story focusing on the layoffs.

That story was co-authored by Ralph Vartabedian, a veteran reporter whose work through the years has qualified him for membership in an elite category known as the Corporate Assassins. These are hard-nosed skeptics who take no prisoners in the executive suite and usually write stuff that slices through euphemisms like "organization transition plan" with ease. According to *TJFR Business News Reporter*, a media newsletter which created the category, Corporate Assassins are respected but seldom loved

21

in the executive suite. There aren't many of them around and their prose isn't always pretty, but their reporting rarely falls victim to the mystique.[6]

Business news that does fall victim tends to be murky and off-target as well as solemn and deferential. It dutifully amplifies the exhaltations of economic celebrants or the latest pronouncements of financial visigoths, or it heaps praise on those who talk a good line while running their firms into the ground and lining their pockets with cash. The press is often accused, not always unfairly, of sounding excessively negative themes, and there are times when it deserves criticism on that score. However, as Galbraith suggests, it also can undermine its credibility when it resorts to fuzzy language and accepts the blatherings of big shots while glorifying their importance and wealth and ignoring their mistakes and transgressions.

A good illustration of this was the failure of the media to hop on the savings and loan scandal in the 1980s and ride it hard from start to finish. The scandal turned out to be a blockbuster, but it was underreported at the outset. To many journalists, the situation looked like another numbers story in an industry where not much happens, the kind of dry piece that gets buried deep in the paper. The overriding presumption was that the care of our giant S&Ls was entrusted to men of consequence and integrity, pillars of their communities in many cases. They were proclaiming that their problems were minor or manageable; regulatory officials were echoing the same theme, and many in the press were buying it and being careful to steer clear of scare stories.

Until Charles Keating and his supporting cast of senators surfaced much later, this also was a tale without recognizable villians. Moreover, it had no protagonist — another essential for any good story — save for a few gadflies like Congressman Henry Gonzalez, who spoke up early about the troubles at the S&Ls but was largely ignored. In Gonzalez' home state of Texas, reporter Peter Brewton of *The Houston Post* also was sounding the alarm. However, the Fourth Estate's aristocracy seldom pays much attention to the writings of people in the hinterlands, and in this case the neglect was made easier by the fact that some of Brewton's articles were not smooth reading. A few other journalists such as Steve Pizzo and Mary Fricker of the *Russian River News* in Guerneville, California, also did some decent work on the story in its early stages; but on the whole it was never given the kind of non-stop attention that is typically lavished on, say, a sex-and-politics scandal.[7]

What we got instead was mostly soft reporting. Gonzalez and the handful of others who were ringing the tocsin proved to be right with their warnings that the industry was spinning out of control. In the lax regulatory environment prevailing at the time, wrongdoers were looting one savings institution after another — in Texas and elsewhere — and sticking the public with a huge tab for the mess. Most of this came to light after the damage had been done. Then, everyone pounced on the story and ran with it. However, for a long while it was shrugged off as too complex or too dull to get excited about.

It is hardly surprising that over the years this branch of journalism has gotten itself saddled with something of a castor oil image, a perception that it deals with the dismal science and with mushy concepts and dreary matters such as deficit figures, monetary policy and the balance sheets of financial institutions — "tiresome matters" H.L. Mencken once called them. This image, while less pronounced than in Mencken's day, lingers on despite significant changes, including many positive ones, that have taken place in the way the press covers the money world. These changes, and the origins of the image and the mystique, can be seen more clearly as we review a little history and locate a few bearing points.

NOTES

1. These stories ran in *The Wall Street Journal* and *The New York Times* on June 25, 1986.

2. The sofa referred to here is one of Washington's less celebrated landmarks, the Edwin Dale Memorial Couch. It was named after a former *New York Times* reporter who at one time camped on it regularly. Dale covered the Treasury and the Washington economic beat in the 1950s and early '60s, when very few newspapers assigned reporters to that beat on a full-time basis. Later, he became a spokesman for the Office of Management and Budget.

3. The four articles on Greenspan's testimony appeared on July 19, 1990.

4. Wall Street consultant and writer Charles R. Morris points out that "Americans have been trained for so long to believe in economics as an exact science that it is disquieting to realize how inexact the basic statistics so cherished by Wall Street really are." Referring to such stats as the Consumer Price Index and Gross Domestic Product, Morris has written in the *Los Angeles Times*: "Most economic data are inherently imprecise, often misleading and sometimes just wrong. . . . The notion of an 'economy' itself is a highly abstract metaphor for the stew of day-to-day transactions that occupy all our lives. There is no big adding machine in the sky that tots up everything we buy and everything we sell, every dollar we spend or every penny we save. Instead, an army of diligent bureaucrats take surveys, compare seasonable patterns, make heroic guesses, interpolate, prognosticate and cobble together the best numbers they can — then revise them over and over again as the months go by."

5. *Business Week*, August 13, 1979. "The Death of Equities" claimed

that the downward trend "can no longer be seen as something a stock market rally — however strong — will check." It ended with a quote from an unnamed "young U.S. executive" who declared: "Have you been to an American stockholders' meeting lately? They're all old fogies. The stock market is just not where the action's at."

6. The Hughes article, co-authored by David Olmos, ran in the *Los Angeles Times* August 26, 1989. *TJFR Business News Reporter*, which monitors developments in business journalism, was started by Dean Rotbart, a former *Wall Street Journal* reporter; it is produced by TJFR Publishing Company in Ridgewood, New Jersey.

7. Pizzo and Fricker expanded their investigative work into a book: *Inside Job: The Looting of America's Savings and Loans* (New York: McGraw-Hill, 1989). Peter Brewton also expanded his reporting into a book: *The Mafia, the CIA and George Bush: The Untold Story of America's Greatest Debacle* (New York: S.P.I. Books, 1992). For additional perspective on news reporting of the S&L crisis, the reader is referred to an analysis by Ben Bagdikian in the May/June 1992 issue of *Mother Jones*, which criticizes the coverage—and to another article with a different viewpoint: "S&Ls: Blaming the Media," *Newsweek*, June 25, 1990.

$

II
YESTERYEAR

3 The New Era

In 1929 America was preoccupied with making bathtub gin and lots of money. The talk was of speakeasies and Al Capone, the Stutz Bearcat and the romance of aviator Charles Lindbergh and Anne Morrow. Books about stocks and business excellence were popular. Fortunes were being amassed in the market, and there was very little in the press that hinted of big trouble ahead. The decade that ushered in prohibition and the Jazz Age would soon end on a sour note. But through much of the year, the mood was upbeat. The economy still looked reasonably healthy, and some commentators were suggesting that the old boom and bust cycle might be a thing of the past. On inaugural day in early March, Calvin Coolidge and his successor wore top hats and waved at the photographers and the crowds gathered along Pennsylvania Avenue. In his initial address to Congress, the newly elected President pledged that his administration would not interfere with private initiative and enterprise. After the speech, according to a gushy account in *The Wall Street Journal*, "Washington and its thousands of visitors continued to make merry in carnival spirit over the inauguration of Herbert Hoover."

A few weeks later, stock prices took a bad spill before recovering and bubbling upward during the summer. By Labor Day they were at record levels, and so were the temperatures along the eastern seaboard on that warm holiday weekend. When the market opened for business on Tuesday, New York was sweltering and the Street was awash in rumors and tips about new stock pools and schemes for manipulating prices and getting even richer in the autumn. One popular market forecaster, Evangeline Adams, predicated that "the Dow Jones could climb to heaven."[1]

As the week wore on, however, stock prices headed the other way. A decline that would eventually turn into the Crash of '29 got underway in earnest on Thursday September 5. It was triggered by what would prove to be a prophetic warning from analyst Roger Babson that stocks were about to collapse, just as Florida land values had collapsed a few years earlier. *The New York Times* put the story on page one:

**Stock Prices Break
On Dark Prophecy**

**Drop in Hectic Last Hour as
Babson's Prediction of a
Big Slump is Printed**

As the article made clear, what troubled Babson was the fact that a majority of stocks were no longer rising along with the hottest ones, as they had for a couple of years. This failure to follow the leaders pointed to deterioration, but *The Wall Street Journal* buried the story of the break on page 22 and put a positive spin on Babson's findings:

> However, many experienced Wall Street observers feel that this selectivity has been the market's greatest safeguard. It is argued that so long as such marked discrimination is exercised, the general list may go along for some time before any reversal of trend is seen.

The "experienced Wall Street observers" in this case included some of the paper's own editors, who were philosophically in tune with the bulls as were many other journalists of that day. The *Journal* had become one of the main cheerleaders, waving the market onward and upward and telling its readers at one point in July that "some traders are so bullish they have stopped naming tops for certain stocks and are saying they will never stop going up." This unabashed rooting for the bulls continued in the *Journal* and elsewhere after the September 5 break, although as trading became more ragged traces of skepticism began appearing here and there. With interest rates on stock market loans at 10 percent, the wisdom of continuing to borrow to play the market was questioned by a writer for the Hearst newspapers during the week of September 19:

> Wall Street had a tear in each eye yesterday, because 'call money,' the kind with which you gamble, cost 10 percent. The thoughtful gambler says to himself, 'if I borrowed that kind of money for ten years, all my original money would be gone, and interest on the interest would leave me about 50 percent in debt.'

The next day, the lead item in the *Journal*'s "Review and Outlook" column took the Hearst writer to task:

Whether a man "gambles" when he buys stock and carries it on borrowed money is a matter of motive. No one but himself can say what his intentions were, but at least there is a tangible consideration, in the form of stock, which logically precludes any such question-begging epithet as "gambling." Even in general newspapers some accurate knowledge is required for discussing most things. Why is it that any ignoramus can talk about Wall Street?

In the weeks that followed, the news didn't get any better. Dynamite and stink bombs were tossed into brokerage offices in Chicago by unhappy racketeers who had borrowed to play the market and were called upon to ante up cash for their margin accounts. Although bigger losses lay ahead, share prices had already dropped far enough below their September highs to trigger margin calls on a broad scale, exonerating the ignoramuses and Roger Babson. *Time* magazine, which was six years old then, reminded its readers on October 14:

> Mr. Babson was flayed by all the financial writers in New York whose pleasure it is to reflect the views of their friends, the brokers. "A statistician who has always been wrong"—"A man for whose opinion the market has no great regard"—"A chronic bear always predicting disaster" — were typical introductory sentences to Babson-flaying opinions.

Those opinions had been voiced several weeks earlier. Now, in mid-October, *Time* could report that, "vindicated, Mr. Babson said nothing."[2]

With the cataclysm drawing near, the specialized business periodicals mostly clung to the belief that more good times lay ahead. While no longer ignoring the bearish argument entirely, they affirmed that fluctuations in the market should not be taken as a sign of an impending business downturn. In mid-October, *Dun's Review* proclaimed:

Nothing has happened to indicate that widespread trade recession is underway, and statistics of railroad freight traffic show, week after week, that distribution of merchandise remains at a notably high level.

Many newspapers cast skepticism aside during that period and echoed a similar theme. In the *Washington Star*, these two exemplary headlines ran on successive days during the week of October 20:

Trade Held Sound
In Spite Of Breaks

Nation's Business
Believed Sound

The *Journal* was in the forefront of this last-ditch effort to reassure, and its Pollyanish comments during those final days before the crash hit with full force warrant a closer look. On October 21 it declared:

There is a vast amount of money awaiting investment. Thousands of traders and investors have been waiting for an opportunitity to buy stocks on just such a break as has occurred over the last several weeks, and this buying, in time, will change the trend of the market.

The next day the *Journal* said:

Fundamentally, conditions in both trade and credit continue sound. . . . it was generally believed that the recent sweeping declines had created attractive opportunities for the purchase of selected stocks for the long-pull.

The morning of October 24, a day when stocks would tumble sharply, the *Journal* played up a sunny speech given the night before in Washington by Irving Fisher, a Yale economist with a wide following on Wall Street. His optimism, he explained, was inspired partly by a wave of corporate mergers that the country had been experiencing under Coolidge and Hoover. Although many of the mergers were financed with heavy debt and followed by widespread layoffs, Fisher saw this as good news. He said:

> These mergers have effected great economies, and have therefore increased the profits of corporations to a great extent. Every merger boosts the stock of the merged companies because of this expectation.

Earlier, Fisher had said that stock prices were reaching a permanently high plateau. He would subsequently prove to be a better scholar than market analyst. But in the autumn of '29, his chimeric pronouncements were what the bulls and their allies in the press wanted to hear. His faith in corporate amalgamations and the belief that the economy was on solid footing were central to the party line that prevailed in the early months of the Hoover Administration. It was a doctrine of everlasting prosperity, often called the New Era.[3] This soon to be discredited idea held out the promise of jam today and more jam tomorrow. Rough moments in the market could safely be ignored. All was well. The mantra was incanted at every occasion. On October 26, the *Journal* declared:

Hoover Asserts
Business Sound

On the morning of the 28th, as stock operators and their victims walked the final steps to the financial gallows, the *Journal* was still comforting them and preaching the same old shibboleth. A "Review and Outlook" column entitled

"Sound Conditions" assured readers that there was no reason for worry, or for Congress to consider investigating the inner workings of Wall Street.

Such, then, was the sanguine view that prevailed in the *Journal* and elsewhere. In fact, the market was infested with thimbleriggers and heavily indebted speculators, as it had been during prior periods of extreme weakness. Trouble was brewing in international finance, with uncollectible loans sliding toward default. The raccoon coat and Stutz crowd was engaging in garish overconsumption — "glittering swineishness," in Mencken's words. The gap between rich and poor was growing wider. Farmers and textile workers were suffering. The steel, auto and construction industries were slowing down. Banks were shaky, and the Federal Reserve was pursuing questionable policies. Privately, the administration was troubled by the deterioriating situation. Hoover was edging away from his pledge of non-intervention and starting to push for farm relief and restrictions on loans to stock speculators, and he was exploring ways to increase public works spending. Publicly, however, the White House sang a different tune, issuing one encouraging statement after another. These canards, which would draw ridicule for years to come, were dutifully recorded and amplified in the press.[4]

NOTES

1. In *Only Yesterday*, Frederick Lewis Allen's informal history of the 1920s (New York: Harper & Row, 1957), Allen wrote that by September 1929 "grocers, motormen, plumbers, seamstresses and speakeasy waiters were in the market . . . literary editors whose hopes were wrapped about American Cyanamid B lunched with poets who swore by Cities Service, and as they left the table, stopped for a moment in the crowd at the broker's branch office to catch the latest quotations; and the artist who had been eloquent only about Gauguin laid aside his brushes to proclaim the merits of National Bellas Hess. The Big Bull market had become a national mania." Allen served as editor of *Harper's* from 1941 to 1953.

2. This is taken from the "Finance" section of *Time*, which appeared regularly starting with the first issue of the magazine in March 1923.

3. Hoover in later years tried to disassociate himself from the term New Era, which had come to signify Coolidge-Hoover prosperity and the prospect of ever-rising corporate profits and stock prices. In *Herbert Hoover: A Public Life* (New York: Alfred A. Knopf, 1979), biographer David Burner wrote that "Hoover came to employ the term with sarcasm and contempt" and once implored a writer to "please do not use me as a whipping boy for the New Era."

4. Written long after he left office, Hoover's own account of this period painted a picture of deep concern about the spiraling market. In *The Memoirs of Herbert Hoover* (New York: MacMillan, 1952) he wrote: "The stock boom was blowing great guns when I came into the White House. Being fully alive to the danger inherent in this South Sea Bubble and its inevitable reaction, my first interest was to get it under restraint." To this end, Hoover says he tried to orchestrate a campaign involving government officials, financial leaders and the press. "To create a spirit of caution in the public," he wrote, "I sent individually for the editors and publishers of major newspapers and magazines and requested them systematically to warn the country against speculation and the unduly high price of stocks." The campaign, he conceded, met with no success.

$

4   *Tumbling Toward Chaos*

There was plenty of economic news to cover as business began to stumble and cracks in the nation's financial structure started to appear, but on the whole very little except the bullish view on Wall Street commanded attention. "Most magazines and most newspapers in 1929 reported the upward sweep of the market in admiration and awe and without alarm," J.K. Galbraith wrote in *The Great Crash 1929*.[1] While researching that book, Galbraith spent a summer in the Dartmouth College library reviewing the financial reporting in various publications from that fateful year. Most of what he saw, he said, was "ridiculously poor" — a judgment borne out much later by my own review of various periodicals.

There were exceptions, of course, and in his book Galbraith identified two of them. One was *The Commercial & Financial Chronicle*. Its editor "was never quite shaken in his conviction that Wall Street had taken leave of its senses," according to Galbraith. In March, the financial weekly had played up a provident warning by Paul Warburg, a prominent international banker, that "unrestrained speculation" in stocks could produce a collapse that would "bring about a general depression involving the entire country." Warburg's fears were centered on the potentially destabilizing activities of investment trusts, which he called "incorporated stock pools."[2]

The other exception cited by Galbraith was *The New York Times*. Its financial page "was all but immune to the blandishments of the New Era," he wrote. "A regular reader could not doubt that a day of reckoning was expected. Also, on several occasions, it reported, much too prematurely, that the day of reckoning had arrived." The *Times'* financial coverage during that period was guided by Alexander Dana Noyes, whose journalistic career had started in the 1880s and had included encounters with other bouts of euphoria and panic prior to '29. Reflecting on the awkwardness of sounding a cautionary note as the market bubbled upward, Noyes later observed:

> The speculative mania seemed by 1929 to have neither geographical nor social bounds. There were occasions, even in social conversation, when expression of disapproval or skepticism would provoke the same resentment as if the controversy had to do with politics or religion. It was not in all respects an agreeable task to point out in the *Times* what seemed to me the very visible signs of danger. As in the similar circumstances of the short-lived speculative mania of 1901, expression of such comment had to meet the denunciatory comment that the writer was trying to discredit or stop American prosperity.[3]

The belief that skepticism bordered on the unpatriotic contributed to the mediocre reporting that prevailed during the period leading up to the crash. However, even among those who seemed wedded to that belief, there were occasional lapses into sobriety. *Forbes* at one point warned investors against buying heavily on margin. *Barron's* advised readers that the movements of the Dow Average could be interpreted as a signal that the bull market might be ending. On October 21 editor William Hamilton wrote: "There is an interesting development in the price movement, as shown by the two Dow Jones averages since the industrial high of 381.17 on September 3 and the railroad high of 189.11 on the same date." Hamilton went on to explain that if the two averages fell further and reached certain levels, "the bearish indications would be strong." He also acknowledged that speculators probably would ignore any negative signals from the Dow.[4]

One reason so much of the reporting during that period lacked a measure of doubt was the curious view that business journalism had of itself. It saw itself not so much as a tough-minded chronicler of events as it did an extension of the community it wrote about. Pliant editors and reporters ingratiated themselves with stock operators and adopted their upbeat perspective. Hobnobbing and long liquid lunches were the rule. Tips and rumors were seldom investigated, and press releases and other handouts frequently were printed without critical comment. As Galbraith has said, "Many of those who were writing about Wall Street and business in those days were drunks and incompetents."[5]

On all but the very best papers, the financial news or "biz" section was a journalistic backwater. It attracted piddlers and diddlers more interested in gathering cash than news, and it bestowed favor on "two-hatters" — newspapermen who sold ads and wrote favorable stories about the advertisers. It also was a dumping ground for burned-out city-side reporters and others looking for a place to camp until retirement. Younger reporters sometimes started in "biz" before escaping to more prestigious beats, and those who got stuck there did not always bother to acquire deep knowledge of what they were writing about. Very little space was set aside for their stories in any event, and there was very little opportunity to display them on page one. It was reserved for news of politics, gangsters, tragedies at sea — just about anything, in fact, except the drab, opaque subject of economics. Or so the thinking went at the time.

Thus it was hardly surprising that when the bottom fell out on October 28 and 29 — two days that erased nearly a fourth of the market's value — much of the press was poorly prepared and found itself chasing a tale that had been unfolding for weeks.[6] The result was a spate of misleading headlines like this one, which appeared the morning of the 30th in *The Wall Street Journal*:

Stocks Steady
After Decline

Like the headline, the lead paragraph of this article tried to put a good face on bad news:

> The stock market passed through its record day of business on Tuesday with the general level of prices reaching new lows. There were signs of support buying, however, as well as investor purchases having some effect on the widespread break.

The reporting elsewhere in the *Journal* that day wasn't much better. Instead of dealing with the crash, the "Review and Outlook" column led off with a discussion of the Russian revolution, followed by a lecture on the evils of the Federal Farm Board's program of loans to wheat farmers. Readers who got as far as page 20 were given a little more information, including the news that a 39 percent drop in the Dow Jones Industrial Average since early September was surpassed only by a 45 percent plunge over a span of 11 months during the panic of 1907. The "Broad Street Gossip" column gossiped about attractive buying opportunities, while the rest of the paper was filled with irrelevant articles such as the one that ran under this headline:[7]

Pig Iron Outlook
Is Encouraging

The obligation to sound a constructive note was felt in newsrooms elsewhere as well. The result was similarly Panglossian in some instances, less so in others. In a few cases, which are included in this sampling, the reporting was fairly straightforward.

In Washington, the *Post* declared:

Dizzy Stock Plunge Halts
As Strong Interests Buy;
Klein, On Radio, Reassures

Along with numerous other papers around the country, the *Post* that day carried this Associated Press account of the crash:

> Huge barriers of buying orders, hastily erected by powerful financial interests, finally checked the most frantic stampede of selling yet experienced by the securities markets and which threatened at times to bring about an utter collapse in prices.

The AP went on to report the soothing remarks of Julius Klein, Hoover's Assistant Secretary of Commerce, who assured a nationwide radio audience that most Americans were unaffected by the market's "speculative gyrations."

The New York Times' front-page headline on October 30 leavened the grim facts with a note of optimism:

Stocks Collapse In 16,410,030-Share Day, But Rally At Close Cheers Brokers; Bankers Optimistic, To Continue Aid

The opening paragraph of the story, however, was unyielding:

Stock prices virtually collapsed yesterday, swept downward with gigantic losses in the most disastrous trading day in the stock market's history. Billions of dollars in open market values were wiped out as prices crumbled under the pressure of liquidation of securities which had to be sold at any price.

After noting the attempt to shore up prices during the late afternoon, the *Times* observed:

From every point of view, in the extent of losses sustained, in total turnover, in the number of speculators wiped out, the day was the most disastrous in Wall Street's history. Hysteria swept the country and stocks went overboard for just what they would bring at forced sale.

Three related articles on page one reported the views of the hopeful and the news that the day had passed without an expression of concern by the nation's central bankers. Inside, the *Times'* financial section contained details on the trading and the fate of individual stocks that were slaughtered after being pushed higher for many months by market operators. When the closing gong finally sounded at the stock exchange, according to one article, a spectator in the visitor's gallery was heard to remark, "There's the knell of many a bank account."

The *Chicago Tribune*'s lead was among the more lucid to appear on the 30th:

New York, Oct. 29 — [Special] — An incredible stock market tumbled toward chaos today despite heroic measures adopted by the nation's greatest bankers. At the end there was an erratic rally . . . but no one as yet knows the full temper of this history-making market.

Later that day, the *San Francisco Chronicle* ran this headline across the top of page one:

Rally Checks Record Stock Slump

The *Chronicle* was one of the few papers west of the Mississippi that made a serious effort to cover the money world in 1929. The main thoroughfare of the city's financial district, Montgomery Street, was commonly referred to then as "Wall Street West," and the *Chronicle*, along with other local papers, paid attention to what was happening there. On page one, it ran the Associated Press account of the crash emphasizing the barrier of buying orders. Inside, on the financial page, additional stories appeared beneath another banner headline:

Headlong Stock Collapse Checked; 16,410,030 Shares Traded

The articles accompanying this headline included another AP account of the debacle:

Powerful financial interests struggled with a panic-stricken public today to save the stock market from complete demoralization, and were finally able to check another headlong collapse of prices, as all trading records were once more broken. . . . No effort was made to check the decline until late in the session, bankers feeling that the selling was a blind mass movement that could not be reasoned with until it had spent its force.

Along with the AP's report of conditions on Wall Street, the *San Francisco Chronicle* carried a locally written story describing the effect of the crash on Montgomery Street:

> In practically every brokerage house it was the same. Tired clerks toiled through the night, getting out statements, striking balances and recording sales and purchases, and after only a few hours rest were forced to drag themselves back to the job again.
>
> Restaurants and cafes in the financial district, ordinarily open only for breakfast and lunch, remained open for dinner, and many of them remained brightly lighted all night, supplying the midnight lunch needs of the thousands of weary workers in the buildings which house big business.
>
> And in many of these restaurants yesterday were seen groups of two or three men sound asleep over their coffee, their heads pillowed on their arms. . . . Cafe proprietors watched them solicitiously, permitting them brief naps and then awakening them so that they could return to their offices.

The following Saturday, *The Commercial & Financial Chronicle* rendered a terse and sobering judgment on all this:

> "The present week has witnessed the greatest stock market catastrophe of all the ages."

That same week, *The New Yorker*'s "Talk of The Town" column observed:

> The collapse of the market, over and above the pain, couldn't help but be amusing. It is amusing to see a fat land quivering in paunchy fright. The quake, furthermore, verified our suspicion that our wise and talky friends hadn't

known for months what they were talking about when they were discussing stocks.

Business Week didn't see any humor in the situation. It had started publishing earlier that fall, and after the crash it weighed in with commentary that was typical of many who claimed expertise in finance but totally misread what was happening:

> The hysteria that accompanied the market upheaval will pass away in a few days. . . . The trouble at this moment is not with business but with businessmen. They are still trying to translate their stock averages, paper gains and losses, and shrunken private check books into terms of fewer automobiles, radios, cigar lighters, corn flakes, caviar, flannel shirts and silk underwear for the millions who merely read about the panic in the evening paper and went to bed to go to work in the morning.

In the years to follow, fewer millions would go to work in the morning, and the press would find itself scrambling after that story as well.

NOTES

1. *The Great Crash 1929* (Boston: Houghton Mifflin, 1955).

2. Warburg's warning the week of March 18 also was reported in a straightforward manner in *Time* and in a few metropolitan dailies, including the *Chicago Tribune* and *New York Herald Tribune*.

3. *The Market Place* (Boston: Little Brown, 1938).

4. Another member of *Barron's* editorial staff, Philip Carret, had sounded a warning on mortgage bonds some years earlier. In his 1924 book, *Buying a Bond*, Carret wrote: "A day of reckoning in mortgage securities is undoubtedly ahead." That day didn't come until after the '29 crash, when holders of many of those fixed-income securities took a beating as did most stockholders.

5. The practice of paying journalists to print tips and rumors was not unusual in the 1920s, as it had been in earlier decades. Robert Sobel has written about this in *The Great Bull Market* (New York: W.W. Norton, 1968). He mentions reporters who were in the pay of publicists hired by market operators to plant items in the press. "It was common knowledge," concluded Sobel, "that newspapermen were being paid, newscasters were working in conjunction with speculators, and that formerly trusted news sources were in all probability linked with one syndicate or another." Another interesting book by Sobel that touches on this subject is *Panic on Wall Street: a history of America's financial disasters* (New York: MacMillan, 1970).

6. On October 28, the Dow Jones Industrial Average fell 12.8% (38.3 points, to 260.6). On the 29th it went down another 11.7% (30.6 points, to 230.1) in the heaviest trading day up to that time; while the volume was put officially at 16.4 million shares, it actually was larger since many trades went unrecorded in the hectic action. The two days together produced a percentage decline roughly equal to a 24.4% drop (17.4 points, to 54.0) on December 12, 1914, at the outset of World War I. After the October 1929 crash, the Dow and other averages kept sliding until mid-November, when a rally began that lasted well into 1930 and retraced about half of the October loss. This rally proved to be a bear-trap and a prelude to a longer decline that continued until the summer of 1932, when the Dow (which had been over 300) hit its all-time monthly low of 46.2.

7. Of the *Journal's* inability to give a proper accounting of the crash, Edward Scharff wrote in *Worldly Power: The Making Of The Wall Street Journal* (New York: Beaufort Books, 1986): "Readers would have been much better off with *Variety*, the show business newspaper. Its headline read: Wall Street Lays an Egg."

$

5   *Vanished Billions*

In 1930, when the economies of the U.S. and Europe were sickly but still alive, *The Saturday Evening Post* carried an essay entitled "Economic Possibilities for Our Grandchildren" by John Maynard Keynes, the British economist and money manager who would later break with traditional economic thinking and put forth the activist theory bearing his name. Keynes was a prolific contributor of articles on business and economics to periodicals in both the United Kingdom and the United States.[1] In His *Post* essay he wrote:

> It is common to hear people say that the epoch of enormous economic progress which characterized the nineteenth century is over; that the rapid improvement in the standard of life is now going to slow down; that a decline in prosperity is more likely than an improvement in the decade that lies ahead of us. I believe this is a wildly mis-

taken interpretation of what is happening to us. . . . I
would predict that the standard of life in progressive countries 100 years hence will be between four and eight times
as high as it is today.[2]

Keynes' long-range prophecy of sharply higher living
standards is coming true in most parts of the world, but
his prognosis for the decade of the '30s proved far too
optimistic. "Economic Possibilities" appeared just before
the Great Depression hit with full force, at a time when the
stock market was still trying to rally and when the steel
mills were still operating full shifts. A favorable economic
forecast sounded halfway reasonable then. Prices of many
products, from Victrolas to Model-Ts, were softening; but
it was felt that consumers would shortly resume their
spending. Wages, too, were declining; but they were expected to reach a level where companies would start hiring again. Slumps were supposed to end that way, and
much of the reporting suggested that this one would follow the conventional pattern.

Signs of recovery were sighted often and doomsayers
were scolded for their lack of faith. Announcements that
the worst was over continued to emanate from the Hoover
White House, along with assurances from Wall Street that
the losses sustained in the 1929 crash would soon be
erased. Financial columnists — including some of the
same ones who had said stock prices wouldn't collapse —
encouraged investors who had any money left to shovel it
into the market, and they printed lists of bargain stocks
that were to be bought without delay. Other writers
touted high-yielding bonds that had been hammered and
were thought to be attractive values. Meanwhile, reports
of bank failures and foreclosures were played down. The
crash had tempered some of the more flagrant cheerlead-

ing — no one crowed about a New Era anymore — but for a while the memory of good times lingered on, and those in the press who had misread the markets in '29 reported that prosperity would soon return.

In his syndicated newspaper column, Calvin Coolidge showcased his belief that the business of America is business and urged the captains of industry and banking to do something to help the economy. These so called "big men" were thought to have primary responsibility for shoring it up whenever it faltered. They had done so in the past, most recently during the early 1920s, and Coolidge, along with a lot of other people, felt they would come through again. Only this time conditions worsened and the "big men" seemed baffled. More than a few of them were in bad financial shape themselves, having been walloped in '29 along with the institutions over which they presided. Their stature and clout deteriorated measurably during that time. Frederick Lewis Allen described the situation this way:

> The Depression sharply lowered the prestige of business-men. The worst sufferers were the bankers and brokers, who found themselves translated from objects of veneration into objects of public derision and distrust — the distrust being sharply increased by the evidence of financial skullduggery which came out in successive Congressional investigations. But even business executives in general sank in the public regard to a point from which it would take them a long time to recover; and in this decline the conscientious and public-spirited suffered along with the predatory.[3]

In this troubling environment, the search for antidotes shifted to Washington, and news organizations hired extra reporters there to cover pronouncements and policy moves that were being made even before the Republicans left office. Although Hoover too looked to the "big men" for help, he also took a few steps that represented a departure from the hands-off approach of the Coolidge Administration. He pushed for a tax cut and additional public works programs as well as for more aid to agriculture and industry. He persuaded Congress to set up the Reconstruction Finance Corporation, a Federal agency that loaned millions to troubled businesses. Over the protests of the more extreme hardliners in his cabinet, he also urged corporate leaders to refrain from mass firings and severe wage reductions, and some of them did, for a while.

As the pressure to shore up profits intensified, however, layoffs and pay cuts became more widespread. The breadlines lengthened and the apple sellers took to the streets. Fearful of the future, many who still held jobs trimmed back their spending. This led to further declines in sales and earnings, and to more cutbacks in production and more layoffs. As if that wasn't enough, financial tremors in Europe produced nasty aftershocks in this country at a time when the public was losing faith in the banks and hoarding cash. Milton Friedman's analytical work three decades later would reveal that the Federal Reserve's response to the crisis had been totally inadequate.[4] Money was being drained out of the banking system faster than the Fed was pumping it in. However, that wasn't fully understood at the time, certainly not by most members of the press. Nor were the full consequences of other unwise policies that were being pursued, including higher tariffs and, later, a determined effort to balance the budget just when the country needed the stimulus of more spending rather than less.[5]

Much of the reporting during this period revealed a lack of understanding of the economy's inner workings. It also reflected a gradual retreat from optimism and a developing sense of dismay. Forecasts of an imminent recovery were replaced by a darker mood as commentators began to wonder what the future held for a democratic, capitalistic America. Were its problems self-correcting, they asked, or was it time for drastic action? Newspaper editorials in the fall of 1931 and the spring of '32 generally held to a conservative view on this issue, while news stories in the same papers showed sympathy for greater activism. Liberal periodicals like *The Nation* and *The New Republic* set forth their agendas for radical change, while others, notably those with broader audiences, continued to favor a steady-as-she-goes approach.

Two years after the Keynes essay appeared, in an article entitled "Vanished Billions," *Saturday Evening Post* readers were cautioned that neither the government nor the "big men" could be counted on to recover the large sums of money disappearing from the economy. The article advised against legislation to help the poor by raising the taxes of the rich, arguing that the rich had already suffered enough. The author of "Vanished Billions," Edwin LeFèvre, suggested that a period of economic pain might do some good if it could shock people into managing their affairs more prudently. The heart of the problem, as he saw it, had been foolishness and greed; thus hard times could serve as a financial cathartic, cleansing the system and proving beneficial in the long run. That there would be a long run LeFèvre seemed to have little doubt. His article dismissed the notion that "the world, so wonderful during the boom, is going to pot via the lost-money route," along with the idea that "the way to recover from hard times is to keep on hoping that somebody else will do something about it, preferably the politicians or the bankers."[6]

However, instead of ebbing as LeFèvre might have wished, the clamor to do something intensified. It culminated, less than a year after "Vanished Billions" appeared, in the presidential election that ushered in the New Deal and put Franklin Roosevelt in the White House. His inaugural parade on March 4, 1933, was described in somber terms in *The New York Times*:

> The drive from the White House to the Capitol was through lines of people who watched with serious, rather than enthusiastic faces. A sense of depression had settled over the capital so that it could be felt. The two men, side by side, were looked upon as symbols of a government trying to cope with dangers which were as subtle as they were treacherous. The few cheers were for Roosevelt rather than Hoover.

The day after the inaugural the *Washington Star*, which had been charitable to Hoover, reported that "only the first induction into office of Abraham Lincoln offers a likely parallel to the events of yesterday." Hours before he was to be sworn in, the *Star* noted, Roosevelt had awakened in his hotel suite "to find his far-flung fellow countrymen looking toward him with an almost childlike appeal, as the economic crisis had deepened and darkened overnight." In the same issue of the *Star*, Mark Sullivan, a Hoover supporter who had criticized FDR frequently during the campaign, was moved to declare:

> Any one who tries to go through the coming months and years hoping with one part of his soul for his own and the country's prosperity, and hoping with another part for failure of Mr. Roosevelt as President — any such person is

going to have an unhappy time, be in an impossible position. He is going to be at war with himself, his soul a
battlefield racked and torn by struggle between contending
desires.

The only way for national prosperity is success for the
Roosevelt administration. The only way for individual happiness, so far as it can be affected by politics, is success for
the Roosevelt administration. This is true not only for
America. Measurably it is true for much of the world.

That same day, the *Chicago Tribune*, which would later
heap scorn on Roosevelt and the New Dealers, offered a
sobering analysis of the mess confronting them as they
took office. Its lead editorial urged the reader to "pray for
their success in the trial of statesmanship which is before
them and the nation." The main news story on page one
conveyed a similar tone, noting the forceful reminder in
FDR's inaugural address that the country had "nothing to
fear but fear itself." The *Tribune* story also pointed out that
the speech "shadowed forth the possibility of the creation
of a dictatorship to accomplish the far-reaching reforms
essential to wiping out the evils which have caused the
present plight of the nation."

The notion of creating a dictatorship to treat economic
malaise in this country may sound far-fetched today, but
at the time there were those who wondered if this was
what the New Dealers had in mind for the land of the free
and the poor. The spector of an authoritarian government
waging all-out war against the Depression without regard
for the Constitution was unnerving but within the realm
of the plausible in 1933, considering how bad things were.
The day FDR and Hoover donned top hats and rode down
Pennsylvania Avenue to the inaugural, the fires were
banked in most of the nation's steel mills. Automobile

assembly plants were shutting down, and the soup lines were growing longer. Unemployment was pushing 20% of the labor force, the stock market was sinking again, and the banking system had collapsed. Depositors were withdrawing cash at a furious pace, forcing the government to take the unprecedented step of closing all banks temporarily. On the Monday morning after the closure, the *New York Herald Tribune* reported:

> A day of conferences between bankers, business men and government officials with the future course of business uncertain and the entire nation looking to Washington for leadership made yesterday a memorable Sabbath in the country's history.

Those who chronicled the worsening economic situation during those years had no trouble locating its most acute victims. They could be found in small towns and large cities, camped in shacks under railroad bridges or fighting over garbage outside restaurants. Journalists could and did find them huddled on the mountainsides of Appalachia, living off dandelions and roots. Other despairing victims, homeless and broke, were interviewed and photographed as they were led away after being caught stealing in grocery stores.

Because human response to adversity varies greatly, in those years — the most adverse the nation had known since the Civil War — the responses produced many stories of deprivation and acts of desperation. These were leavened with occasional tales of fatuity, such as the one about the aristocrat who suffered a loss of dividend income and proudly declared he had solved his money problems by laying off most of his servants. Meanwhile, millions of victims of the tumult in the money world found themselves somewhere in between these two extremes. They had no servants to dismiss, but neither were they forced to subsist on dandelions. There was little visible evidence of their privation, though their standard of living was falling. The ordeal of trying to manage while waiting for hard times to end was described at some length by a woman writing in *Commonweal*:

> It is distressing to abide in a damp, chilly house during those first cold days of autumn, because coal is precious and must be hoarded until winter is unmistakably with us. It is hard to deny your children so many of the simple things they long for, the possession of which gives them standing with other children. It is a bitter thing for a woman to see the man she loves growing sadder, grayer and more silent day by day, as he goes, fear-haunted, to his office job.
>
> But I am not altogether without hope that my imagination will function again and eventually will idealize what is now so cruel and so real. Perhaps, some day, when I am no longer desperately hanging by my fingernails to this precipice of hard times, I shall look back and the space, or time — whichever it is — between then and now will give the whole thing a different perspective, so that this portion of my life will seem less like an endurance test and more like the interesting crisis in the life of a woman in a story.
>
> For it is one of the true things that all earthly states and conditions must come to an end. Stocks, crushed to earth, will rise again; salaries, like other down-and-outers, will stage a come-back; restored bonuses will take on all the magic and thrill of the first one ever received; and our children, bless them, will emerge from all this welter of the world's distress. And they will face the new prosperity with greater wisdom for having known what it means to be poor.[7]

Such accounts of hardship struck a familiar chord and helped give the coverage of events a human dimension.

With Coolidge-Hoover prosperity coming unglued, the country looked to the press for solace as well as for information. Interest gradually subsided in the kind of frothy journalism that had characterized the '20s, with much attention devoted to fads, fashions and celebrities. The public developed an appetite for features about how people were coping, for news of government's actions, and for commentary on political-economic affairs. Syndicated columnists such as Walter Lippman, Drew Pearson and Westbrook Pegler began building audiences by offering a steady flow of punditry about the situation confronting the country. So did radio commentators like H.V. Kaltenborn and Gabriel Heatter, who regularly included in his nightly reports the reassuring words, "Ah, there's good news tonight."

Meanwhile, the newsweeklies increased their readership by condensing events in a breezy style that was enjoyable to read, even if the news itself wasn't. Both *Time* and *News-Week* (the hyphen disappeared later) provided concise accounts of the downturn, written from a national perspective. Here is how *Time* rounded up items from various places for an overview of what it called "the race against human misery" during a period when the race was just getting underway, shortly before Christmas in 1930:

* In New York, John Davison Rockefeller & son gave Chairman Seward Prosser's committee $1,000,000, providing 200,000 days of work for the jobless. With Edward Stephen Harkness's gift of $500,000, the committee's total passed $4,000,000. This sum was what made it possible for little knots of men to be painting Central park benches, digging sewers in The Bronx, performing clerical work in city hospitals, pitching manure on Park Avenue's thin central strip of grass. Total thus employed: 17,300.

* New Orleans jobless began hawking Louisiana oranges on the streets. Manhattan's unemployed fruit vendors sold tangerines two-for-5 cents. In Elizabeth, N.J., the idle sold celery.

* Duluth, whose plan has been organized in thoroughgoing fashion, card-indexed its unemployed, set them to sweeping brush out of the parks, repairing two naval vessels, building a municipal golf course.

* Patrick Cardinal Hayes ordered every pastor in the archdiocese of New York to add a prayer for relief in all masses where the rubric permits.

* In Minneapolis and St. Paul, the jobless paved streets, shoveled snow.

* Chicago cleaned up its alleys, hired hundreds to repair and extend the Lake Michigan breakwater. Many found work preparing the site of the 1933 World's Fair.

* In San Francisco, the idle planted grass, cleaned sand from streets, build roads, paths, cut fire-breaks in the woods. Women stitched at sewing centers.

* Kansas City, Mo. fixed it so that 400 men would have 16 days a month cleaning streets, guarding public works, "doing something."

This round-up, which included several other items, was followed two weeks later by a story about a petty Congressional debate that dragged on through the holidays over how to handle relief for destitute farmers and unemployed factory workers. In a language of its own that would later become its hallmark, the magazine described a climactic moment in that debate:

> Then up rose Idaho's Senator William Edgar Borah crying: "For God's sake, get something done to feed the people who are hungry."[8]

While *News-Week* was getting underway and still struggling in 1933, *Time* was already ten years old and a commercial success. It continued to flourish throughout the Depression, further surprising those who had expected it to fall short from the outset. Biographer Robert Elson has noted that *Time*'s founders, Henry Luce and Briton Hadden, were warned in the early 1920s that their new publishing venture "would almost surely fail because readers did not want to be instructed, but to be entertained."[9] By the '30s the magazine had settled on a pattern of presenting stories in an entertaining manner while instructing or informing the reader, and it followed that dexterous pattern thereafter. *Time*'s coverage of the economy wasn't especially deep, but it was readable and understandable, and it dominated the magazine's Nation and Business sections for more than half a decade, until the war clouds gathered and Hitler's actions became Topic A. By then, *Time* had put one New Dealer after another on its cover, including Labor Secretary Frances "Ma" Perkins and General Hugh Johnson, who ran the NRA's ambitious Blue Eagle program of centralized planning until it was scrapped by the courts.

All of this coverage appeared at a time when the prolonged downturn and government's attempts to end it overshadowed all other topics. Luce's innovative newsweekly prospered in that environment, while periodicals offering their readers entertainment and little else suffered losses of circulation and advertising. It was an interesting period in journalistic history, a period when, as Elson has pointed out, "the definition of news changed; the demand for facts and explanations of what was happening increased." This proved to be a change that benefited *Time*'s new sister publication as well.

NOTES

1. Keynesian theory, which stresses the role of government spending as a tool for reducing unemployment and stimulating growth, was set forth by Keynes in *The General Theory of Employment, Interest, and Money* (New York: Harcourt, Brace & Co, 1936). British author Wayne Parsons has calculated that Keynes wrote some 300 articles, mostly in support of his views, for numerous publications including the *New York Post*, *The Nation*, and *The New Republic*. According to Parsons, "Journalism enabled Keynes to have a ready command of public (outside) and policymaking (inside) opinion." See *The Power of the Financial Press* (New Brunswick: Rutgers University Press, 1990).

2. *The Saturday Evening Post*, October 11, 1930. A longer excerpt from "Economic Possibilities for Our Grandchildren" appears in the Appendix.

3. *The Big Change: America Transforms Itself* (New York: Harper & Row, 1952).

4. *A Monetary History of the United States 1867–1960*, by Milton Friedman and Anna Schwartz (Princeton: Princeton University Press, 1963).

5. Many books have delved into the causes of the Depression, including *A New Economic View of American History*, (New York: W.W. Norton, 1979). Written by Peter Passell and Susan Lee, the book summarizes and critiques various explanations for the severity of the slump, including those of monetarists and Keynesians.

6. *The Saturday Evening Post*, February 13, 1932. Readers will find additional passages from "Vanished Billions" in the Appendix.

7. From "Meeting the Salary Cut," *Commonweal*, February 10, 1932.

8. These *Time* excerpts are from the issues of December 15 and December 29, 1930.

9. *Time Inc.: The Intimate History of a Publishing Enterprise 1923–1941* (New York: Atheneum, 1968). Elson's book is part of a three-volume corporate history and elaborates on a number of the points made about the birth of *Time* and *Fortune* in this chapter and in chapter 6.

$

6 What's to Become of Us?

In memos outlining his plans for the creation of a new business magazine, Harry Luce promised that it would be "beautiful" and "brilliantly written." He assured the directors of his publishing company, who were being asked to approve an expenditure of $50,000 for its development, that the magazine he had in mind would be "authoritative to the last degree." It would be called *Fortune*, he said, and one day it would be achieve the status of a national institution.

Surveying the competition, Luce came to some nippy conclusions. *Forbes*, he declared, was "piddling and inexpressively dull." *Nation's Business*, published by the U.S. Chamber of Commerce, seemed to be "enslaved" by the idea that any article by a business leader "is per se entertaining reading no matter what the Great Name may tell his ghostwriter to say." In conversations with business associates, Luce dismissed these competitors as "the cheapest, least distinguished of magazines."

From the outset, *Fortune* lived up to its advance billing. The first issue was described in *The New York Times* as "sumptuous to the point of rivaling the Pearly Gates." It appeared just as the Great Depression was beginning in 1930 and sold for $1 a copy, which was a lot of money then. It contained more than a dozen comprehensive articles on topics ranging from the riches of the Rothschilds to a profile of the meatpacking business, illustrated with striking photographs taken by Margaret Bourke-White. There was a first-of-its-kind photo essay by Bourke-White on the subject of shipping on the Great Lakes, together with articles on privately-owned islands, the economics of operating a New York hotel, and the innovative use of color to market consumer products. The only dry reading in the entire 184-page issue was a 10,000-word magnum opus on the banking industry, co-authored by Luce.

Luce had pledged that *Fortune* would be devoid of "stock market fluff," and it was. It also was mercifully devoid of self-praise. Volume 1, Number 1 did not carry any introductory material extolling the virtues of the new publication. Meanwhile, its oversized (11″ × 14″) pages provided an attractive showcase for advertising a wide range of products and services — including cars like the Packard Custom Eight ("ask the man who owns one"), hotels such as New York's Lexington ("one person $4, two $5"), and sites for commercial development like the city of San Francisco ("in California, where life is better").

While it had a prosperous look, editorially the new magazine offered no hint that prosperity for the country as a whole was coming to an end. Like the rest of the Fourth Estate and most business analysts, *Fortune* failed to anticipate that the slowdown which was underway foreshadowed a depression. However, as conditions worsened, it responded to the growing demand for information about the situation by running fewer articles on companies and products and more policy stories. A good example was "What's to Become of Us?" which ran in 1933 and explored the issue of where the New Deal was taking the country. The lengthy sub-head of this 7,000-word piece, written by Archibald MacLeish, summarized *Fortune*'s answer:

> Roosevelt only knows. Who is Roosevelt? The American tradition. But does Roosevelt know? He knows what he wants. What does he want? Industrial democracy. What is industrial democracy? Neither Wall Street in 1929 nor the Kremlin in 1934 but . . .

This article appeared at a time when *Forbes*, *Barrons* and most other business publications were casting a skeptical eye toward the New Deal and urging their readers to have faith in the nation's corporate leadership. In "What's to Become of Us?" *Fortune* took a different view. To the surprise of some of its more conservative subscribers, it argued that while FDR was the product of a culture favoring private enterprise and individual initiative, the grim condition of the economy left him no choice except to expand the role of government. Federal action was needed, the magazine said, to deal with the crisis at hand and to "prevent the exploitation of society by the unprincipled" as well as to "prevent the exploitation of labor by employers" and to "protect the nation as consumers not only against greedy price rises but against the disasters caused by selfish competition." MacLeish's article contended that while Roosevelt's brand of industrial democracy did not portend a Soviet-style dictatorship, as the *Chicago Tribune* had feared, it would require extensive regulations aimed at preserving the profit system. Such regulations, said the article, were in the country's best interest and would irk "only those who are irked by any limitation upon sheer industrial banditry."[1]

Even in the midst of a Depression, this was heady stuff for a business magazine to be telling its readers. Terms like "industrial banditry," "greedy price rises" and "selfish competition" were, and still are, largely the province of more liberal journals. However, *Fortune* was leaning well to the left in those days. Further evidence of this can be found in its published definition of liberalism — "an attitude which sets human rights above property rights at every point of conflict" — and in its commentary following Roosevelt's landslide victory over Republican Al Smith in 1936. After analyzing the vote, the magazine observed:

> There is unfortunately no reason whatever for supposing that the election of November, 1936, proves the country has completed a mass migration to the Left.

The operative word in this passage is "unfortunately." Roosevelt's election to a second term in '36 signaled a continuation of policies which by then no longer seemed particularly radical to *Fortune's* liberal writers. While they found the New Deal worth writing about, a number of them favored bolder moves toward socialism. This group was made up of poets and other literary folk who felt they knew enough about business to know what they didn't like. Along with MacLeish, it included Ralph Ingersoll, who later started *PM*, a leftist New York newspaper, and Dwight Macdonald, whose experience studying companies for the magazine soured him thoroughly on private enterprise.

Macdonald in some respects personified *Fortune* during that era. Literate, a New Yorker and a Yale graduate, he had enrolled in a training program at Macy's and tried his hand at selling neckties for a while before deciding that merchandising wasn't his métier, whereupon he switched to journalism. At *Fortune*, he became one of the most prolific writers on the staff. His crowning achievement was a series on the United States Steel Corporation that took several months to prepare, ran more than 30,000 words and expanded the boundaries of business journalism. For one article alone — on the company's labor relations — over 200 steelworkers were interviewed by Macdonald and other members of the editorial staff. In that piece, the third in the four-part series, Macdonald wrote:

Now it is most certainly not in the mind of Chairman Myron C. Taylor, a well-intentioned and charitable man, that Steel's 196,000 workers should suffer the loss of free speech today — or that they should suffer from any oppression whatever. His associates presumably share that view. Yet oppression there is. Much freedom, much security, much happiness, much good will vanishes never to appear again in the ramifications of that puzzle that thoughtful Corporation executives describe as "the problem of the overzealous minor official." The overzealous minor official is the great, overgrown Peck's Bad Boy of U.S. Steel. In his zeal for tonnage he trips over the delicate structure of employee relationships and thoughtlessly kicks it out of the road. In his desire for a harmonious working force he puts his brothers, uncles, in-laws, and close friends in key spots throughout the plants. Sometimes, missing the last few signals from afar, he sets detectives to shadowing newspaper editors or bewildered journalists in the same way they shadow Communists and labor leaders. If the comedy of

American capitalism is ever written, the overzealous minor executive, well meaning and awkward, ambitious and blundering, must emerge as the liveliest character, a mixture of Falstaff and Sancho Panza, with a streak of prudent cunning in his make-up.[2]

This third installment, together with the two that preceded it, added up to a scathing indictment of not only U.S. Steel's labor policies, but also its press relations and monopolistic pricing practices. The author's draft of a fourth and final installment was even pricklier. It led off, as Macdonald recalled later, "with a cheerful quotation from Lenin's *Imperialism* to the effect that monopoly was the last state of capitalism and led 'inevitably' to socialism." The magazine's readers, however, never saw this version. It proved too much for Luce and his editors, who scuttled it and replaced it with a milder, less opinionated piece.

That prompted Macdonald to resign in protest. Subsequently, writing in the *Nation*, he took *Fortune* to task, calling Harry Luce a "great mouthpiece" for business. Still later, in his memoir, he explained that his sojourn at *Fortune* had made him highly skeptical of private enterprise, and he described the prevailing ethos on the magazine's closely-knit editorial staff:

The New Deal was inspiriting to me as to my fellow writers on *Fortune*. To Luce's dismay we became increasingly liberal; we wanted to write about Roosevelt's farm program, about the NRA, the CIO, the Wagner Act, unemployment, social security, anything but business. Luce was divided between his pro-business convictions and his journalistic instinct, which told him the CIO was news and that the wonders of American Cynamid Co. weren't; his typically American pragmatic fascination with Power and Success told him the same thing. He compromised (as did we) and for a few years *Fortune* was a pastiche of mildly liberal articles on "social" themes and reluctantly written "corporation pieces" dealing with enterprises that had somehow managed to make a profit.[3]

Macdonald's articles on U.S. Steel stirred up considerable reaction. They irritated the company's management and pleased labor activists who were struggling to organize its work force. The articles also generated a great deal of comment in financial circles — "a truly enormous clattering in the streets" was the way another member of the staff, Eric Hodgins, described the response. He added: "Whereas hitherto we were 'the mouthpiece of the House of Morgan,' we now became 'paid with Moscow's gold.' We certainly shook the pillars of the temple and shook them hard — and I privately think it was very good for the temple."[4]

The U.S. Steel series served to intensify criticism that was being leveled at *Fortune* because of its leftist views. The complaints came from subscribers and advertisers and from the magazine's ad salesmen. Their task wasn't made any easier by articles openly disdainful of capitalism such as a piece on European weapons manufacturers — "Arms and the Men" — written by Hodgins for the March 1934 issue. Here is an excerpt:

According to the best accountancy figures, it cost about $25,000 to kill a soldier during the World War. There is one class of Big Business Men in Europe that never rose up to denounce the extravagancy of its governments in this regard — to point out that when death is left unhampered as an enterprise for the individual initiative of gangsters the cost of a single killing seldom exceeds $100. The reason for the silence of these Big Business Men is quite simple: the killing is their business. Armaments are their stock in trade;

governments are their customers; the ultimate consumers of their products are, historically, almost as often their compatriots as their enemies. That does not matter. The important point is that every time a burst shell fragment finds its way into the brain, the heart, or the intestines of a man in the front line, a great part of the $25,000, much of it profit, finds its way into the pocket of the armament maker.

Shortly after "Arms and the Men" was published, *The New Yorker* was moved to declare:

> Today, for radical reading, turn not to the *New Masses*, or to the *Daily Worker*, or to the *Nation*; turn to *Fortune*, that well-groomed organ of Big Business which sells for a dollar and to which we award the 1934 Pulitzer Prize for its article, "Arms and the Men." It is something when *Fortune*, born into the lap of capitalism and nurtured at the breast of salesmanship, begins taking the profit system apart.

J.K. Galbraith is often associated with this era of fervent liberalism at *Fortune*. In fact, he arrived there toward the tail end of it. A sardonic debunker of business shibboleths and an extraordinarily gifted writer, Galbraith made a strong contribution as a member of its editorial staff, but that was after the leftward drift had been tempered by Luce. Aided by the departure of a few of the most ardent radicals such as MacLeish and Macdonald, *Fortune*'s editor-in-chief managed to prevent his magazine from becoming totally Marxist and he steered it back in the direction of what he had in mind in the first place, which was a chronicle of the achievements as well as the shortcomings of business.

This change did not amount to a whole lot at first, largely because business was still floundering and there weren't that many achievements to chronicle. But it was enough of a rightward turn to calm down some of the more irate critics, and it was made easier by the fact that government activism wasn't producing many wonders either. While it alleviated much suffering, it did not end the Depression. The economy didn't fully recover until midway through World War II.

By the time Galbraith joined *Fortune* in 1943, defense plants were humming, unemployment had all but vanished and the recovery was well underway. The magazine still ran articles with a liberal flavor — by writers such as Hodgins, John dos Passos and Bertrand Russell along with Galbraith — but they stopped short of calling for a Marxist revolution. Prior to joining the staff, Galbraith had done a wartime stint as Roosevelt's chief price-fixer at the OPA (Office of Price Administration). His first *Fortune* piece — an 8,000-word analysis of the economy's post-war prospects — advocated a major role for government in planning for demobilization. The article did not show great confidence in business's ability to manage the transition to a peacetime economy. However, compared with what other staff members had written a decade earlier, it was tame stuff indeed. Here is how it summarized the situation facing the country at the start of 1944:

> Brave words to the contrary, many Americans (including, apparently, a lot of worried soldiers) expect to return after the war to a good old-fashioned depression. This state of mind is more than unfortunate. It is dangerous. Should a like mind control private and public planning through demobilization, then the U.S. will return to 1939. Plan boldly and we can't.[5]

Galbraith's recollections of that article and his experience at *Fortune*:

"When I turned in the manuscript for the post-war planning story, Ralph Paine, the managing editor, thought enough of it to rearrange the January issue and put my article in the lead position. That did a great deal for my self-confidence. After that I was removed of any doubts about my journalistic skills.

"Looking back, I can see that making the transition from government and academic life to being a practicing journalist was risky, but I didn't feel that way at the time. I had developed an agreeable view of journalism as it was practiced at the better publications. And I had acquired a high regard for several of the reporters I knew in Washington, some of whom, such as Scotty Reston and Walter Lippman, paid attention to our activities at the OPA.

"I always looked upon the time I spent at *Fortune* as an interlude and felt that at some point I would return to academic life and government, but my years on the magazine were one of the most instructive periods of my life. I enjoyed them enormously. They gave me an intimacy of exposure to the structure, goals, and influence of the modern corporation that I could not have gained any other way. No small part of my instruction came from Harry Luce, who was a superb editor. With a few sweeps of a soft black pencil, he could remove excess verbiage from a manuscript without losing anything of consequence.

"Although I was well to the left of Luce, I didn't feel particularly confined in what I wrote because he was extremely curious and always willing to entertain ideas other than his own. He had gone through a long period when he found himself having to choose between socialists who could write and conservatives who couldn't. That era, which was mainly over by the time I got to *Fortune*, was one of the more extraordinary episodes in the history of business journalism."

NOTES

1. "What's to Become of Us?" — *Fortune*, December 1933. A longer excerpt can be found in the Appendix. MacLeish, the author of the article, left the magazine in 1938 and later remarked that in the early '30s it had turned its attention to broader topics after being "released from its preoccupation with big business."

2. "The U.S. Steel Corporation: III" ran in the May 1936 issue. It was subtitled: "An account of the two hundred thousand people who depend on the Corporation for their livelihood. And an analysis of the most severely criticized and most uncompromisingly defended position ever taken by the corporation: its labor policy."

3. From Dwight Macdonald's autobiobraphy, *Memoirs of a Revolutionist* (New York: Farrar, Straus and Cudahy, 1957).

4. Eric Hodgins became managing editor in 1935.

5. "The Job Before Us," *Fortune*, January 1944. A longer excerpt is reprinted in the Appendix. In the more than 40 years that have passed since he left *Fortune*, Galbraith has been one of his profession's most prodigious writers of articles and books. His most recent books are *Culture of Contentment* (Boston: Houghton Mifflin, 1992) and *A Short History of Financial Euphoria* (New York: Viking, 1993).

$

7 *Toadyism*

Fortune succeeded during hard times because it offered a superior editorial product and a counterpoise to the servility and blandness of its competitors. Nearly all of them had started during the Industrial Age, a lengthy span bracketed at either end by major calamities, the Civil War and the Depression. By the time Luce's new magazine arrived on the scene, most of its older, more supplicant rivals had been running fluff and fawning over the titans of the money world for so long that it would have seemed out of character for them to do anything else.

Interestingly, the first business publication born during that era, *The Commercial & Financial Chronicle*, was somewhat of an exception, although its conversion to healthy skepticism, evident during the 1929 crash, came at a rather advanced age. When it began in 1865 the *Chronicle* was a dedicated fawner. In fact, it promoted itself as an antidote for a poor image which the business community was suffering from. The first issue of the *Chronicle* declared:

> The pursuits of industry have been looked upon too exclusively in their money making aspects — too little in their social and political ones. The great influence which they have always exercised upon the fortunes of our country and which they must always continue to exercise, have been forgotten in the strifes of petty politicians and in the heat of personal discussion. No comprehensive paper devoted wholly to the great mercantile and commercial interests has yet appeared. Taking the entire press of the country together we shall find that these interests have to a certain extent obtained public recognition; but in no single journal have they received undivided attention.
>
> It is to fill this place in the ranks of the public press, and supply this want, that *The Commercial & Financial Chronicle* aspires.[1]

The "strifes" and "heat" referred to in this florid passage deserve a closer look. They were, ostensibly, an important part of the reason for launching the new weekly, which took birth during an eventful period in our history. The divisive war between the states had ended and the reconstruction of the South was underway. The taming of the West had resumed, with caravans of prairie schooners carrying settlers across the Great Plains. Major inventions like the telegraph and the cotton gin were coming into wider use. In California, horse-drawn coaches bearing the Wells-Fargo insignia clattered across the desert and miners who had fought in the war were back panning the rivers for gold. San Francisco and Los Angeles were starting to become centers of commercial activity. If *USA Today* had been around then, it might have responded to these and other developments with one of its patented feel-good headlines, perhaps something like:

Get Ready for Era of Possibilities as USA Progresses Westward.

An upbeat article along those lines would have been appropriate in the main, though not without a caveat pertaining to the money world. For this also was a time when business interests — the audience the *Chronicle* would appeal to — were coming under increasing criticism and acquiring notoriety that the new weekly wanted to counteract. There had been accusations of unfair profiteering during the war. After Appomattox, carpetbaggers had begun roaming the southern states, exploiting unsettled conditions there in search of easy money. In the industrial Northeast, the satanic factories and grimy sweatshops were gearing up for post-war production with a poorly paid labor force that included large numbers of children. Meanwhile, bankers were printing and circulating paper currency of questionable value, and railroad barons were cutting shadowy deals with politicans and grabbing vast amounts of land. Surveying the economic scene in those days, *New York Tribune* editor Horace Greeley repeatedly aired the warnings of socialist Charles Fourier that the U.S. was in danger of becoming a nation of soulless corporations, millionaires and beggars.[2]

As if all this wasn't inglorious enough, Americans also were struggling to shake off the effects of a severe panic that had rocked the country a few years earlier. It had followed one of those periods which seem to recur every so often in our history, when the gathering and spending of riches dominates until all participants have expended themselves, as in a gymkhana, at which time the illusion of financial invincibility fades quickly.

As we have seen, in 1929 and at the start of the '30s most

of the business press had trouble recognizing this course of events. That appears to have been true as well in the specialized periodicals during the years immediately prior to the Civil War, when the illusion was fueled by euphoria over mining schemes and railway deals and by loose lending practices and speculation in low-grade securities. However, not a whole lot can be said about the role of these periodicals back then, since there were very few of them: some tacky newsletters plus the *The Journal of Commerce*, the nation's oldest business paper, which started in 1827; and the *American Banker*, which had begun in 1836 and was devoted chiefly to banking matters. Both of those were bonafide publications, but they reached very limited audiences, as did the nation's first financial periodical, *The Shipping and Commercial List and New York Prices Current*, which began in 1795 and had disappeared by the late 1850s. In the specialized press, and in some of the harsher stories that were beginning to appear in the general press, the reporting was a blend of traditional English approaches to political-economic journalism together with the American emphasis on making a fast buck.[3]

Although the coverage was sparse, this nonetheless was an instructive period in the history of the press and the money world. The gathering and spending of riches ended abruptly in August of 1857 following the collapse of Ohio Life and Trust, a prominent financial institution based in Cincinnati. The news of its demise traveled far and wide by telegraph, and the ensuing debacle produced a steady flow of stories which continued until the outbreak of the Civil War and set the stage for *The Commercial & Financial Chronicle*'s debut later as a prolocutor for business interests.

Until August 25, 1857, the day Ohio Life closed its

doors, it had been doing business with banks and companies throughout the Ohio and Mississippi valleys and eastward to the Atlantic Seaboard. Thus the reverberations from its failure were felt throughout the Midwest (which was then considered the West) and in New York. There, uneasy lenders began calling in loans, including those of John Thompson, a securities dealer who had clients in Ohio and nearby states. Unable to pay up, Thompson was forced to suspend operations. Soon several other dealers also closed their doors, and from then on it was all downhill. Stocks fell and frantic depositors flocked to their banks and demanded gold coins or "specie" in exchange for the paper money in their pockets. The *New York Herald* reported during the week of August 27 that "Wall Street was in a fever of excitement" and noted that "the panic was deep and widespread."

News reports of the debacle were typically laced with pungent commentary. Here is how Ohio Life's demise was described in the *Chicago Daily Tribune*:

> The failure of the Ohio Life and Trust Company was the subject of general conversation in commercial circles yesterday. Everybody was astonished to hear the news. That company had sustained the highest reputation for solvency and responsibility. Capitalists placed perfect confidence in its soundness. It was an institution of many years standing, and had generally been managed with prudence and fidelity, at least so the commmunity believed. This company handled a capital of more than six millions of dollars. Its legitimate business was to loan money on bond and mortgage, for terms of years, at reasonable rates of interest.
>
> But its managers were not satisfied to let well enough alone. The frenzy of speculation got among them. They threw themselves in the way of the bears and bulls of Wall

Street, loaned vast sums at high rates of interest to kiting railroad companies and received their worthless or depreciated securities therefor. When the bottom fell out of those railroad stocks and bonds, the Life and Trust Company had to suffer the loss, and thereby have brought ruin upon hundreds of confiding guardians, widows and children.

The *Tribune* showed no sympathy for the troubles of John Thompson, who published a newsletter called *The Bank Note and Commercial Reporter* in addition to dealing in the financial markets:

> We presume that the failure of Mr. Thompson will not cause that general feeling of sudden and poignant regret which would be elicited by the withdrawal of other parties from the financial world. We think that the influence he asserted in respect of the paper currency of the West was altogether deleterious — that Thompson's Reporter was mainly a Reporter for Thompson — that his tricks with shinplasters were little better than other people's tricks with cards and thimbles — that he kept a menagerie for wild cats of dangerous ferocity, which we are not sorry to see temporarily closed . . . We understand that his office is for the present in the keeping of the Sheriff.[4]

A few days later, *Harper's Weekly* articulated its view of the situation:

The Financial Storm

> The week which was ushered in by the astounding failure of the Ohio Life and Trust Company closed with . . . a gloomier state of things in the financial world than has been known for years.
> It has long been evident to every thoughtful person that a great portion of this country, and especially the Western States, have been 'burning the candle at both ends,' vis, spending money in foreign dry goods, comforts, luxuries on an unexampled scale, and at the same time investing

every dollar they earned, and more besides, in the construction of railroads and other works of improvement, in opening new lands, and laying the cornerstone of new cities . . .

The reproach lies at our door too. Our extravagance engendered the extravagance of the West; our costly houses, our expensive furniture, our ruinous habits of dressing and living generally, are just as unsuited to our progressive condition as the two-fold expenditure of the Western people is to theirs. No city in Europe is so extravagant as New York. Dukes and princes on the Continent spend less money and live in less splendid style than our common merchants. Our young women spend as much on their toilet as their fathers would lay out on the whole family in England or France.[5]

Meanwhile, *The New York Times* weighed in with this analysis:

The great productive resources of the Union, the cotton, and sugar, and rice, and tobacco plantations, the wheat, and the corn, and the hayfields, the coal mines, the iron mines, the lead mines, the gold mines, the forests and the orchards — these are the sources of our prosperity and greatness, and while they are unharmed, no mere financial revulsion can affect the general prosperity . . .

Indeed, we are not sure but the country at large would profit immensely by the utter prostration and extinction of the whole brood of gamblers, whose reckless and unprincipled transactions are ruining thousands of innocent victims, and bringing disaster and disgrace upon the commercial and financial character of the City.

The Stock Exchange, as at present managed, is very little more than an enormous gambling establishment — and the whole scale of its operations is quite as ruinous, quite as demoralizing, quite as infamous as any of the Broadway hells which have recently enjoyed the attention of the Metropolitan Police. When an Exchange is devoted to its legitimate use — that of facilitating the exchange of real values and serving as an agent between buyers and sellers who lack the leisure, the skill or the knowledge to transact business of this kind for themselves — it is undoubtedly a useful and laudable institution.

But the New York Stock Exchange does just enough of this kind of business to keep up appearances. The principal occupation of its members is gambling, and they carry it on by a systematic cheating, more infamous than playing with loaded dice, or any of the devices which brand the professional and law-hunted gambler. They swindle not only the men who play the game with them, but they rob every person who happens to have his savings invested in the stock which supplies the material for their nefarious schemes.[6]

While criticism was being directed at hanky panky on the stock exchange — as well as the public's lavish spending habits and mismanagement at Ohio Life — *The Journal of Commerce* turned poetic during those fateful days. After surveying scenes of tumult in the financial district, with angry mobs threatening to storm the exchange and the banks, it urged readers to petition the Supreme Being for assistance:

> *Steal awhile away from Wall Street*
> *and every worldly care,*
> *and spend an hour about mid-day*
> *in humble hopeful prayer.*

NOTES

1. *The Commercial & Financial Chronicle*, July 1, 1865. The *Chronicle* was an amalgamation of four trade journals: the *Bankers' Gazette, Commercial Times, Railway Monitor* and *Insurance Journal* (the oldest of which dates back to 1839). The introduction to the first issue, elaborating on the publication's aspirations, is reprinted in the Appendix together with a portion of one of the main articles.

2. Horace Greeley wrote frequently about business affairs in the *New York Tribune*, which he founded in 1841. In 1835 James Gordon Bennett, a former economics teacher, founded the *New York Herald* and created its "Money Page." The two papers were combined into the *New York Herald Tribune* in 1924.

3. For more on the influence of British periodicals and editors on early American business coverage, the reader is referred to *The Power of the Financial Press* (see notes to chapter 5). For a portion of our historical data, we are indebted to Robert Shabazian, author of a chronology of milestones which appeared in the 50th Anniversary Journal of the New York Financial Writers' Association. According to Shabazian, *The Shipping and Commercial List and New York Prices Current* was started in 1795 by James Oram, a New York printer.

4. From the *Chicago Daily Tribune* (the word Daily was dropped later) of August 26, 1857. "Shinplasters" was a derogatory term applied to paper currency issued by bankers; its name stemmed from its resemblance to the paper used in plasters on sore legs. At the time, some 1,500 banks were circulating more than 6,000 different types of currency.

5. *Harper's Weekly*, September 5, 1857.

6. *The New York Times*, August 26, 1857.

$

8 Parvenu Feudalism

As the Industrial Age progressed through the late 19th century and into the 20th, its excesses as well as its achievements continued to attract attention in the general press. Each new specialized business periodical that came along, meanwhile, focused heavily on the achievements while catering to the ethos of its readers.

Few topics were worthy of more attention in those days than the consolidation of wealth and unrest among working people who felt they were being denied a fair share of the nation's growing prosperity. In steel, railroading, garment manufacturing and several other industries, pressure was building for higher wages and better working conditions. This led to riots and confrontations that became front-page news. After one particularly turbulent week in 1886, for example, the *Chicago Tribune* filled six of seven columns on page one of its Saturday edition with strike news. One story headlined "To Shoot the Workers" described a tense situation in Kansas City where striking Missouri Pacific employees were reported to be in danger of being gunned down by the local militia. A day later, the *Tribune* devoted a full page to the views of business and labor leaders and others on the eight-hour workday, one of organized labor's key demands at the time. The result was a wide-ranging discussion that compares favorably with the best op-ed page forums that can be found in the press today. Nearly a dozen contributors argued for the eight-hour day. Dissenters were in the minority, but their views, too, were laid out. Here are two brief excerpts:[1]

Henry George, author of "Progress and Poverty," which was published in 1874 and dealt with the widening gap between the haves and have-nots in American society:

> The movement for the reduction of the working day to eight hours deserves earnest support. It is a step toward securing to the masses something of the benefits which advancing civilization ought to bring. . . . The few hours of the working day which remain to the man whose faculties have been on the strain for ten or twelve hours a day are not leisure; nor yet is there leisure in the days and weeks and months of involuntary idleness which the vicissitudes of our industrial organizations force upon hundreds of thousands — idleness accompanied by weary uncertainty and racking anxiety more exhausting than toil.

Leland Stanford, founder of the university that bears his name and, at the time, a California senator and railroad executive:

> Labor is a commodity; its value depends upon the demand for it and its power of production, and cannot

be regulated by legislation. If one man can produce as much in eight hours as another man can produce in ten, he ought to be paid as much; not by the length of time he is employed, but by the amount that he produces. To pay the men by the day is often a premium upon idleness; and the idle, worthless man will naturally shirk when he knows he is to receive as much compensation as the industrious man who is next to him.

The Wall Street Journal made its first appearance during this period of labor unrest. The *Journal* was primarily the handiwork of Charles Dow and Edward Jones, who had been publishing a financial bulletin, the *Customer's Afternoon Letter*, which was hand-delivered around New York to business executives and stock market traders.[2] When they decided to create a newspaper, Dow and Jones aimed it at essentially the same audience. What they brought forth, in the summer of 1889, was a far cry from the *Journal* of today. There was no op-ed page with pro and con commentary on labor issues or any other subject, no comprehensive analysis of political developments or foreign affairs, and no personal money management news or reviews of books and plays. Like *The Commercial & Financial Chronicle*, the *Journal* catered mainly to the concerns of the privileged, though it didn't start doing that in earnest until after it had been publishing for a while. The first edition on July 1 was all of four pages and contained a mishmash of data such as the going rate for a bale of cotton, along with a few scraps of non-financial information like the latest word on a John L. Sullivan boxing match. Page one featured a report on a stock market index — forerunner to the Dow Jones Industrials — that had been developed earlier by Dow.[3]

Average Movement of Prices

The bull market of 1885 began July 2, with the average price of 12 active stocks 61.49.

The rise culminated May 18, 1887, with the same twelve stocks selling at 93.27.

Prices gradually declined for about a year, reaching the net extreme low point April 2, 1888, the 12 stocks selling at 75.28.

The report went on to track the ups and downs of the index into 1889. It offered no interpretation or background information to guide readers, and the writing style was dry as dust. This was true of the rest of the paper as well. Even so, from inception the *Journal* had its share of savvy devotees, and the maiden issue drew mostly favorable reviews like this one in the *New York Star*:

Wall Street is a large and growing field for journalistic enterprise, and it can be said that the plans of the enterprising proprietors of *The Wall Street Journal* seem eminently calculated to meet the requirements of the investing and speculating public.

When the *Journal* introduced editorial comment on a regular basis a few years later, the country was going through another economic upheaval. Excessive borrowing and a whoopee atmosphere along Wall Street were followed in the early 1890s by a panic not unlike the one that had savaged the nation in the late 1850s. The news coverage was similar too, with the better quality periodicals voicing concern about avarice and calling for a return to financial sanity. During this period the *Journal* spoke mainly for the wealthy, though as the years went by it showed occasional compassion for the labor movement. For example, it weighed in with editorial support for

Pennsylvania coal miners engaged in a bitter strike over working conditions shortly after the turn of the century. On the whole, however, the paper's sympathies lay firmly with business and with the trend toward consolidations and mergers. This can be seen in the following extract, which typifies the *Journal*'s editorial tone at that time:

> The extent to which a handful of men are able to control the great bulk of the wealth of the country is extraordinary and even startling . . . but alongside of these facts must be put also the other fact of a larger degree of average prosperity than there was ever known before.[4]

At the other end of the political-economic spectrum, small left-wing periodicals decried the rough-and-tumble of the profit system just as outspokenly as the *Journal* came to the system's defense. This passage is from *Arena*, a monthly that has long since gone wherever old flaming liberal gazettes go after they expire:

> Apologists for corporation rule are just now very loud in their claims that laboring men were never so well off as today; never did they receive such high wages as now; and one of the more daring mouth-pieces of plutocracy has had the hardihood to declare that the belief that the capitalist has received too large a share of the benefits that have arisen from invention, machinery, etc., is not true, but that the masses have received as fair a proportion of such benefits as the rich. The absurdity of this last proposition is such that it is not necessary to take space to notice it, and it is only mentioned to show the brazen hardihood of lawyers and other special pleaders for corporation rule in their effort to shackle present-day civilization with the new parvenu feudalism.[5]

A few years after this essay appeared, in 1907, the country experienced still another panic, one that was exacerbated by the concentration of financial power and which led ultimately to the creation of the Federal Reserve System.[6] That same year, taking aim at the critics of giant trusts, the *Journal* displayed predictable indulgence:

> The outcry against financial concentration today is not much different than the same outcry which was heard thirty or forty years ago. When the first consolidated railroad system was created between New York and Chicago, the warning was raised that such power in the hands of private capitalists, irresponsible to the public, was dangerous indeed. Nevertheless these consolidations have been of unquestionable economic advantage to the country. They have extended its trade and increased its financial power.[7]

Like the *Journal* and *The Commercial & Financial Chronicle*, other periodicals of this genre that started between the Civil War and the '29 crash were faithful to the idea of untrammeled free enterprise. Their loyalty remained unshaken during the busts that followed the booms, and it stayed resolute in the face of disillusionment that spilled over into the political arena and radicalized portions of the electorate. *Dun's Review* (which began in 1898), *Financial World* (1902), *Nation's Business* (1907), *Forbes* (1917) and *Barron's* (1921) each in varying degrees offered a benign picture of the country's growing economic power. Readers were seldom exposed to the view that government should play a more active role in succoring the commonweal. Instead, they were assured that business was the proper agent for achieving public ends, and business leaders were given benedictory treatment.

This tendency to kiss the hem of the garment showed itself in bold relief when B.C. Forbes started his own magazine as America was entering the First World War. B.C. was Bertie Charles, a Scottish immigrant and former printer's apprentice who had been a writer for the *Chronicle* and financial editor of both *The Journal of Commerce* and Hearst's *New York American*. Along with considerable writing and editing experience, Forbes had acquired good instincts for the value of stories about the rich and the famous. He also had acquired a knack for mingling with business people, flattering them and persuading them to respond to his questions. Here is how the first issue of his new magazine adulated over John D. Rockefeller in promoting an upcoming article:

> The man who built up the most wonderful business the world has ever known, not only tells, in the next issue of *Forbes* magazine, how he got on, but gives pointed advice to the young men — and the older men, also — of America, on how to succeed and how to live. This authoritative interview with John D. Rockefeller is the most intimate, the most self-revealing, the most inspiring he has ever given a writer.[8]

The first issue, which sold for 15 cents a copy, also carried a story entitled:

How Forbes Gets Big Men to Talk

In this piece, B.C. Forbes cautioned that a reporter cannot simply drop in on "the greatest businessman in the world and get him to discuss any or every subject at order." On the contrary, he explained, such interviews required careful advance preparation, including contact with Rockefeller's public relations advisers. Here is how B.C. Forbes characterized Rockefeller in the profile that ran two weeks later:

> John D. Rockefeller is the most impressive, the broadest-visioned, the most fundamental thinking man I have ever met. Napoleon 'thought in Empires,' Cecil Rhodes

'thought in Continents.' John D. Rockefeller thinks universally; his yardstick is the world, the whole human family. His invariable test is: How will it affect mankind? He looks and acts beyond parochialism, beyond provincialism, even beyond nationalism.

In another story that same month, B.C. Forbes used buttery verbiage and prolix writing in coming to the defense of financial chieftans who were accused of a lack of patriotism during the country's preparations for war. With characteristic certitude, he wrote:

> The most patriotic spot in America is not Washington, not Kokomo, but Wall Street.
> The men of Wall Street are no more grasping, no more money-mad, no more self-seeking than the average farmer, the average cotton grower, the average corner grocery man, the average artisan.

Periodically, the early *Forbes* leavened its servility by showing concern for laborers. Just as the *Journal* had voiced support for striking miners, B.C. Forbes, by all accounts a highly moralistic individual, scolded companies that were quick to lay off workers when profits fell and times got tough. On the whole, though, his publication courted the "big men" that he was fond of writing about and expended much of its energy fulminating against left-leaning politicans, particularly in the 1930s, when the country was turning to liberalism. In the process *Forbes* weakened its credibility and, for several years, its viability as a publishing enterprise.

Forbes, the *Journal* and most of the other specialized business periodicals born during the Industrial Age have long since toned down their toadyism. It has been replaced, in some instances, by a refreshing irreverence.

John Quirt

Meanwhile, *Fortune* no longer occupies the position of eminence it enjoyed for several decades on the strength of its impressive start in the 1930s. As we shall see, its slide from supremacy is traceable to tougher competition, to its own internal difficulties, and to the influence of television, which has fractured our attention span, drastically altered our reading habits and supplanted the printed word as the main source of news about the money world for most Americans.

NOTES

1. *Chicago Tribune*, May 1, 1886.

2. Dow and Jones, together with a third partner at the *Journal*, Charles Bergstresser, began their careers in financial publishing with the Kiernan News Agency, which started in the 1860s. For more on the *Journal's* early history, the reader is referred to Lloyd Wendt's *The Wall Street Journal* (Chicago/New York/San Francisco: Rand McNally & Co., 1982) and to *Worldly Power: The Making Of The Wall Street Journal* (see notes to chapter 4).

3. Charles Dow's first index, created in 1884, covered 11 stocks. The number was increased to 12 in 1886 — three years before the *Journal* began — and to 20 in 1916 and 30 in 1928.

4. *The Wall Street Journal*, January 24, 1907.

5. *Arena*, December 1903. A less polemical view of the average American's situation in the early 20th century appeared several years later in the "Investments & Finance" column of the *Literary Digest*. It reported that in 1914 the typical family of four had an annual income of $847, rented a small house and paid $140 in taxes. That same year, *Investment* magazine blamed softness in the economy partly on the "motor car," which it called an "extravagance." The column criticized the prevailing habit of replacing old cars with new ones. Today, this would be considered favorable economic news.

6. The Panic of 1907 saw a run on the nation's banks and a sharp upswing in unemployment to around 16% of the nation's work force. It ended after a group of influential bankers and other "big men" led by J.P. Morgan intervened to prevent the situation from getting worse.

7. *The Wall Street Journal*, January 6, 1907.

8. *Forbes*, September 15, 1917. Along with more than a dozen articles and B.C. Forbes' column, "Fact and Comment," the first issue contained a feature called "Woman In Business" written by an associate editor, Marian Glenn. *Forbes* correctly called her feature "unique." At the time, business journalism was dominated entirely by men.

$

III
TELEVISION

9 Ninety Seconds

On a gray winter evening shortly after the start of his second term, Ronald Reagan celebrated the waning hours of his 74th birthday on Capitol Hill, delivering one of his most memorable State of the Union addresses. It was a rouser, relentlessly upbeat and unashamedly rhapsodic. Articulating a mood of national optimism, Reagan declared victory over the troubles of the Carter years and offered a grand vision of even better times to come. He hailed the dawning of a "second American revolution of hope and opportunity" and proclaimed that a "new freedom" was alive throughout the land. The speech was onward and upward all the way, interrupted 28 times by applause and capped off by a loud chorus of Happy Birthday and a final burst of teary-eyed cheering that seemed to echo forever through the cavernous House chamber.

That evening, in February 1985, mid-way through

Reagan's eight-year reign, represented the quintessence of the nation's first truly theatrical presidency. It was Hollywood on the Potomac, a night of bangles and baubles that even liberal Democrats in the chamber found intoxicating. An unnamed White House aide later described it in *Newsweek* as "boffo political theatre."

As a journalist, my job that day was to look into what the President was saying about the state of the economy. While the assignment was a fairly routine one, the story of how it was handled is worth recounting in some detail because it speaks to the issue of television coverage of the money world.

First, though, a brief word about State of the Union addresses. Along with the gimcrack and the geegaw — the inspirational remarks and standard applause-getters left over from the campaign trail such as the pledges to eliminate poverty forever and work toward prosperity for all — a President often will use this nationally televised mid-winter speech to reveal a few of his priorities and predilections. Clinton did this in his 1993 State of the Union, when he came out in favor of higher taxes on the rich and the middle class, and other Presidents have used the speech in similar ways. Sometimes they'll hint which way they are leaning on the major economic trade-offs confronting their administration. At the start of a four-year term, for example, they may be thinking of prescribing distasteful medicine early in hopes that the economy and the voters will be feeling better by the time the next election rolls around. This is a favorite gambit among political strategists of both major parties who dream of manipulating the economy like a puppet on a string. It seldom works very smoothly, though the Reaganites could claim some success along those lines during their first term, when they endorsed an effort by the Federal Reserve to cure inflation with a severe dose of tight money. That led to a nasty recession which was over well before the voters returned to the polls in November of '84.[1]

By the time Reagan's second term began, inflation was under control, the money spigot had been turned back on, and business was expanding again. Some Americans were still struggling as if hard times had never ended. Debt was becoming a major concern, along with a growing imbalance in international trade. Many manufacturers were feeling the pinch of foreign competition and starting to trim their work forces. Overall, though, business was chugging along and doing well enough so that a few White House insiders were starting to wonder if it might run out of gas later in the term, thereby reversing the pattern of the first four years. However, there was no strong conviction that this would happen, and no inclination in any case to criticize the Fed for being overly generous. Nor was there much enthusiasm for proposing a bigger dose of spending cuts or more taxes, either of which, if enacted, could have reduced the amount of fiscal adrenalin being pumped into the economy.

These and other aspects of the situation were potentially relevant to our coverage of Reagan's State of the Union speech, depending on what he intended to say. The task was to figure out what that was and report it on Cable News Network before he said it. The report would be an "advancer" — a kind of sneak preview which assumes that audiences gather in front of their TV sets well before something is due to happen, hoping to get the early word on it. How much of this gathering actually goes on is debatable. My own hunch is that television favors advancers not so much because audiences expect them, but out of a sense of inner frenzy. It is wrought into the fiber of TV news operations and begets other contrivances like instant analysis at political conventions or campaign interviews which frantically implore candidates to rehash what they have just told their audiences. In the case of the President's speech, the inner frenzy was signaling for an advancer in the expectation that something would turn up to justify putting it on the air. At lunch time we had very little to go on, but the newscast was still several hours away. As Washington economics correspondent for the network, my charge was to see if I could get a line on what the Congress and the country were about to be told.

In other circumstances — a commencement address, say, or an after-dinner talk at Rotary — the sensible way to approach this would be to telephone the person giving the speech, tell him you're a reporter working on deadline, and ask what he planned to say. He might cooperate right away or you might have to badger him a little, but the odds are you probably could gather enough information for a story. With the nation's Commander in Chief, this direct approach seldom succeeds. Celebrity journalists and prominent editors occasionally get through to the oval office, but rarely the worker ants in the press corps. When they try to solve their reporting problems by ringing up the President, on his birthday or any other day, they typically find themselves talking to his press secretary or a deputy press secretary or an office secretary who works for the press secretary or the deputy press secretary. These White House press people are skilled at keeping the ants away from the boss.

On this occasion they proved adept as usual at fielding the key question. I posed it to the press office around noon: "Can you give us a line on what the President is going to say about the economy tonight?" "No," came the reply. "We have nothing on that." It was explained that a few excerpts from the speech might be made available later that afternoon. While these could be of some help, I suspected they would contain mainly drum rolls and rhetorical flourishes rather than any worthwhile insights into Reagan's current thinking. It was time to look elsewhere.

In a situation like this, one saving grace is that Presidents not only are too busy to take calls from the ants; they also are so busy that other people draft speeches for them, while still others review the drafts and suggest changes. A major address like the State of the Union can pass through a half-dozen or more hands — writers and advisers and cronies from Congress or from outside the government. The more the merrier, of course, since that increases the chances of finding someone who will talk about the contents.

Infighting at the White House over what should be said in a speech can help the cause too. In a clash over policy, the gladiators have been known to phone the media to leak information favorable to their point of view. Especially when the battle is young and support has to be built up quickly, the more earnest among the combatants tend to call and leak with a fecklessness matched only by the eagerness of reporters who grab at every scrap in hopes that it might be a scoop.

There have been many practitioners of this black art, and much has been written on the subject. On matters of economic policy, two accomplished leakers come immediately to mind. One was David Stockman, who chose opportune moments in the midst of great battles to parcel out newsworthy tidbits, often favoring *The Wall Street Journal* editorial page or a columnist such as Robert Novak who generally could be counted on to give Stockman's views a thorough airing.[2] The other was Walter Heller, when he was head of the Council of Economic Advisers under President Kennedy. In the early 1960s, Heller rallied support for a tax cut in the face of opposition by adroitly spooning out information that reinforced his arguments and usually had some news value. In dealing with reporters, he drew on his skills as a teacher, explaining patiently what he thought his plan might accomplish and how it could help meet JFK's goal of getting the country moving again. While Stockman was bold in his use of the technique, Heller was a cautious leaker who usually held back until he felt he had tacit approval from Kennedy to go public.

Worthwhile leaks come along less frequently after the infighting over policy has stopped or the content of a major presidential speech has been decided. At that point the gladiators are spent and reporters must rummage around for sources who will talk even though there may no longer be much in it for them if they do. The job becomes especially difficult in economics reporting because, in any administration, the number of people who know their stuff is small, and the number who will reveal what they know is even smaller. It gets very tiny indeed if you eliminate those who cozy up to journalists and expect them to enter into a symbiotic relationship and act as a mouthpiece in return for access and dinner party invitations.

Meanwhile, the challenge of finding decent sources and getting information from them is kept interesting by the tendency, common among leakers and press relations people, to practice spin control, another of the darker arts. This is a technique, also employed in the corporate arena, for claiming victory in defeat or making down seem like up. The use of spin control to influence economics reporting is well illustrated by an incident that took place a few months before this particular State of the Union address. At the time, steel imports were in the news, and the administration announced it was rejecting a proposal by the International Trade Commission for new tariff protection for the nation's steel industry. The announcement generated banner headlines like these:

Reagan Declines Strict Steel Import Controls
U.S. Says No To New Steel Tariffs

Reflecting the spin the White House had placed on the story, most of the headlines conveyed the impression that the administration was taking a hard line against protectionism. Radio and TV newscasts echoed that theme, which was in keeping with the free trade and free market image the Reaganites were anxious to foster. However, the truth of the matter was quite different. While rejecting the ITC proposal, the White House simultaneously set in motion a course of action aimed at giving the steel industry a different type of protection against low-priced imports. The U.S. trade ambassador was ordered to negotiate voluntary restraints, and steel exporters were warned that any country failing to restrict its sales to the U.S. would be barred from our market. While this information was included in most of the stories, it was played down just enough so that it never made it into the lead or the headline. At the time, William Niskanen was on the Council of Economic Advisers. He recalls:

"Among the newspapers I was following, only one paper and one reporter got it exactly right — Clyde Farnsworth at *The New York Times*. The others were influenced to one degree or another by the smoke and mirrors act orchestrated by our trade ambassador's office. It was a good example of a technique which I happen to believe is a legitimate device for government to use, and in this case everyone felt it worked pretty well. By the time the other papers figured out what was happening a day or so later, the story was off page one and buried on the inside."

The morning after the announcement, the accuracy of Farnsworth's reporting was reflected in the *Times* headline:

Reagan Seeks Cut In Steel Imports Through Accords[3]

Returning to our account of that day a little over four months later when we were preparing our advancer, I managed to reach a source in the afternoon who was familiar with the content of the President's speech. He had a nickname, Waffle, which owed to his habit of vacillating when confronted with hard questions. Whether he waffled because he didn't know or because he didn't want to say I could never be entirely sure. Probably it was a combination of both. He was a congenial guy who liked to dabble at spin control and had a good sense of where the President stood on the economic issues of the day. Waffle enjoyed a toddy now and then. Occasionally, across the street from the White House in the English Grill at the Hay-Adams, I would ply him with one or two in hopes of loosening his tongue. The best that can be said for those efforts is that occasionally they met with modest success. At other times the hair of the dog appeared to have the opposite effect, causing him to talk less, perhaps for fear of embarrassing himself by slurring his words.

As Washington sources go, Waffle wasn't in the same league as Woodward and Bernstein's Deep Throat, capable of whispering a few words in a garage that could bring down an entire government. But he was estimable enough to rate a nickname, and in the shorthand of the trade he was always referred to as "a source close to the administration." Respecting his wishes, I assiduously shielded his identity from viewers and from my colleagues at the network. Waffle and I had known each other from earlier days in California.[4] While I never felt he was quite the hot shot insider he presented himself to be, he was reasonably helpful on many occasions, including this one. True to form, he portrayed the speech in glowing terms. Future generations might well remember it, he said with only a trace of a smile, as "practically another Gettysburg Address." Waffle gave me fewer specifics on the content than I had hoped for. However, he supplied me with enough to get me started on a script that would eventually run about 90 seconds — which was my allotted air time.

NOTES

1. The notion of manipulating the economy with an eye toward the ballot box had been an issue in 1980, when Jimmy Carter tried to accelerate the pace of Federal spending during the primary campaign in an attempt to blunt Senator Ted Kennedy's argument that government wasn't doing enough. During the 1972 campaign, the press reported that the Federal Reserve was pumping up the money supply in an effort to help re-elect Richard Nixon. What actually happened was a little more complicated: Fed officials in the spring of '72 were conscious not only of the upcoming election; they also were concerned that wage-and-price controls might be extended to interest rates if the central bank failed to pump and rates were allowed to rise.

2. In *The Triumph of Politics* (New York: Harper & Row, 1986) Stockman acknowledged using the media to argue his case in public. More than once he referred to the syndicated newspaper column by Evans and Novak as his "bulletin board." During a 1981 struggle over budget strategy with Senate Finance Committee Chairman Pete Domenici,

Stockman said he "posted a message on the Bob Novak bulletin board and had a little conversation with my friend Bob Bartley, editorial page editor of *The Wall Street Journal*. The next day there appeared on that gray dignified page a searing editorial entitled 'John Maynard Domenici.' It accused the Senate Budget Chairman of single-handedly attempting to destroy the Reagan Revolution out of a benighted affection for the failed Keynesian policies of the now medieval past."

3. From *The New York Times*, September 19, 1984. Farnsworth's story began: "President Reagan today ordered actions that the White House said would reduce steel imports and help the American steel industry. The President directed his trade negotiatior, Bill Brock, to negotiate 'voluntary restraint agreements' with steel-exporting countries." The article went on to explain that "the White House, seeking to assure the industry that it would get protection, added that it would act to block access to the American market for countries that refused to agree to limit their steel shipments to the United States."

4. Waffle at one time had slipped word to me that Reagan was under consideration at CBS as a commentator and Eric Sevareid's successor. Upon hearing that I expressed mild disbelief. Later I learned it was true; he was among those who were being considered, though nothing ever came of it. My initial reaction was to chuckle and ask if CBS wouldn't be better off turning to Jane Fonda, who also had experience in front of the camera and a strong political orientation. Waffle replied: "The country needs to be exposed to the wisdom and insights of Ronald Reagan because someday he will be our President." If memory serves, I chuckled at that too.

$

10 The Credo and The Clicker

Let's take a sidelong glance at an eventful year that has relevance for our story of the advancer on the State of the Union speech. The year was 1932. The union and the economy were in a dreadful state then, a mess that was making headlines every day — and there was other news as well. In 1932, Amelia Earhart became the first woman to fly alone across the Atlantic. Babe Ruth homered after allegedly pointing to the wall at Wrigley field, and the Yankees swept the Cubs four straight in the World Series. Vitamin C was discovered, and General Mills introduced Bisquick. On Broadway "Americana" opened at the Shubert Theatre, featuring the hit song "Brother, Can You Spare a Dime." It was a year for political upheaval. In Germany, unemployment passed the five-million mark and Adolf Hitler prepared to assume power. With the number of jobless rising in this country too, voters gave Roosevelt a mandate to try to put an end to hard times.

That was in November. A few months earlier, on a warm sunny day on the campus of a small college in Eureka, Illinois, a little-noted event took place that also would make its mark on history: the young student who would one day become our 40th President was awarded his bachelors degree in economics.

It would have been interesting to have been there with young Dutch Reagan in his cap and gown, extending congratulations and asking him how he felt about the way things were going. His years at Eureka College were a remarkable time to be studying economics and forming impressions. The year he earned his degree, more than 12 million people were out of work, including his father and quite a few others in his hometown of Dixon, where they queued up every morning outside Newman's Garage for bread and coffee. Nearly everywhere, bankruptcies were on the increase. Trade with other countries was slowing down. The stock market was moribund — the Dow Jones Industrial Average hit its all-time low not long after graduation day. And all the while, among Republicans and Democrats, there was talk of raising taxes to balance the budget; it was out of whack and this was thought to be one reason for the growing number of jobless.

In that atmosphere, Reagan took to wearing a Roosevelt button. His politics tilted mildly to the left and stayed that way for several years, during which time he generally supported the notion of affirmative government. Later, after studying the world as it looked from Hollywood and Sacramento, and after becoming a newspaper columnist, his views began to change. Along with greater wealth, he acquired new ideological certitudes and articles of faith.

Article One was keep taxes low while preaching the virtues of a balanced budget and hailing the magic of the marketplace. Article Two was borrowed from an old French king who assured his people that it was okay to grow rich. "Enrichez-vous" is basically what he told them. Reagan offered similar encouragement, reminding all who questioned the wisdom of worshiping personal wealth that the less fortunate stand to benefit if the go-getters are allowed to go and get, with minimal interference from Washington.[1]

This was essentially the same credo that lost favor when the Coolidge-Hoover era ended in 1932 and when the Reagan-Bush era ended 60 years later. And it's the credo that Eureka's most famous alumnus was getting ready to expound on once more the day I was preparing to report on his fifth State of the Union address. He would phrase things differently, of course, using more eloquent language and drawing on his exceptional communications skills. Based on what I had found out about the speech, and on a few excerpts that surfaced in the White House press room in the afternoon, I began writing my story in the form of a script. It noted that Reagan would give his blessing to a Treasury plan for revising the tax code, without committing himself to a specific timetable for action. In the skirmishing that had taken place during the drafting of the speech, Treasury officials had argued for a firm commitment, while others had wanted Reagan to make only a few general remarks about the tax plan. Waffle told me the Treasury had lost that little internecine battle. Since this was newsworthy, I included it in the script.

By mid-afternoon I had put words to paper, taking pains to provide some perspective on the victories the President was preparing to celebrate. With the economy bouncing back from recession, he had a favorable story to tell. However, Presidents habitually stretch their tales of progress, and Reagan was no exception. A few months earlier he had made the eagle scream extremely hard in campaign speeches. Having reported on several of those, I had some idea of what might be coming and felt that a counterpoint would be in order. After summarizing the palmy scenario he would describe that night, I said:

> Presidents invariably get blamed whenever the economy goes sour and take credit when times are good, even though they seldom deserve either full credit or all of the blame.
>
> Tonight, Mr. Reagan will benefit from this tradition. The economy is not completely healthy. . . . but inflation is under control, the recession is history, and times are a good deal better than they were when he first took office.
>
> In his speech, the President will take credit for this improvement, claiming his policies have turned the nation into nothing less than a "reborn industrial giant." And he will celebrate what he considers his achievements on a night that's made for celebrating — his 74th birthday.[2]

Those 112 words took about 30 seconds to say aloud — which meant they consumed roughly one-third of my script. The rest had to be devoted to the business about tax revision and one or two other points the President would make — the fresh news, such as it was, from the economic portion of his speech. Once that was done, we were out of time. Our 90 seconds were used up. There was no time left to mention that lower inflation was due to the efforts of the Federal Reserve, or that the reduction had come at the expense of a nasty slump. Nor was there time to say more about debt, foreign trade, the nature of the recovery, or the large number of service jobs being created and the debate over whether we were turning into a nation of hamburger servers. There were no spare seconds left for a discussion of policy options or for a comparison — which would have been favorable to the Reaganites — with prevailing economic conditions in other countries. And there certainly wasn't time to strike a balance with the President's high praise for less government by explaining how deregulation had started under Carter and had led to discommodities like weaker airlines and a debilitated financial system. On such matters Reagan by then was on his way toward becoming a modern-day Zeus, positioned above the shores of Troy. However, there wasn't room in the script for analogies either, since they too can require a bit of explanation.

The situation was frustrating from a journalistic standpoint but tailor-made for a President who was an experienced and persuasive TV pitchman. Reagan could step in front of a camera and sell almost anything, including economic policy. It sounded terrific the way he described it, until you paused to say, hey wait a minute, what's this all about? His televised performances on Capitol Hill were spellbinding. Bush was never able to match them, but Clinton has come close. His 1993 State of the Union performance was superslick in its own way, setting forth an economic program that repudiated promises made during his campaign and differed radically from those of his two Republican predecessors. Advertised as an all-out assault on the deficit, it featured old-fashioned Democratic spend-and-tax policies plus spending cuts. His program too cried out for a critical look, which began filtering through in some of the better newspaper and magazine pieces and television commentaries in the days and weeks following the speech. However, as in years past the critical look was on the feeble side in most of the TV reporting the night of the address.[3]

But that's the way it is in commercial television. Even when the nation's Commander in Chief is making what is arguably his biggest speech of the year, news reports have to be sandwiched in between ads for the Heartbeat of America and Hemorrhoids Relief. The subtleties and complexities of a story get squeezed out. Ideas become truncated, and analysis is short-changed in the rush to form judgments and offer instant wisdom. This happens all the time in TV news, and with distressing regularity in economic news, where reports are normally kept very brief to avoid boring the viewer.

They also are often scripted well before air time to enable videotape editors to dress them up with stock footage of money being printed, factories belching smoke, shoppers parading through stores or other shots illustrating economic activity. Unlike stories about riots or rocket launchings, for example — which can be told with action-filled pictures — coverage of the money world seldom lends itself to easy visualization. Thus a variety of devices are employed to enliven stories, including cartoons, colorful graphics that zoom or spin around, and fever charts with moving lines that wiggle their way across the screen.

These visuals are not altogether frivolous. They can be used to emphasize important figures and dramatize worthwhile points. Even when they fail to do that, they perform a service simply by entertaining viewers and discouraging them from switching channels. The computer is making it easy to create these visuals, and they are welcomed by network executives who live in fear that an audience will disappear unless it is constantly being amused. Their paranoia about this has intensified with the advent of the dreaded clicker, the hand-held remote control device that makes changing channels extremely easy.[4]

To give Cable News Network's tape editors time to spruce up my advancer on Reagan's fifth State of the Union address, I narrated part of my script onto an audio track in the White House press room shortly after 4 pm, about three hours before air time. This was done in a sound-proof booth equipped with a direct line to CNN's tape-editing facilities, located a few miles away in another part of Washington. The remainder of the report, known as the "stand-up close," would be delivered live during the newscast, in front of a camera on the White House lawn, where I also would be asked to respond to questions on the air.

At this stage things were going about as well as could be expected. Pictures and graphs were being matched up with my words. Meanwhile I was still calling around trying to learn more about the speech and sharing some of what I had dug up with two veteran journalists whose judgment I respected: Charles Bierbauer, Cable News Network's White House Correspondent, and Dan Schorr, an old colleague from CBS days who had become a correspondent and analyst at CNN. Both were involved in the coverage of the speech, though neither was concentrating solely on its economic content. That, for better or worse, was my job.

Shortly before 7 pm, with the wind whistling through the barren trees near the north portico, we went to work. My producer, Larry Moscow, pointed me toward a dry spot on the lawn where our camera crew was setting up its gear. The location, directly in front of the west wing, represented a further bow to the dictates of show business. It gave us a visually appealing backdrop and conveyed the impression that our information might have been relayed to us moments earlier by high-level sources located only a stone's throw away. By delivering the report live rather than taping it in advance, we enhanced this sense of immediacy.

Final preparations were underway. A tiny microphone was clipped to my tie, and another tiny gadget that looks like a hearing aid was placed in my ear enabling me to hear directions from the network's master control room in Washington as well as questions from the newscast's anchor, who was in a CNN studio in New York. There was a last minute microphone check. The camera lights were switched on, bathing us in a white glow and drawing a few curious onlookers outside the gate along Pennsylvania Avenue. Invigorated by the evening air and surrounded by small mounds of snow, we were ready for prime time.

Seven o'clock came and the newscast, *Moneyline*, led off with the taped portion of our report. Through my earpiece I could listen to my audio track, interrupted only by periodic reminders from master control that we were only so many seconds away from starting the live portion. 20 seconds . . . 10 . . . 5. I heard the Go signal and chattered away into the camera in my most earnest tone of voice. As soon as I stopped talking, the rehearsed portion of our beanfest was over. Next came the Q&A or debriefing, which is a rather peculiar ritual.

A reasonable person might conclude that it would be almost superfluous to pepper a reporter with questions at this point. Assuming he did his job properly in the first place, there shouldn't be all that much left to talk about. What's more, a journalist can be made to look a little silly if he is confronted with a stream of unanswerable questions, or if the interrogator adopts a tone of superiority and says, in effect, Now I Want To Know The Real Story. Forget the Gobbledygook and Tell Me, What Does This Really Mean to Mr. and Mrs. America?

But debriefings also have their advantages. They permit two people to relate to each other and engage in a dialogue, which is usually livelier than a monologue. Moreover, debriefings give a correspondent additional air time. This was especially welcome that night, since I had much more to say than I could squeeze into my allotted 90 seconds. The debriefing would allow me to unburden myself of some of the information I had been forced to leave out and to include contrapuntal music that I felt should be played alongside the President's cantata. In keeping with established practice, I fed a few questions in advance to the anchor, Lou Dobbs. While this is always wise when dealing with newscasters who do not know the difference between a Treasury Bill and Gunga Din, in Dobbs' case it wasn't really necessary; he too had studied economics in college and was perfectly capable of posing good questions without any help. However, by prompting him with a few of my own I felt I might be able to steer our conversation toward some points that needed to be made.

Having finished my on-camera narration, I stood there on that chilly evening waiting for the first question. Only it never came. No question. No Dobbs. No commands from master control. No sounds of any kind. Only an awkward silence. Instinctively I fiddled with my earpiece, and that became a signal to those who were masterminding our electronic adventure that the anchor's words were not getting through. The control room responded by quickly switching away from the White House — and presto, we were off the air.

Larry Moscow tried to get us back on in a hurry. Using a portable telephone, he called master control and asked what had gone wrong and how fast it could be fixed. When the technicians on the other end of the line flunked this impromptu quiz, he asked to be patched through to CNN in New York, where he raised similar questions in an urgent tone but again failed to get satisfactory answers. Moscow is an experienced and persistent troubleshooter, the sort of unheralded foot soldier who plugs away and usually succeeds; but it quickly became clear that this time he had met his match. As the seconds went by, and then the minutes, hope faded for a return to the air. The camera crew eventually turned off the lights and the lawn went dark. I surrendered my microphone along with the ear-piece — and we were out of business.

The post-mortem that invariably follows a mishap such as this got underway the next morning. Messages flew back and forth between Washington and New York as the network's technical experts sought to identify the cause and escape direct blame. After participating in a few phone conversations and reviewing several explanations, Moscow approached me at the water cooler shortly before lunch, ready to report the final verdict.

"Somebody," he said, "threw the wrong switch."

NOTES

1. With the press once again reporting on the Democrats' proposals for more affirmative government, Reaganomics is starting to seem like a distant memory; but it wasn't that long ago, 1987, when, in a speech to members of the World Bank, Reagan declared that his policies had helped trigger a "revolution in economic thinking" and produced a

growing feeling that private markets can do more to solve economic problems. Reporting on his remarks, Leonard Silk wrote in *The New York Times* on September 10: "Mr. Reagan contended that even economists had learned something from his record. 'You know,' he quipped, 'it is said that an economist is the only professional who sees something working in practice and then seriously wonders if it works in theory.' Then, as though to lighten his attack, he added, 'I can say that because my degree was in economics.'"

2. That evening the three major broadcast networks also carried advance reports on the State of The Union address. They emphasized its economic aspects but also touched on foreign policy and other issues, which was the way CNN handled the story on other newscasts.

ABC led with an advancer that was a minute and forty-five seconds long and concluded with an on-camera close by Sam Donaldson, who said: "So the President goes up to Capitol Hill tonight to lay out his vision of a second American revolution. But if one begins to hear the stirring sound of fife and drum in the background, it's well to remember that there are plenty of modern day redcoats waiting in ambush."

CBS and NBC aired their advancers following lead stories about a controversy stirred up by David Stockman, who had called for cuts in Federal assistance to veterans and farmers. The CBS report by Bill Plante ran one minute; the NBC story by Andrea Mitchell was 90 seconds long and aired after the first commercial break.

3. An example of the kind of specific critical assessment that was hard to find on network coverage the night of the Clinton's speech but began appearing in the printed press later was a piece by syndicated columnist David S. Broder on February 24, 1993. He wrote that some $54 billion of Clinton's claimed spending reductions were "actually increases in taxes or fees." Broder also scoffed at the idea that Clinton's backtracking on a promise to cut taxes for the middle-class was justified by the "unexpected" $346 billion Federal budget deficit he inherited. The columnist suggested that Clinton knew all along the shortfall could be that large and noted that in July 1992 he had "told *Business Week* that the deficit would approach $400 billion." (In the July 6 issue of *BW*, Clinton was quoted as saying, "When I began the campaign, the projected deficit was $250 billion. Now, it's up to $400 billion.")

4. This device can be especially detrimental to news coverage of a topic such as economics, which requires explanations that aren't always entertaining, and it has had an influence on TV programming in gen-

eral. In an interview in *USA Today*, Don Hewitt of CBS told Larry King: "The clicker. That damn little thing millions of people hold in their hands and punch with sheer delight. If they don't like what they see, they can make a decision to hit the clicker in a matter of mini-seconds. And if you were on the screen, now you are gone. You better be constantly interesting." ABC's Ted Koppel has said in the *Los Angeles Times*: "When you are in competition for a large, live audience, it's who can make it the fastest, the most enjoyable that counts. We keep speeding it up, throwing out images faster and faster to get viewers and hold them. We're desperately afraid of losing the audience."

$

11 First Rattle

It would be easy to write off the episode on the White House lawn that evening as merely another example of electronic journalism short-circuiting itself. As is often the case in television, we were preoccupied with the visual. The same words could have been spoken just as easily into a camera in one of the network's studios, where fewer things tend to go wrong. In the finest showbiz tradition, we were stretching ourselves and taking risks to entertain our audience — but only small risks. The vast majority of the time, performances such as this come off smoothly. The equipment works; the brightly-lit White House provides a splendid backdrop; and viewers at home feel they are getting the latest inside dope. This particular time, misfortune struck and our final act was a flop. The incident seems almost metaphoric and in some ways an apt denouement, but there is a little more to it than that. From start to woeful finish, the saga of our ill-starred 90-second advancer illustrates several of the exigencies surrounding TV coverage of business and economic news. And the fact that we were doing the story at all, however imperfectly, is indicative of the effort the medium has been making over the past decade or so to try to pay more attention to the money world.

This effort is worth a closer look for a couple of reasons. One of them is that most people get most of their news about money matters from television. That may seem anomalous to those of us who grew up reading newspapers, but experts who have conducted polls and studies swear it's true and there is no longer any cause to doubt them.[1] Today, tens of millions of Americans rely on the glitter box for information that influences their attitudes toward business, their economic values and their ideas about borrowing, saving and investing. Television thus finds itself with an obligation to cover these topics and an opportunity to strengthen its news programming if it can do so in ways that are credible and appealing. This poses a challenge with which the medium is still grappling.

There is another consideration that enters in, and, depending on your turn of mind, another anomaly as well. In the age of electronic journalism, officials often pay more notice to views expressed on TV than to those set forth in print. This applies to the economy as well as to other spheres like politics and foreign affairs. It means that someone striking a pose in front of the west wing and babbling into a microphone stands a better chance of being heard on policy issues than a newspaper reporter or magazine writer who labors mightily and brings forth a carefully crafted article on the same topic. Social critics grieve over this condition, which has led to a decline in the quality of public discourse, and one can sympathize with their lamentations.[2] My own superannuated reference system is such that it was an eye-opener to discover that now and then I could trigger a much stronger reaction in the corridors of power with brief reports on the air than I had with more elaborate stories written for publications like *Fortune* or *Time*. This is a peculiarity of the medium that evidences itself in the inordinate amount of notice our society pays to nearly all who appear on TV.

Primarily, of course, television reflects an agenda set by others. It reinforces a public consensus while influencing policy at the margin. In economics, its basic role is to amplify ideas and events, and the degree to which it has begun recognizing that it has a role represents a small breakthrough. For many years, it should be remembered, television largely ignored the money world, and it wasn't until the 1960s, when network TV news operations were more than a decade old, that attempts were made to rectify the situation.

One of those who tried to do something about it back then was Louis Rukeyser, now the host of *Wall Street Week*. He had switched from a newspaper job to ABC and in 1968 became its economics correspondent. Rukeyser appeared on the evening news and did a number of special reports, including "The Great Dollar Robbery: Can We Arrest Inflation?" His contributions were of a high caliber, when he could get them on the air. Years afterwards he told an interviewer he felt his efforts were hampered by network supremos who thought the subject of economics was "too dull and too complex for viewers used to sitcoms and shoot-'em-ups."[3]

For several years before Rukeyser's tour of duty at ABC, I was under contract in the CBS organization, having gone there in 1962 from the *New York Herald Tribune*, where I had been a financial reporter. At CBS, the situation wasn't much different. As an independent contractor, I was called on to contribute several times a week to network radio, less frequently to television. Usually it took a plunging stock market or some other momentous happening before the producers of the *CBS Evening News*, anchored by Walter Cronkite, would invite me to go on the air with a brief report summarizing what had happened. Now and then the morning newscast, anchored in those days by Mike Wallace, would decide to do a business or financial story, usually in the form of a feature. On one occasion, for example, I flew around the country for them preparing a report on investment clubs. It ran nearly four minutes, much longer than the average report, and showed club members in several cities gathered in living rooms discussing stocks. The piece gave the viewer a look at the process of reaching a consensus about which ones to buy and sell.

Although seemingly innocuous, such reports were among the first of their kind on television, and we found ourselves in uncharted territory, trying to figure out the rules and establish guidelines as we went along. Securities and Exchange Commission officials were less than thrilled at the idea of my discussing specific stocks on the air. It is done routinely now, but at the time there wasn't much precedent for it. Over lunch one day in Washington during the early '60s, SEC General Counsel Philip Loomis explained that the nervousness stemmed mainly from an earlier experience with Walter Winchell, the columnist and radio broadcaster. It seems that Winchell had taken to the airwaves and spoken kindly about a stock that subsequently rose in price, thereby benefiting insiders who allegedly had loaded up on shares in advance. Sylvia Porter had exposed the caper in print, and Loomis was clearly rankled by the incident.[4] "Just don't pull a Winchell," he cautioned me over lunch, "that's one thing we'd be concerned about." With that admonition firmly in mind, I returned to New York and continued to mention individual issues on the air whenever it seemed newsworthy, taking care all the while never to recommend or "pull a Winchell."

While the network made occasional use of my reports, its flagship station in New York was a steadier customer. WCBS-TV dispatched me frequently to photogenic locations such as the balcony of the New York Stock Exchange for a minute or two of on-camera chatter against a backdrop of hub-bub on the trading floor. Between assignments for the station and the network, I teamed up with camera crews to do more than 200 reports from the New York and American stock exchanges between 1962 and 1968. I cite this as evidence that a certain amount of money news was going out over the air in those days. Much of it played heavily to the viewer's presumed need to know about the ups and downs of stock prices. It included brief interviews with some of the more excitable Wall Street hagglers, usually the ones who could be counted on to give snappy, plausible explanations for what was happening in the market.

At times it seemed as if what we were doing was the equivalent of setting up a camera alongside a gaming table and reporting on the winners and losers. Among the winners one could occasionally spot a few buckoes who were adept at spreading rumors and jumping in and out of stocks at propitious moments. They were quick, smart and ruthless and they played with serious money. The losers more often than not included those who listened to the rumors, bought when they should have been selling and sold when they should have been buying. Many of them never should have been playing in the first place, at least not on a day-to-day basis. The longer time periods that made sense for them — and which still make sense for most people — unfortunately do not make for exciting television. So in those years we bowed to the exigencies and covered the day-to-day or week-to-week swings, the short-term action in the casino, squeezing in a few words about more profound matters whenever possible.

All pioneering efforts have to start somewhere, however. This one had part of its origins on the balcony of the stock exchange, and it might have led to more substantial results except that one of its stronger supporters, Fred Friendly, left CBS abruptly at a time when we were starting to explore ways of expanding beyond Wall Street and doing more reporting on the economy for the network. Friendly, who was president of the network news operation, got into a flap with his superiors over their refusal to air live coverage of a Congressional hearing on the Vietnam War. The incident has since been written about at length; it involved a decision to show a rerun of *I Love Lucy* instead of the testimony of George Kennan before the Senate Foreign Relations Committee in February 1966.[5] As it happened, I had just returned from Saigon, having worked on some special projects there, including a report on the Vietnamese economy for the *CBS Evening News*. That report, which described how Vietnam's country was being ravaged by inflation and economic mismanagement, drew measured praise from Friendly, and the prospects for doing more and better stories were improving, or so it seemed. However, by the time I unpacked my suitcases, finished some writing I had started in Asia and turned my attention back to television and radio, one of the leading advocates of economics coverage within the CBS hierarchy had quit.

In the years that followed, I did fewer rather than more stories for the network, while the flagship station continued to make regular use of my services. Its evening newscast, anchored in those days by Robert Trout (and later by Jim Jensen and Reid Collins), called on me several times a week for reports. The majority of them were uncontroversial as well as brief, but some were discordant, and these did not always thrill the oligarchy at corporate headquarters on Sixth Avenue, in the building known as Black Rock. In principle the overlords there favored the idea of expanding news coverage to include the money world. However, they were seldom enthusiastic about having their peers — many of whom were lions in that world — treated with anything but the highest respect.

On one occasion, I aired reports on both WCBS-TV and the network citing the failure of Johnson Administration policymakers to come clean with the public about the inflationary dangers of their initial guns-and-butter program, which involved spending heavily on the war and on domestic programs without raising taxes to pay the bills. The reports contained accusations of obfuscation and were, without a doubt, censorious. And, as I learned later, they were not a big hit with all members of the oligarchy, one or two of whom were known to be on a first-name basis with LBJ's inner circle. Another time, William Paley, the network's paterfamilias, passed along word that he was unhappy with a story I did on Third World indebtedness and the policies of the World Bank's soft loan affiliate, the International Development Association (IDA). The story raised the possibility that the debts

121

of many developing countries were building toward dangerous levels, and that overly generous lending practices were contributing to the problem. Paley, who was no stranger to the banking fraternity or IDA, did not see it that way, and he instructed one of his lieutenants to tell me as much.[6]

Fortunately, such impediments to covering the money world were not a common occurrence. Paley's meddling in the nitty-gritty of my banking report did not reflect good judgment on his part, but the vast majority of the time there were no intrusions. On the whole, the overlords at Black Rock and the princes and dukes who ran WCBS-TV deserve credit for their willingness to let me plumb new territory with some of my early reporting. Though by no means extensive, it represented a first rattle out of the box. I was doing graduate study in economics and applying what I was learning to my work. My on-the-job training included lessons from Trout on how to read a script and tie a tie for television, along with games of tic-tac-toe with Frank Gifford as we waited in the wings to do our respective reports, sports and business, on the evening news. Frank's familiarity with the diagramming of Xs and Os during football season served him well in those games, which were played on nights when it was decided I should skip the trip to the stock exchange and perform live in the CBS studios on West 57th Street.

All in all, it was a pleasant interlude and a period of experimentation with mixed results. Progress was generally fitful, and the coverage was toddling. It would finally start growing out of that stage, but not until several years later.

NOTES

1. The first study on this subject that caught my attention was a Roper survey of 2,000 adults in 1982 which found that 60% rely on TV news as their prime source of "information about business." Other studies since then have pointed to similar conclusions, and this dependency has been cited frequently in the literature of media criticism. In *Ninety Seconds To Tell It All* (Homewood, Illinois: Dow Jones-Irwin, 1981), A. Kent MacDougall observed that "polls show that most Americans get most of their news, including business news, from television, and that is where the trouble lies." Other statistics relevant to this trend include a steady decline in the number of newspaper subscriptions per household.

2. A good example of the grieving appears in Neil Postman's *Amusing Ourselves To Death* (New York: Viking, 1985). Postman called his book "an inquiry into and a lamentation about the most significant American cultural fact of the second half of the twentieth century: the decline of the Age of Typography and the ascendancy of the Age of Television." He wrote that "as the influence of print wanes, the content of politics, religion, education and anything else that comprises public business must change and be recast in terms that are most suitable to television."

3. From an interview in *Playboy*, April 1987. Rukeyser also reflected on his days at ABC in *What's Ahead for the Economy?* (New York: Touchstone/Simon & Schuster, 1983). In that book he said of TV journalism, "economic coverage remains the number one failing of our profession."

4. The episode centered around a tip that a company called Pantapec Oil would be a good investment. After Winchell mentioned it on the air, Pantepec stock rose in heavy trading, prompting government investigations and a series of probing articles by Porter, who went on to scrutinize other stocks that had been mentioned on his broadcasts.

5. Fred Friendly's own account of the incident appears in his book, *Due To Circumstances Beyond Our Control* (New York: Random House, 1967). Friendly wrote: "It was not a matter of deciding between two broadcasts, but a choice between interrupting the morning run of the profit machine — whose only admitted function was to purvey six one-minute commercials every half-hour, all of which had been viewed hundreds of times before — or electing to make the audience privy to an event of overriding national importance . . ."

6. The lieutenant was Robert Wood, whose job was to oversee the CBS owned and operated stations, including WCBS-TV. He told me that Paley felt my report bordered on the irresponsible. Many years later, after Wood had retired, we ran into each other in California and the subject came up again. By then, lax lending practices and the debt burden of developing countries had become major issues, and Wood acknowledged that in hindsight top management might have overreacted at the time. However, he still felt it had been unwise for me to draw my sword on a topic where the sensitivities at Black Rock ran high. My response was that, unwise or not, it wasn't in my nature to confine myself to easy targets.

$

12   *Proliferation and Credibility*

Money news began blossoming on television following the success of *Wall Street Week*, which built a loyal audience on PBS starting in the 1970s. At the major networks, more journalists with experience in this area were brought in to do on-the-air reporting. After Rukeyser left ABC to devote more time to his new weekly show, in 1974 ABC hired as its economics correspondent Dan Cordtz, who had written for *The Wall Street Journal* and *Fortune*. Later, ABC brought in Gordon Williams from *Business Week* along with Steve Aug, who had been business editor at the *Washington Star*. Other seasoned pros who were put to work during that period include Ray Brady (CBS), former editor of *Dun's Review*, and Mike Jensen (NBC), who had plied his trade as a business reporter at *The New York Times*. Meantime, NBC's early morning newscast began offering regular analysis of business and financial topics by Alan Abelson of *Barron's*.[1]

The decade of the 80's saw the start-up of a number of shows devoted solely to money news, including *Nightly Business Report* and *Adam Smith's Money World* on PBS, *Business World* on ABC, *This Morning's Business* on CBS, *Nation's Business Today* on ESPN and *The Wall Street Journal Report*, an independently produced program. During this time Financial News Network began providing continuous coverage of the markets from dawn to dusk. Later, its TV operations were merged with another '80s start-up, the Consumer News and Business Channel (CNBC), a subsidiary of NBC. Meanwhile, Cable News Network launched *Business Morning*, *Business Day*, *Inside Business*, *Your Money*, *Pinnacle* and *Moneyweek* along with *Moneyline*.

Several other endeavors started in the '80s and failed, including *Business Times* on ESPN, *Business Day* on the Disney Channel, and *Strictly Business*, which aired on several NBC stations.[2] Even after allowing for the casualties, however, the decade was still a generative one, not only at the networks but also at local stations around the country. KDKA-TV in Pittsburgh, WTVJ-TV in Miami and WDVM-TV in Washington, D.C. were among those that began reporting business news regularly. Most of this expanded coverage, on the networks and local stations, remains on the air, and it has been augmented in the '90s by a few other new shows and performers. To be sure, not all of it airs at convenient times. Some of it competes with old movies or other pre-dawn fare, especially in the western time zones. Where I live in California, for example, weekdays at 3:30 a.m. *Nation's Business Today* and *Business Morning* for many years have gone head to head with *Faith 20* and *Zoobilee Zoo*.

Radio also has been doing more with money news, aiming chiefly at those who watch comparatively little television and at commuters tuning in during drive time. There is evidence of this on the all-news stations, on syndicated talk shows and on public radio programs like *All Things Considered* and *Morning Edition*. American Public Radio pioneered two programs in the '80s devoted solely to the money world: *Sound Money* and *Business Update*. *Update*, prepared by CBS News, was succeeded by *Marketplace*, an independently produced half-hour daily show that was anchored at the outset by Michael Creedman, a writer who had penned articles for *Money* and other financial periodicals. FNN also moved into the field of radio along about this time, supplying summaries of business news to stations in several metropolitan markets. In a few places, all-financial news stations have started up. They are ambitious undertakings whose success is by no means guaranteed. One has to expect that there may be more casualties like KDAY-AM in Los Angeles, which found it couldn't make it with an all-financial format and became a Korean talk-radio station.

On both radio and television, the more consequential advances have come in those areas where programming can be targeted at smaller audiences. This contrasts with the approach long favored by the major networks, where, especially in television, the emphasis has been on shows that can earn big ratings, thereby impressing the makers of mass-merchandised products such as toothpaste and beer. It's no accident that much of the better reporting appears on PBS, which is less constrained by the ratings game, and to some extent on cable, where technology and lower costs have made it feasible to do more with specialized shows. In a 1992 Harris survey, PBS received top marks for its business coverage from 30% of all executives who were polled and 45% of all journalists. Interestingly, these were the highest percentages in the survey, which suggests that many of those polled were not overly thrilled by what they saw, not even by some of the better coverage. CNN garnered top marks for its business reporting from only 27% of the executives and 31% of the journalists, while CNBC fared even worse, receiving them from just 4% of the executives and 12% of the journalists.[3]

The term "better coverage" as used here deserves elaboration — it is reporting that goes beyond a recital of the latest numbers and headlines and includes worthwhile analysis and comment. Unfortunately, a fair amount of what airs from day to day on TV does not measure up to this definition. Instead, it is spartan, superficial and innocuous, an incantation of financial froth, rattled off by smartly coiffured ladies and gentlemen who don't always inspire confidence that they know what they're talking about.

This type of coverage comes afflicted with several maladies indigenous to the medium. By now the litany may be starting to sound familiar. It includes bewitchment with conflict at the expense of understanding and with personalities at the expense of issues, as well as self-aggrandizement and an overemphasis on exclusive interviews that lend themselves to hype and are in vogue as a measure of success in bigtime TV journalism. A. Kent MacDougall, who has written disparagingly of the networks' attempts to report on the money world, puts his finger on two other familiar maladies when he points to stories that are "condensed to the point of incomprehensibility" and others that are "cluttered with show-and-tell gimmicks designed to compensate for the fact that what a viewer hears registers less readily than what he sees."[4]

Even among the more accomplished ringmasters of the the televison carnival, economic news is often a hole in the coat. We get a hint of this from an anecdote relayed to us by economist Barry Bosworth. When he was in the Carter Administration, Bosworth was sent forth by the White House to make TV appearances and answer questions about Carter's policies, especially in the area of inflation, which was a hot issue at the time. As he recalls the incident, during a commercial break on a show hosted by Barbara Walters, after reviewing a list of questions that had been prepared for her interview with Bosworth, Walters declared, "I don't understand these questions." To which one of the show's producers replied, "You don't have to understand them. Just ask them. He'll explain them."

That, of course, is not the way it's supposed to work. Journalists, including hosts of interview shows, are expected to know their subject matter well enough to understand the questions, ask the right ones and follow up if necessary. During her career Walters has demonstrated that she has those skills and has used them in interviews on numerous topics. Economics just doesn't happen to be one of them, or it wasn't in this case. And that isn't particularly unusual among anchors and talk show hosts. Economics is a subject with which they often appear uncomfortable. With a few exceptions such as Bernie Shaw at CNN and Jim Lehrer on PBS, it's a weak spot where the mystique and the castor oil image have managed to linger on. Evidence of this also can be found on business shows where anchors who should know better wing their way through live interviews now and then without adequate preparation, making unenlightened inquiries and fishing for controversy rather than engaging in thoughtful discussion.

One other invidious malady that belongs in our litany is a propensity for gloom and doom when the reporting gets beyond the headlines and numbers. George Bush complained about this during the 1992 presidential campaign, and other political and business leaders have voiced displeasure about it in the past. It has been the object of study for some time. In a survey of news aired by CBS, NBC and ABC over a five-year period, Ted Smith III found that those three networks "consistently emphasized economic problems and de-emphasized or omitted economic successes." His survey found that "stories reporting economic losses or failures outnumbered stories reporting economic gains" by a wide margin. He concluded that during much of this time it was "difficult or impossible for even the most regular and attentive viewer to form an accurate perception of how the American economy was performing." Smith's study quoted NBC's Irving Levine as having told an interviewer: "My reports on Reagan's economic program focused on their deficiencies and contradictions . . . For producers and reporters, bad news is good news."[5]

This inclination toward the negative is sometimes construed as a bias toward liberalism. Bush's supporters saw it that way. They bewailed the fact that the networks played up the economy's deficiencies until right after the votes were counted, when they began reporting that the statistics were starting to look better. The Smith study, which covered an earlier period and dealt with the media in general, found that "liberal/Democratic" views dominated the reporting but left open the question of whether this reflected bias in the selection of stories or the course of political developments or both. The Harris survey also looked into the liberalism issue and found that 78% of all executives polled felt too many reporters let their leftist political views color their reporting, and only 27% said business journalism is "fair, balanced and accurate." Not surprisingly, among journalists who were polled a smaller share (22%) acknowledged that liberal views influence the reporting, while a huge majority (84%) held that business journalism is "fair, balanced and accurate."[6]

Another study, coordinated by Holmes Brown of the Institute of Applied Economics, examined the nightly newscasts of the major networks in 1983, a year not unlike 1992 when the economy was recovering from recession and the Republicans were in office. His study found a readiness to accompany news of a decline in the monthly unemployment rate with a warning that pockets of joblessness still exist, followed by a feature reinforcing that point. According to Brown, "it was typically a depressing feature on some forlorn guy in Ohio who was about to commit suicide because he couldn't find work. By the time viewers got through watching it they forgot all about the fact that the unemployment rate went down instead of up." This type of reporting may or may not prove the existence of a strong bias, but it certainly represents poor editorial judgment and probably a lack of understanding of economics as well. Much the same can be said for the other examples citied here.

Still another item that belongs on our list is a willingness to doctor the truth for the sake of exciting pictures. This was exemplified by NBC's use of remote-controlled incendiary devices to ensure that a fire would erupt in a staged test crash of a General Motors pick-up truck on one of the network's news programs. It was an especially flagrant flirtation with believability. NBC later apologized for it. However, it's the sort of thing that's bound to happen in a medium where there is constant pressure to add pizazz and news-related decisions are being made by people with a show business orientation.[7]

The list goes on. Another shortcoming that belongs on it is the interview or report which serves little purpose other than to hawk stocks or newsletters. The absolute worst that television has ever offered in this realm was some of the early programming on Financial News Network featuring commercials packaged to look and sound like news. These "infomercials" or "advertorials" damaged FNN's believability during its formative years, when it relied on them to help generate cash. Its authenticity as a news network was impaired further by the appearance on the air of what I would judge to have been miscast young Hollywood hopefuls trying their best to sound informed as they articulated the latest figures on pork belly futures and the movements of the yen. The end product was so inexpert that it probably should have carried some kind of warning label on the screen, like the "Death of Equities" cover story mentioned in chapter 2. In time, the "advertorials" were downplayed; and the arrival of better informed reporters such as Robert Metz, who had covered finance for *The New York Times*, served to elevate FNN's newscasting by a notch or two. However, by then the damage had been done, and FNN's TV operation proved in the end to be a lame critter that was finally relieved of its misery through the merger with CNBC.[8]

One final addition to the litany is a practice that also weakens credibility and can add to the medium's woes if left unchecked: moonlighting by financial journalists in testimonial ads or promotions touting services or institutions that the journalist is supposed to be monitoring with a critical eye. This practice isn't new; it has precedents in newspaper and magazine reporting that date back many decades, and it has spilled over into television. An example of the practice was the appearance by CNN's Lou Dobbs in promotional videos for stock brokerage firms and the Philadelphia Stock Exchange in the early '90s.[9] Like the "infomercials," the gloomy features on suicidal job seekers and the other errata mentioned here, participation in such promotions reflects an obvious lack of good sense.

Drawing up indictments against TV news is an easy pastime, of course, especially in this domain, which has long been characterized by trial, error and trumpery. Back in the days when CBS thought it could boost ratings by having ex-Miss America Phyllis George co-anchor its morning newscast, Bill Moyers wrote that the network's once hallowed news operation had succumbed to the encroachment of entertainment values to a point where "stories about tax policy had to compete with stories about three-legged sheep, and the three-legged sheep won." Anyone who was around then can sense that an increase in the quantity of money news has been accompanied, at CBS and elsewhere, by some improvement in quality, spotty as it may be. One is hesitant to go much further than that, however. As Marshall Loeb, a frequent broadcaster on radio, has observed: "The situation is remindful of a comment that's often made about the economy in some Third World countries. It's getting better, they'll say, definitely better. Now, why for once can't it just be good?"

A closer look at one of the more noble attempts to make it good may provide a few clues. It took place over a period of several years at ABC, which set out early on to be the front runner in economic news. Its determination to improve led to positive results in the '70s and early '80s, with Dan Cordtz taking to the airwaves and winning awards for his work. The addition of Williams and Aug further strengthened ABC's competitive edge in this area, and the whole effort progressed to a point where all three reporters were getting on television or radio regularly, with Cordtz doing a stint on TV every evening. His summary of the day's events was brief but authentic.

Alas, in commercial television that type of performance, steady but glitzless, isn't always fully appreciated by those who decide what the viewer gets to see. Meanwhile, the inner frenzy that is innate at all networks keeps signaling for change. Thus the formats of newscasts are revamped periodically to create the impression that something new and exciting is happening. The sets in the studios are altered from time to time, along with the lighting and sometimes the wardrobes and hairdos of the on-the-air performers. Correspondents are showcased for a while and then bedwarfed, while the anchors who read the news gain and lose favor like courtesans. There is seldom much rhyme or reason for any of this. But it goes on all the time, at local stations and at the networks. One day ABC's nightly business summary disappeared from the screen. Subsequently, so did Cordtz. His reports began appearing less and less often. Eventually he was bypassed as anchor for a new Sunday show, *Business World*, in favor of Sander Vanocur, a political journalist. For Cordtz, this was the nethermost level, just as the daily summary had been the apex. Afterwards he reflected on the course of events at ABC:

"The main reason we had a reputation for being a leader

in business news is that for a while we were doing some very good stuff. This established a perception in the viewing public's mind about who was on top, and that perception lingered on. But times change, and you have to ask yourself, how serious is any organization that starts a business show and puts it in the hands of people who know comparatively little about the subject?

"To top it off, ABC scheduled a press conference to promote its new show and at the last minute I got a call telling me I should be on hand, presumably to lend credibility to the project. So there I was, standing on the sidelines at their press conference, playing shill for people who couldn't possibly understand exactly what they were about to put on the air.

"I was ticked off, of course. But the fact is, that kind of thing goes on all the time in television. One reason is that those who run network news operations are, almost without exception, executive producers or producers who have the notion that they know how to do any kind of show all by themselves. That may work okay if the subject matter is very general, but it doesn't work well when you get into an area like business, where substance really counts."

More than a year after the Sunday show episode, which occurred in 1986, Cordtz bade farewell to ABC and returned to magazine journalism as chief correspondent (and later managing editor) at *Financial World*.[10] In fairness to those who were left behind to soldier on, it should be added that *Business World* survived for quite a while. It continued to benefit from the contributions of Williams and from the work of Aug, who eventually became its anchor; and it lasted until the Spring of 1993, when ABC took it off the air.

Cordtz' departure from the network deprived that show of a solid performer and reduced ABC's margin of superiority over its main rivals in terms of daily business coverage. On their evening newscasts, all three broadcast networks provide basically a headline service plus sparse, workmanlike reports on a limited number of money-related stories and an occasional short interview or debriefing, or a feature that is often given a consumer angle to maximize its appeal. To be sure, this represents an advancement from the days of tic-tac-toe and the three-legged sheep. However, calm, leisurely analysis and commentary on the major economic issues of the day clearly remain at a premium.

NOTES

1. NBC's first move in the direction of expanded coverage was to assign economic stories in the early 1970s to Irving Levine, who had been reporting political and other news. The network's flagship station, WNBC-TV, made a pioneering move in the same direction a decade earlier when it hired Warren Berry, a financial writer at the *Herald Tribune*, to cover business and the markets during the 1962 New York newspaper strike.

2. James Crimmins, former chairman of *Business Times*, which failed in 1985 after an impressive start, later told an interviewer that he believes one of the obstacles to success in television business news programming is that executives and managers — a key part of the audience advertisers are hoping to reach — are "very light TV watchers." Crimmins added that televised business reporting generally suffers from a shortage of "subtlety and analysis."

3. This study, by Louis Harris and Associates for John Hancock Financial Services, covered 125 executives and 125 journalists.

4. *Ninety Seconds to Tell It All* (see notes to chapter 11). This book deals mainly with corporate news and grew out of a series of articles written for the *Los Angeles Times*.

5. From *The Vanishing Economy: Television Coverage of Economic Affairs 1982–87* (Washington, D.C.: The Media Institute, 1988). Ted Smith III examined stories that appeared on the three networks between 1982 to 1987, a period when the economy was on the upswing. The quotes attributed by Smith to Levine are from an interview with Dinesh D'Souza for a 1986 article in *Policy Review*.

6. On two key points a majority of the executives and journalists polled by Harris were in agreement: 92% of the executives (and 72% of the journalists) expressed concern about the problem of reporters lacking familiarity with the industries they cover; and 76% of the executives (98% of the journalists) said business journalism has improved over the past quarter-century.

7. The General Motors test-crash story aired on *Dateline: NBC* in November 1992. After GM exposed the shabby way the piece had been handled, the network's apology was expressed on the air by the show's anchors, Jane Pauley and Stone Phillips, in February 1993.

8. Following a bidding war with Dow Jones & Co. and Group W Satellite Communications, FNN (which had more than 30 million subscribers) was acquired in 1991 for $154 million. While CNBC's programming is an improvement over FNN, it includes an odd assortment of non-business shows and emphasizes the recitation of numbers plus some useful economic analysis, chiefly by William Wolman and William Seidman. CNBC was run for a while by Albert Barber, a GE financial executive with experience in the railroad car business who was put in charge of the news network and thereafter became known among some employes as "Boxcar Al."

9. *The Washington Post* reported on July 29, 1992, that Dobbs was reprimanded by CNN President Tom Johnson for making the promotional videotapes and agreed to return more than $15,000 in fees he received for doing them. The story of his tape-making activities broke in *The Wall Street Journal* four days earlier; the *Journal* story noted that other financial journalists had done similar work in the past.

10. A few years before he left ABC, Cordtz jousted with his friend Holmes Brown over the 1983 study pointing to a negative bias in network coverage of economics. The two traded gentlemenly punches on the op-ed page of *The Wall Street Journal* and took part in a conference on the issue sponsored by the U.S. Chamber of Commerce.

$

13 Tracing the Lineage

When he was chief economist for the U.S. Chamber of Commerce a few years ago, Richard Rahn found himself in Ardmore, Oklahoma, participating in a panel discussion on the subject of economic growth. "It was a good lively session," he recalls, "but of course you always worry about how much is getting through to the audience and the journalists who are there." Rahn articulates his views in understandable language, and if he feels he has to worry, that isn't a good sign. In this instance his concern was not misplaced. After the panel discussion ended, a local TV reporter came up to him and asked, "Tell me, Dr. Rahn, do you think we need a war to keep the economy growing?"

"That was very discouraging," Rahn said later. "The reporter, who was in her early 20s, seemed to have the idea that without a war the only way to keep people employed in peacetime is to build tanks by the thousands and push them into the sea. This was her vision of how the economy worked, and she brought that vision to the story she was covering. She simply didn't know what she was talking about."

Rahn's experience in Oklahoma is a severe example of an unfamiliarity with economics that's not uncommon among television journalists. There are any number of them who approach their assignments with quaint ideas about what makes the economy work, and others who seem to have no particular ideas at all, quaint or otherwise. They mostly draw a blank, and when their lack of familiarity with the subject is matched by a lack of reportorial experience, that is a very bad combination.

Those who do a credible job in this area, by contrast, tend to be seasoned reporters with deep roots in newspaper or magazine journalism. The experience they gain there, wrestling with a wide range of complex stories year after year, proves invaluable when it comes to making the quick judgments that have to be made in television. Unlike, say, weather forecasting, where one can step before the camera and be wrong or sound a little foolish and get away with it, in reporting on the money world there isn't much margin for error. A reporter can't afford to ask too many irrelevant questions, misinterpret the facts, draw the wrong conclusions or convey the wrong message. Viewers can easily be misled, alarmed unnecessarily or lulled into a false sense of security. A lengthy tour of duty in print journalism doesn't guarantee that these things won't happen, but it can cut down on the more egregious errors and improve one's chances of being able to project the right tone and make sensible comments on the air. Especially on live television, there is

139

no way to fake it. Either you know your stuff or you don't.

Before citing examples of veteran print journalists who do know their stuff and who have done commendable work on TV, we might remind ourselves that television is a fluid business. By the time you read this, any of the names mentioned here may have disappeared from the screen for one reason or another, following in the path of Dan Cordtz, whose departure from ABC was noted earlier. Or one or more of the programs may have died or been altered beyond recognition. These things happen regularly and are the nature of the errant one-eyed monster. With that caveat, we can proceed with a few names.

The first one is George J. W. (Jerry) Goodman, host and chief architect of *Adam Smith's Money World*, which is broadcast in the former Soviet Union as well as in the U.S. Goodman manages to inform and entertain without oversimplifying. He reports on the markets, companies and the economy, concentrating on one topic each week. A typical show, on specialty retailing, toured a Banana Republic store in California and introduced viewers to the founders of that company as well as to the creators of Esprit and another innovative specialty firm in Italy. Extensive travel was required to do the interviews and gather videotaped footage of the three apparel-manufacturing operations. The program, which aired in 1987, was structured in a way that appealed to different groups of viewers, including investors, retailers, aspiring entrepreneurs and consumers who frequent apparel shops.

Another typical *Adam Smith* show took viewers behind the scenes of the multibillion-dollar country music business in Nashville. In this episode, which aired in 1991, Goodman interviewed record industry watchers along with moguls and aspiring singers. He explored the subject of merchandising the music of Barbara Mandrell, who explained how she packages her songs for sale. The program itself was packaged to hold the attention of those who are curious about what makes a business tick as well as music lovers and would-be songwriters who dream of getting rich with a hit tune about drinking or cheating. As the show's host explained to his audience, those two themes are among the more reliable moneymakers in country music.

Adam Smith's Money World also tackles weightier matters such as monetary policy and taxation. Whatever the topic, Goodman's message is always conveyed in a dour, low-key manner. He isn't silver-tongued and deep-voiced like game show hosts or the anchors on Action News, but he brings to television a powerful background that translates into well above average credibility.

Goodman's first book penned under the "Adam Smith" nom de plume was *The Money Game*, a best seller about investing published in 1966. He has managed investments on Wall Street, written for *Barrons*, *Fortune*, *Time* and *Esquire*, and served on the editorial board of *The New York Times*. Goodman was one of the founders of *New York* magazine, where he observed innovative reporting and writing techniques and adapted them to financial news. His first *New York* article — "The Day They Red-Dogged Motorola" — was an engaging account of a sudden shift in mood among Wall Street analysts who were told at a meeting that Motorola's profits for 1966 would be lower than expected. ("Red-dogging," as some readers undoubtedly know, is an old football expression that has to do with surprising the opposition and creating pandemonium.) At the meeting, Robert Galvin, Motorola's president, assured the analysts that his company was doing well, except that its earnings for the year would rise to only around $6 a share, or $2 less than anticipated. The article revealed the startled reaction of the analysts as they scraped back in their chairs and elbowed each other in their rush to phone the bad news to their colleagues. Goodman wrote about this again in *The Money Game*:

> The sage and august analysts look at each other for a moment: $6? $6? What happened to the other $2? Then it is like the end of the White House news conference, except that nobody has even said, "Thank you, Mr. President." They are all running for the phones. Except that they are security analysts, not newsmen, so they use the Olympic heel-and-toe walk instead of the outright sprint. There is a question-and-answer period, but Mr. Galvin's audience has been depleted.

After that, Motorola's stock declined sharply, and so did the market. Its downward spiral prompted Goodman to describe what had happened:

> This is what the French sociologist Emile Durkein called *anomie*. In market terms it means anxiety builds up as the market drops, and than as you get all the noise about "resistance levels" and so on, and the market goes plunging through them, and you get *anomie*. It's like alienation, only it means "Where's the bottom? Where's the bottom?" Nobody knows where the bottom is; nobody can remember where the top was; they're all the way out there in the blue, riding on anxiety and a shoeshine.[1]

In his book *In Search of History*,[2] Teddy White concluded that Goodman's lively style revolutionized the field of financial writing. A similar point has been made by Peter Landau, who points out that Goodman's work in the 1960s "changed the way we think about financial journalism. Instead of being told that the Dow Jones Industrials declined two points or something equally boring, all of a sudden we were awakened to the fact that exciting things happen on Wall Street." Landau later succeeded Goodman as editor of another magazine he helped launch in the '60s, the *Institutional Investor* or *II*, a monthly dealing with professional money management. Goodman and a small band of innovators enlivened that magazine with the same verve that had worked well at *New York*. The result was similarly entertaining and informative. For many years after its birth in 1967, *II* was the hottest periodical in its field.

Since it bears directly on what he accomplished in television, it may be worth digressing to offer a brief overview of some of the goings-on at *II* during his editorship. At his suggestion, I began doing some work for it in 1969, shortly after leaving the CBS organization and moving to Europe; from there I wrote for the magazine and edited an affiliated journal published in London. I can still recall Goodman's comment about the manuscript of my first article, a profile of a French investment manager. "I didn't have to put a single pencil mark on it," he told me in a trans-Atlantic phone call. "I think you might have some fun working with us." I did, although life in the *II* organization was, in its own way, nearly as chaotic as life in television. Articles from outside contributors invariably required many pencil marks before they were printable. There was a lot of revising and scrambling around to get issues out on time, and much chasing after overdue manuscripts, some of which came from investment professionals in foreign countries and from academics who had trouble writing for a wider audience. As each new deadline approached, the crisis atmosphere would intensify as the ritual of scrambling and rewriting repeated itself. The whole process was described once by an observant member of the staff as "similar to making snowballs out of shit."

Nonetheless, that epoch, which extended into the 1970s, was marked by a sense of being in on a florescence of financial journalism. Fresh ideas, bright graphics, irreverent headlines and lucid writing were the order of the day. Money managers and industry analysts in the U.S. and elsewhere who had toiled away in obscurity for years were lionized or sometimes plucked by the beard in cover stories. Questionable practices in the investment business were examined with a fresh eye. The staff was talented but small. To make it seem more substantial, the title of Director of Research was added to the masthead and that position was assigned to a fictitious K.F. Ping. Gilbert Kaplan, *II*'s grand sachem, dreamt up the name. Although Ping's presence is no longer required to enhance an image of substantiality, the name remains on the masthead more than two decades later.

Like the magazine itself, the atmosphere around *II*'s offices in Manhattan was unstructured and experimental. The work routine was enlivened with calisthenics and occasional field trips into the bowels of the financial district, and it was all a lot of fun. For me, *II* was a pioneering adventure that bore some similarity to the one I had undertaken earlier for the CBS organization. Both explored new territory and tried to present news and information about the money world in an easily digestible manner, and both were rewarding experiences.

Many years later, over coffee one morning in his Manhattan apartment, Goodman summarized the progression of events from *New York* and *II* to the start-up of *Adam Smith's Money World*:

"If you trace the lineage from the days on *New York*, you should bear in mind that the atmosphere there was terrifically experimental, with writers like Tom Wolfe and Gloria Steinem and Jimmy Breslin doing very creative things. Tom had a strong influence on me. His writing was loose, more metaphoric, more provocative and more impish. It had a whole persona about it.

"The way we got stories was different, too. You didn't just carry a spiral notebook and go out and say 'tell me, sir.' You got a job or you experienced something and then you wrote about it. Gloria got a job as a Playboy bunny. Tom would get down in the car pits with the stock car drivers and recount exactly what happened there.

"I had worked on Wall Street, and that gave me a point of view different from the one that financial reporters had. In fact, they probably never would have written 'The Day They Red-Dogged Motorola' because they probably never would have been at the analysts' meeting. And if they had been there, they certainly wouldn't have written it up in the same way.

"That was the first 'Adam Smith' piece. I needed a pseudonym so that I could go to luncheon meetings on Wall Street without being identified as a reporter, but I certainly wasn't happy with that name. It was chosen by one of the editors at the magazine and it was supposed to be a joke. I thought it was awful, but the whole thing took off, and I was stuck with it."

The journalistic wit and wisdom sharpened on the whetstone of *New York* magazine set the stage for what Goodman feels he achieved at *II* and, later, on public television:

"After I became editor of the *Institutional Investor*, I tried to bring a sense of adventure to that magazine. We took four money managers and dressed them as Superman, Batman, Captain Marvel and somebody else and put them on the cover. Nobody in the financial press had done anything like that, and it created an enormous amount of talk right away.

"When we started the television show, I brought in several early issues of *Institutional Investor* to give the producer an idea of the style I had in mind, and he was able to adapt it easily. When we reported on the Disney organization, for example, we did it as an old Disney show. Once upon a time there was a happy kingdom, but then Walt died. Meanwhile, there was another man who wanted to step in and take over. His name was Saul Steinberg. And with that you heard scary music and saw a beautiful castle representing the Disney kingdom high up on a rock. Again, it was the kind of thing which had never been done.

"I have always believed that if you dramatize a story, you can make it comprehensible while at the same time maintaining a relatively high level of sophistication. When it comes to doing this, remember that *Money World* has an advantage over shows that air on the other networks. Our half hour is about 30% longer than their half hour because we don't have any commercials. We use that extra time to explain the relationships between things."[3]

Before he succeeded in getting his show on the air, Goodman went through an exercise that, in his view, says a lot about what has been happening in television over the past decade or so:

"The antecedent of *Money World* was a weekly financial show that Reuters asked me to help create. We did a pilot and I took it to the broadcasters' annual convention in Las Vegas in 1983 and tried to syndicate it. The station people would come by our booth and look at a cassette of the show and I would suggest that they might want to air it at 8:30 at night. They'd say 'you're crazy, that's prime time. You can't put a show like this on the air during prime time.' I would explain that the only other time my audience is at is home is on weekends, and they'd say 'but on Saturday and Sunday afternoons we've got football.' So I'd ask, 'what about before football?' And they would tell me they had something else that had to be aired then, and so on.

"I began to see that you couldn't do a show like the one I had in mind on the stations of the commercial networks at an hour when your audience wanted to watch. And I came to the conclusion that the best way to reach my audience was on public television, where a program doesn't need massive numbers to do well. Since the late '70s and early '80s, as the big audience that commercial networks depend on has become more fragmented, smaller numbers have become more acceptable on both public TV and cable. That's good for business news, which is a subject that doesn't command a huge audience."

NOTES

1. Both extracts are from *The Money Game* (New York: Random House, 1966). Goodman's other non-fiction books include *Supermoney* (New York: Random House, 1972), *Paper Money* (New York: Summit Books, 1981) and *The Roaring '80s* (New York: Summit Books, 1988). "The Day They Red-Dogged Motorola" appeared in *New York* in October 1966, when that magazine was a Sunday section in the *World Journal Tribune*.

2. *In Search of History* (New York: Harper & Row, 1978).

3. Another assessment of this program and its host is contained in "The World According To Adam Smith" by Richard Scheinin, which ran in *Avenue* magazine in October 1987. I am indebted to Gil Kaplan for drawing my attention to this article. Scheinin described Goodman as smart, skeptical, somewhat dour and dedicated to making *Adam Smith's Money World* worth watching. "When he has Sony chairman Akio Morita talking by satellite to former United Auto Workers President Douglas Fraser in New York about the U.S.-Japan trade wars, that's damn good television," wrote Scheinin. "And when he smiles his trademark smile — pleasant, slightly bored, almost pencil-thin, the smile of a pychiatrist, authoritative yet unthreatening — it encourages Ivan Boesky to flash two beaming rows of predatory teeth and make this pronouncement: 'My motivation's never been the money . . . it's been the desire to do something well and thoroughly' — that's better than good television. That's remarkable stuff."

$

14 *Honing Their Skills*

Another veteran print journalist who made a worthwhile contribution to television starting in the early 1980s is Myron (Mike) Kandel. He became CNN's financial editor shortly after the all-news network was formed in 1980. Before that, he had reported business news for *The New York Times* and edited the financial sections of the *New York Herald Tribune, Washington Star* and *The New York Post*. He also co-authored a syndicated newspaper column on business, edited a law journal, wrote a book about investing and created a newsletter about people in the securities industry.[1]

Along with Reese Schonfeld and others, Kandel was instrumental in moving Cable News Network deeper into business news during its formative years.[2] From the outset he brought to the network a consistently mature view of events. And he has continued to do that ever since the days when CNN was in the trial-and-error stage, making mistakes galore and leaving itself open to ridicule. There were those back then who suggested that its initials stood for Chicken Noodle News.

Kandel weathered that period, which was characterized by an abnormal level of inner frenzy, and managed to emerge from it largely unsullied. At one point I can recall, he was urged by some all-knowing executive producer to get out of the studio and do his reports from the stock exchange. This was suggested in the belief that the trading floor would provide an exciting visual backdrop for his words. (Even the casual reader will recognize that some things in the televising of financial news never change, including the relentless pursuit of visually pleasing backdrops.) The idea of shifting to a new venue wasn't new or especially clever, but Kandel went along with it, and it didn't last. After a while the novelty wore off; the all-knowing producer disappeared; and Mike eventually found himself back in the studio, analyzing the news from there.

Among those of us who worked with him at CNN, he will long be remembered as one of the "grown-ups," a term used to differentiate the network's more experienced hands from those who lack seasoning and are engaged in on-the-job training. Cable News Network has always employed lots of bright young men and women who are willing to work cheaply to gain practical wisdom. They push cameras around, write scripts for newscasts, edit tape and make decisions that would never be entrusted to them anywhere else. The average viewer may not realize it, but people fresh out of college sometimes have more responsibility at CNN than those who have worked for years at ABC, NBC or CBS. It's an unusual way to run a news operation, and it has been modified with the passage of time. While it has caused some anxious moments, on the whole the system has worked remarkably well, in part because pros like Kandel provide a steadying influence. His presentations are devoid of exaggerated self-display, and, like Jerry Goodman, his stock in trade is credibility born of knowledge gained through repeated observation and long practice.

Kandel began his career on *The New York Times* copy desk, and the story of his ascent from there is an interesting commentary on how one got to be a financial journalist years ago. He recounted the tale for me and reflected on a few of the changes that have taken place in business reporting during his career, which spans more than three decades. Here is a portion of our conversation:

You started out on the Times' copy desk, which was certainly a good place to begin. How did you manage to get off the desk?

"What happened was that I heard that three reporting jobs were opening up in the financial section, and my first reaction was, who wants to be in business news? But after five years as a copy boy and copy editor, I was eager to make a change. A friend of mine who had been a financial reporter said 'it's not so bad,' so I thought I'd look into it. I told Frank Adams, the city editor, that I wasn't going to stop bugging him until he let me off the desk, and finally he said that if Jack Forrest, the financial editor, wanted to hire me, he wouldn't stand in my way."

And you persuaded Forrest that you were qualified for the job?

"Well, I went to him the next day. Jack was a Scotsman and a newspaperman from the old school, and the first thing he asked was why did I want to be a financial reporter? I replied, 'because I studied economics.' Which was true. What I didn't tell him was that in college I had only taken Eco One, a required basic course. I've often mentioned that incident when I've given speeches. The moral is, you should always tell the truth in applying for a job, but you don't necessarily have to tell everything."

Editors today are looking at job candidates with graduate degrees in economics and finance. If that had been the case in the days when Hector was a pup, some of us might never have been hired.

"That's very possible. The hiring process in the financial sections of most newspapers was hit or miss. I was told a story once that supposedly took place in Cincinnati. It involved a night rewrite man whose wife had inherited some stock that he followed from day to day by reading *The Wall Street Journal* at work. When the paper's financial editor retired, management was trying to figure out who could replace him when someone suggested that the best solution would be to appoint this guy. 'He's obviously the right man for the job,' they said, 'because he reads the *Journal* every day.'

"The way that beats were assigned to reporters was hit or miss, too. When I was hired, one of the other openings at the *Times* was filled by John Lee, who had reported and edited financial news in Richmond, Virginia. At first he was assigned by Forrest to cover the garment industry and I was told I would be covering steel, which was okay. However, someone took Jack aside and suggested that it might make more sense to have Lee, who evidently knew something about the steel business in West Virginia, cover that industry and let me, a New Yorker, cover the garment business and retailing. So Jack switched our beats."

*Which newspapers and which people in financial journalism
did you look up to then?*

"The *Times* and the *Herald Tribune* were the preeminent
metropolitan papers for financial news. I paid attention to
those two plus *The Wall Street Journal*, and that was about
the extent of it. At the *Times*, I admired three people in
particular. One was Herb Koshetz, an assistant financial
editor who had covered the garment beat. He was knowledgeable, patient and a great source of comfort to me.
Another was Bob Bedingfield, who covered railroads and
was a hard-driving, no-nonsense reporter. And the third
person was Burton Crane, who was practically an institution along with Oliver Gingold at the *Journal* and Norman
Stabler at the *Trib*. All three covered the stock market and
their stories were displayed prominently every day. If you
recall, there was a bull market going on then, with the
New York Stock Exchange promoting the ownership of
shares and people coming into the market in droves and
looking for news about stocks. It was a prestigious time to
be a market writer on those papers."

*Meanwhile, there you were, reporting on the rag trade and
retailing. Did you you find some good stories to work on?*

"Oh yes. That was an interesting time to be covering
those industries, especially retailing. The discount revolution was beginning, and there was a lot to learn and a lot
to write about. One of my first page-one stories was E.J.
Korvette opening a store on Fifth Avenue alongside the
expensive shops. That was a big deal. I also had to compete in those days with Dan Dorfman, who was reporting
for *Women's Wear Daily*. Danny knew how to dig for news,
and he was tough competition. I acquired a lot of respect

for him. Several years later when I took over the financial section at the *Herald Trib*, he was the first person I hired."

In between your tours of duty at the Times and the Trib, you did a short stint as business editor of the Star in Washington. What was that all about?

"That was when the *Star*, which has since disappeared, was a solid competitor to *The Washington Post*. Both papers, however, had terrible financial sections. They did a lot of cheerleading for business and ran lots of favorable stuff about local executives. It wasn't befitting their stature as quality newspapers. I was brought in at the *Star* to try to correct that and build up the section. My title was business editor because no one wanted to upset the financial editor, who was still there and had been there for ages.

"One day shortly after I arrived he came over to me with six photos of newly-appointed vice-presidents of a Maryland savings and loan and said it was customary to run them. I told him we weren't going to run all of them. He got upset and marched into the managing editor's office, where he was reminded that things had changed and that I was in charge. That was in 1963, when you were just beginning to see upgradings in the business sections of one newspaper after another, including *The Washington Post*."

The editor who upgraded the *Post*'s section starting in the '60s was Hobart Rowen, who also happens to be another example of a print journalist who has made a contribution to television coverage of the money world. For many years Rowen was a frequent panelist on *Washington Week In Review*, where his observations were generally insightful.[3] He also has done commentary on *NBR* (*Nightly*

Business Report). His views on such issues as government intervention in the marketplace are more liberal than Kandel's. Like Kandel, he had an abundance of reporting and editing experience before he went on the air. Rowen began at the bottom in the newspaper business and confronted challenges at the *Post* similar to those encountered at the *Star*.[4] Here are some of his recollections:

"I came out of City College of New York just before the Second World War with an ambition to become a reporter. The first job offer I got was from *The Journal of Commerce*, so my specialization in the area of economics was really an accident. For nine months I ran copy on the night shift, and one of my chores was to ride the subway up to Times Square at 11 o'clock and buy the bulldog editions of the *Herald Tribune* and the *Times*. I would then tear back downtown to our offices at 63 Park Row and distribute the papers to our editors, who would scan the financial pages and quickly rewrite any important stories that our small overworked reporting staff had missed.

"I watched this process for a while, and one night I took a yellow pad with me and rewrote a story on the subway ride back downtown. After that night's edition had closed, I felt brave enough to show my rewrite to our managing editor, Arthur Kramer. He asked if I had written it myself. I said, 'sure, on the subway.' The next day I had a job as a reporter and my salary jumped to $18 a week."

Rowen transferred to *The Journal of Commerce*'s Washington bureau for a brief time and then spent a couple of years working in government before going to *Newsweek* in 1944 to cover the Washington economics beat. There, he began writing a "Business Trends" column, which was an innovation in newsmagazine coverage of the economy.

"We started the column because we didn't have any vehicle for reporting on trends that hadn't yet shaped up into a news story. It was similar to the magazine's 'Periscope' feature and to Kiplinger's newsletter. 'Business Trends' had the distinction of being the only piece of copy in *Newsweek* that was written in the Washington bureau. It was popular with readers, but our New York editors didn't like having that copy out of their control, so I wasn't surprised when they dropped 'Business Trends' after I left to go to the *Post*."

Rowen gave up his economics reporting job at *Newsweek* in 1966 and decided to take over the *Post*'s ailing financial section for a couple of reasons.

"One reason I did it was that I had been passed over for the job of Washington bureau chief at *Newsweek*. Another was that newspapers ran bylines rather than the unsigned articles that were common in newsmagazines back then, so there was more opportunity for ego satisfaction. And a big consideration for me was the fact that Ben Bradlee, who had left as bureau chief and gone to the *Post* earlier, took me to lunch and made me an offer I couldn't refuse.

"I was brought in as Bradlee's guy and given carte blanche to improve the section. I established a few conditions relating to things like personnel and the size of the section and getting a cleared front on Sunday, with the prospect of getting one on a daily basis during the week. Bradlee promised I'd get what I needed, and he pretty much kept his promise.

"When I arrived, Oliver Goodman was the *Post*'s financial editor, and his main interest was in local news. He wrote a column called 'Capital Commerce.' There were two full-time reporters, neither of whom lasted very long, and one news aide. The section consisted of only 16 columns of type, of which 13 were taken up with the agate tables (stock and bond prices). That left three columns for news and headlines and art. One of the three was usually reserved for Oliver's column on the local business stuff. There was a Wall Street report and a few other short items, and that was all. It was disgraceful for a major metropolitan paper, and it had to change."

One of the biggest obstacles to change, according to Rowen, was the commercial side of the *Post*.

"The advertising people used to come down to the 5th floor newsroom and distribute company press releases to the reporters. I had to lay down new rules and let everyone know we were no longer going to be running those releases as if they were news. I spelled out a code of ethics, and once the ad guys began to realize that the old days were over we started to get some cooperation. But it was all a very slow and painful process.

"Another problem we had was finding competent people. We didn't have a lot of money to offer. To some extent we drew on other departments. We also relied heavily on outside talent, especially in the Sunday section, which we concentrated on and tried to showcase. I was able to persuade Milton Friedman, Paul Samuelson and others to contribute articles, usually for free. We got a dialogue going on monetary policy versus fiscal policy and tried to provide readers with a more balanced diet of news and comment.

"Gradually we began to get some attention, but it was a lot of work. I was doing reporting, writing a column, and editing the section. I had three jobs and I was killing myself. My wife told me I had to start turning some of it over to other people, so I tried to and eventually I did."[5]

Bart Rowen and Mike Kandel, like Jerry Goodman, honed their skills in print journalism at a time when newspaper and magazine coverage of the money world was coming alive. All three participated in the early stages of that enlivenment and went on to do pioneering work on television. There have been a handful of other journalists who traveled the same path. One of them is Dan Dorfman, the former *Women's Wear Daily* and *Herald Tribune* scribe who once competed for stories with Kandel. At one point in his career Dorfman wrote the *Journal's* "Heard on the Street" column. He currently writes for *USA Today*. In television, he did his basic training at CNN before switching to CNBC. His specialty on the air parallels the turf he has always plowed as a columnist, digging up scoops and tidbits in the investment field. Those who like their financial news spiced with gossip find Dorfman well worth watching. His primary beat is the Wall Street rumor mill. He is good at what he does, and what he does is brisk and snappy and, in many respects, ideally suited for TV.[6]

Lou Rukeyser is another ex-newspaper journalist who has drawn wide notice for his work on television. Along with his ABC experience, his background includes reporting for the *Baltimore Sun* and a syndicated column for Tribune Media Services which he wrote for 17 years. His PBS show remains one of the most popular financial programs on the air. His monologues in the opening minutes may seem a trifle roseate, and a viewer could be excused for growing a tad weary of hearing that Congress rolls the stone of Sisyphus or that stock prices fell while the host of the show was away. But Rukeyser's questions are razor sharp. He knows how to extract information from his panelists and guests — mostly investment managers, analysts and economists — and he rarely lets them serve up inordinate amounts of baloney or merchandise themselves shamelessly on the air.

The deftness with which Rukeyser pleasantly conducts his interrogations and slips in revealing little questions is typified by an exchange that once took place with a panelist who declared that the economy should be put through a recession in order to "take the bad medicine quick and get it over with." Without hesitation Rukeyser asked, "Would you volunteer to be among the unemployed?" To which the chastened panelist replied, "Oh no, thank you very much, I have three in college."[7] On many programs, an insensitive comment about the wisdom of inducing a slump that would throw people out of work might go unchallenged, but that is not likely to happen on Rukeyser's watch.

Although times haven't changed much in the television business when it comes to the pursuit of visually exciting backdrops, they clearly have changed when it comes to mentioning stocks on the air. The days when the SEC fretted about my citing specific securities on CBS have given way to a more permissive atmosphere where buy and sell recommendations are offered with regularity. *Wall Street Week* is an excellent case in point. Panelists and guests routinely name stocks that they deem worthy of purchase and others that they feel should be avoided. Much of the program is taken up with discussion of these tips and the outlook for the market. There are those, Rukeyser not least among them, who would argue that this information has considerable value, and it certainly has some. My own suspicion, for what it's worth, is that most short-range market forecasts are a throw of the dice; and for the average investor who lacks access to thorough research plus the experience and the time to analyze it, picking big winners consistently in the Wall Street casino can be pretty difficult. However, the quest will go on as long as there is a casino that's fun to play in, players to interview, and plenty of press attention focused on the action. Rukeyser helps supply that attention, and he does so with doses of humor that are, for the most part, wholly appropriate. I sometimes think of him as the Andy Rooney of TV financial news.

Before we leave the subject of Rukeyser's show, there is a bit of historical linkage that may be of interest to some of its viewers. When the program was being developed at the start of the 1970s, one of its creators, Anne Truax Darlington, visited the *Institutional Investor* in New York and took a look at *Video Forum*, a series of panel discussions *II* was producing on videotape for clients in the investment community. The program featured a moderator, usually Goodman, asking three Wall Streeters which way they thought the market was going and which stocks they were buying and selling. The format of *Wall Street Week* bears some resemblance to that of *Video Forum*, but the similarity ends there. *Video Forum* met with little success, partly because at the time the technology for distributing the program in a timely fashion was not yet available.

We could probably add another name or two to our list of graying financial journalists who have done pioneering work on television, but this is a full enough measure. It should be pointed out that there are places on TV where one can find respectable business reporting and analysis that isn't necessarily the handiwork of those who paid their dues by putting in long years on newspapers or magazines. One example is the commentary by economists and other outside contributors who appear (along with several journalists) on *NBR*, a show that is otherwise devoted heavily to the daily action in the markets. Another is *60 Minutes*, where viewers who prefer a dash of muckraking with their money news can occasionally find something to their liking. Its reports on the money world tend to be eye-openers and aren't always popular with business people. While they can be laudatory, more often than not they feature corporate chicanery or expose greed and maleficence and portray slick money-making schemes along with their victims.

Still another program that can be a useful source of information is the *MacNeil/Lehrer News Hour*. It does interviews linked to breaking news that provide more background information than one gets on the shorter newscasts of the three major broadcast networks. These interviews are generally superior to the features on business that air on the program, and they work best when structured as one-on-one sessions, less well when they become mini-debates among guests, especially economists, with supposedly conflicting views of the money world. While the show's anchors are not experienced business reporters, they ask good, basic questions and allow a decent amount of time for answers. There are no ten-second sound bites purporting to describe the state of the economy in one fell swoop, and no flashy visuals. The end product isn't fancy, but it lends itself nicely to a subject where events require more than a few seconds of explanation.

Much the same can be said for Bill Moyers' reporting on PBS. While he does not cover economics regularly, when he does the result is almost always a refreshing change from tabloid-style TV journalism. In a similar vein, C-SPAN deserves mention. Its leisurely coverage of governmental proceedings periodically touches on topics such as trade, tax policy and the budget. Now and then, C-SPAN's founder, Brian Lamb, does unhurried interviews with authors or others knowledgeable about economic affairs. These interviews and proceedings represent a triumph of substance over style and are well worth watching when you can find them.[8]

NOTES

1. Kandel's book on investing, written at the start of the bull market of the 1980s, was entitled *How To Cash In On The Coming Stock Market Boom: The Smart Investor's Guide To Making Money* (Indianapolis: Bobbs-Merrill, 1981). The newsletter was the *Wall Street Letter*, which Kandel founded with the help of two other journalists and subsequently sold to the *Institutional Investor*.

2. Schonfeld oversaw much of the initial developmental work that propelled CNN into the field of business news. He had a falling out with Ted Turner and left the network shortly before I began doing some work for it in the summer of 1982.

3. Rowen's successor as the designated economics specialist on *Washington Week in Review* in recent years has been *Wall Street Journal* reporter Alan Murray, who does a very capable job. Like an old movie star who periodically makes brief comebacks, Rowen has been brought back to the show on occasion to provide historical perspective on certain stories. On September 18, 1992, he was given a couple of minutes to explain the decades-old origins of a complicated upheaval in the European monetary system.

4. Rowen and Kandel share another similarity in their careers. Both have been active in a group originally called SABW (Society of American Business Writers), which tries to promote professionalism in this area of journalism. At Rowen's urging, years ago the name was changed to Society of American Business and Economic Writers

(SABEW); later still it was changed again to Society of American Business Editors and Writers. (This latest alteration at least served the purpose of allowing the group to keep the same acronym.)

5. Rowen stepped down as editor of the *Post's* business section in 1975 and continued to write his column.

6. Dorfman, one of the bonafide "grown-ups" during his years at CNN, was an especially valuable asset when the all-news network was trying to establish itself. The fact that he was a recognizable name became less important as other CNN people became somewhat better known, and as the network began making its mark as the nation's leading provider of live news coverage. Dorfman was profiled by another of his former employers, *The Wall Street Journal*, in a page-one article on January 18, 1988. In the piece, "Tireless and Excitable Dan Dorfman Chases Stock Market Scoops," Randall Smith wrote that Dorfman reports "rumors as well as news" and observed that "analysis isn't his strength. What he wants is to be first: with corporate news and coups, with takeovers and make-overs —whatever might move a stock."

7. This exchange took place between Rukeyser and William Waters on December 9, 1988.

8. For more details on C-SPAN and its origins and capabilities, the reader is referred to two articles: "No Sound Bites Here" (*The New York Times Magazine*, March 15, 1992) and "C-SPAN: The Network That Dares to Be Dull" (*Los Angeles Times*, July 13, 1992).

$

IV
BETTERMENT

15 Business Day and the Agate Ghetto

The fortunes of the The New York Times were on the downswing in the early 1970s. Companies were moving out of the city; a recession was underway; and the *Times'* ad revenues and profits were feeling the pinch. The lifestyles and interests of many of its readers were changing, and the *Times* clearly needed to make adjustments. It decided to broaden its distribution, redesign its sections and place greater emphasis on business news. Characteristically, it set out to do all this without radically altering its appearance.

A central figure in the upgrading of the business coverage was John M. Lee, the reporter from Virginia who had been hired with Mike Kandel more than a decade earlier. In 1972, after serving as the paper's financial correspondent in London and Tokyo, he was brought back to New York to help lay the groundwork for the introduction of the Business Day section, which made its debut in 1978, two years after Lee became business editor. Here are his thoughts on the changes which took place during that time, including the sectionalization and the launching of Business Day:

"We wanted to acknowledge the shifting interests of our readers by expanding the *Times* — by throwing a few more potatoes into the stew, as it were — and adding stuff that had not been emphasized as much in the past. Out of this was born the idea of a four-section newspaper replacing the old two-section paper. That might not sound very startling since many newspapers already had multiple sections, but it was for us. It was decided that the first section would be predominately world and national news. The second section would be metropolitan news. The third would feature sports, science and other broad categories, with each appearing on a different day of the week. And the fourth would be a self-contained business section, virtually a separate newspaper within the *Times*."

Section four was given more space than any of the other three, along with its own team of local, national and foreign correspondents and its own graphics specialists. A decision was made to funnel into it virtually all national and international economic pieces in addition to traditional business news. The department's staff was nearly doubled to around 100 people. A number of new reporters and editors were brought in from other publications, including Fred Bleakley from the *Institutional Investor*, Paul Lewis from the *Financial Times*, and Fred Andrews from *The Wall Street Journal*.[1] More than a half-dozen writers were recruited from *Business Week*. Among them: Geraldine Fabrikant, Soma Golden, Anthony Parisi and Winston Williams. Lee said there was a specific reason for tapping *BW*'s pool of talent:

"One of the things we wanted to do was introduce more interpretation of the news. Being a weekly, *Business Week* has always had to add that element to its stories to squeeze more juice out of them. With help from the people we hired from *Business Week*, we found we were able to begin squeezing more juice out of our stories every day. We also tried to do more on a daily basis with the kinds of graphics one ordinarily finds in publications with longer lead times."

The push for more interpretation, according to Lee, was rooted to some extent in his experiences as a *Times* foreign correspondent:

"Part of this, I'm sure, resulted from my having spent five years in London in the 1960s reading the *Economist* and the *Financial Times*. I became intrigued by the idea that people like to have some high-class commentary in their news stories, along with graphics that help explain things and maybe even a bit of gossip. I didn't want to see us go too far in that direction, but I felt we could do a little more, and we did. At a dinner one evening I met a man in the financial markets who told me he didn't like our coverage of municipal bonds because he felt it was 'too gossipy.' I don't recall what I told him but I thought to myself, that's just wonderful.

"Remember, too, that Business Day started at a time when readers were becoming more interested in insider accounts and profiles of people and explanations of why things happened and how. Some of that followed from what you guys were doing at the *Institutional Investor*, where the premise was that everyone can be a star. We were influenced by that, by the idea of taking faceless people from Wall Street and making celebrities out of them. Readers of business news grew accustomed to having those people written about like actors in a drama, and that became a staple of modern financial journalism.

"One of the moves we made very early was to create an M&A (mergers and acquisitions) beat. We put Bob Cole on it. When he would look into a deal and try to reconstruct the negotiations, he would find that the participants had kept careful notes — it was 3:30 a.m. when they sent out for pastramis on rye while their banker was kept waiting in the lobby of the Carlisle as Mr. Getty finished his deliberations in his antique-filled suite on the 37th floor, or whatever. We discovered that readers were fascinated by those details, and we began including them in stories that were written in a more novelistic fashion."

While the introduction of Business Day and a four-section paper didn't solve all of the problems at the nation's most influential metropolitan daily, it was a clear-sighted move that was followed by an equally ambitious effort to make the paper more readily available across the country. Here again, business news played a key role. After a failed attempt at a national edition in the 1960s, the *Times* tried again in 1980, printing by satellite transmission on leased press time in Chicago and later in other cities in the South and the West. The new national edition was launched as a two-part paper (and later grew to three parts). Part one was reserved for national, international, and cultural stories as well as metropolitan stories that were deemed to have news value in the hinterland. Part two, it was decided, would be Business Day in its entirety. Lee explained the thinking behind that decision:

"There was no hesitation about making the second section business instead of sports or something else. The reason is that business news travels well. As you go out across the country, you find that people nearly everywhere are interested in what Wall Street is thinking and what's happening in the economy, as well as in personal finance. And you find that the *Times* and *The Wall Street Journal* are second buys and in competition with each other.

"The *Journal* followed a different course, starting with a business paper and adding other elements like political and cultural news. We moved the opposite way, adding a more comprehensive business section to our established coverage of national, international and cultural affairs. This approach has worked well for us. It has allowed the business section to reflect the values and interests of the paper as a whole. Business Day has a particular quality because it's part of the *Times* rather than a business paper per se, or an investors' paper per se."

Lee acknowledged that what the *Times* did entailed a measure of risk:

"When we were making our plans, Abe Rosenthal (who was then managing editor) said to me, 'This is a marvelous opportunity for you to fall on your face.' And I suppose that was true. Looking back, I guess the single biggest risk we took was that our section might be compared unfavorably to the *Journal*. But that didn't happen. We succeeded in making the transition from a gray page with a stock market lead to something with more substance and more sparkle."

Lee and the others involved in the transition also managed to make it work without adding a lot of twaddle. Although the section grew in size, there wasn't any noticeable retreat from the pull-no-punches reporting that has characterized financial news in the *Times* since the days of Alexander Dana Noyes or even earlier, when the paper was socking it to Wall Street during the Panic of 1857. Here are the headlines and lead-ins of two tough stories from the early 1990s:

Looking Out for No. 1

*Internal Competition for Limitless Bonuses
Bred Fractious Culture of Greed at Salomon*

At Salomon Brothers, trading has always been a form of war in which the opponent is entitled to no pity and the rules are viewed as impediments.[2]

Much the same unyielding approach can be seen in this headline and lead from this piece, which started on the front page and concluded in Business Day:

GM Directors
Do Away with
Rubber Stamp

The General Motors Corporaton — long known as one of America's most smug and insular companies — has abandoned its past in placing an outside board member in charge of a top board committee to monitor more closely GM's management.[3]

Suffice to say, not every newspaper would be willing to risk the ire of a General Motors by calling it "smug and insular" on page one. The change in the committee structure could have been reported without making such a stern judgment in the lead, and many publications handled it that way, inserting their interpretations a little later and using gentler language.

Here is one more example of the pull-no-punches style. James Sterngold, a *Times'* staffer and frequent contributor to Business Day from Tokyo, wrote the article which appeared under this headline in the Sunday magazine:

Japan's Rigged Casino

*The Tokyo stock market is a bridge
to a shadowy financial world in which
politicians, speculators and mobsters
dip into a vast cash machine.*[4]

One of the most popular features in Business Day has been the "Economic Scene" column, written for many years by Leonard Silk and, after his retirement, by Peter Passell and others. The column discusses economic trends and policy and tries to provide straightforward explanations of the issues. That's one of the hardest things to do in this area of journalism, partly because those who do the explaining tend to have definite ideological preferences. The Keynesian-oriented Silk, a Ph.D. economist and former editorial writer, once described the "toughest part" of his job as "separating myself from various schools of economic thought and trying to be a reporter and interpreter of events without becoming the prisoner of a doctrine that is really an ideology in disguise." His perspective on the *Times'* expanded business coverage:

"It has been improving for many years, and certainly the most dramatic change came with the start-up of Business Day. That meant more space for the section and it moved us in the direction of more interpretive writing. It also meant that we had to find a strong lead story for the middle of the page every day. This forced the staff to look at what's really important instead of just covering the stock market or reporting the latest economic indicators. There has been more thinking going on among editors and reporters than in the old days, when the section was mostly reactive and habitual."[5]

In its second try at a national edition, the *Times* succeeded, and that venture was followed in short order by two others involving greater use of business news. In the early 1980s the paper started a quarterly supplement on personal finance and another, entitled Business World, which it runs several times a year as part two of its Sunday magazine.

Taken together, all of these endeavors have added up to a huge increase in the *Times'* coverage of the money world. No other metropolitan paper has gone as far, but many others have moved in a similar direction, starting separate sections that appear once or twice a week or in some cases daily and often play up local and regional stories. A few of the more substantial upgradings, such as those at *The Washington Post* and *The Miami Herald*, occurred well before the start-up of Business Day. At the *Los Angeles Times*, the changes came in a couple of stages. Some of them took place under the guidance of John F. Lawrence and Paul Steiger around the time Business Day was starting. Long before that, however, in 1961, the *Los Angeles Times* crawled out of the dark ages of business journalism when it scrapped a shabby little section called Oil and Mining and began assembling a more respectable one under the direction of Bob Nichols. A former business writer for *Time* and labor correspondent for the *Herald Tribune*, Nichols said afterward that he was brought in with instructions to improve the coverage quickly:

"My mandate was to raise the quality as fast as possible and as cheaply as possible, which was a typical *Los Angeles Times* approach to those things. The day I started work I took the 'Oil and Mining' sign off the door to my office, and what I discovered was an incredibly backward operation. In the composing room there were trays of type — important dividend announcements and news stories — that were gathering dust. They were being held to run in the future because there wasn't any room on the business page that day.

"I also was struck by the fact that our page, like so many others of its kind, was buried deep in the gray agate ghetto, where it was hard to find. As a department, Oil and Mining was considered purgatory for the few people who were assigned to work there. The whole thing was at rock bottom. When you start making improvements from that level — and we made lots of them in the eight years I edited the section — almost anything you do is an upward move."[6]

Although the *Los Angeles Times* meliorated its business coverage in the '60s and '70s, unlike *The New York Times*, for a long while California's largest daily continued to run most economic stories in the main news section. William Thomas, who was editor from 1969 to 1989, explained the thinking behind that policy:

"We were reluctant to put everything in the one basket marked 'business news' because we weren't sure our readers would turn to that section and find all of those stories. We hesitated to force them to dig into the back of the paper for news about things like inflation and major economic trends. However, eventually we did more of

175

that, while continuing to keep some of the most important stories on page one. And then Business got its own section every day, which increased its visibility enormously."

Concerted action to progress beyond the gray agate ghetto and make lasting improvements has been taking place for a long while, not only in New York, Washington and Los Angeles, but also in many other cities. San Francisco is a good example, and the story of what has been happening at the two major newspapers there, the *Chronicle* and *Examiner*, is told in some detail in chapter 25 from the vantage point of two of the principals involved. Meanwhile, one does not have to look hard to find a similar pattern at magazines that were once considered irretrievably somber such as *Business Week*, which was always informative but not easy to read; *Financial World*, which was nearly unreadable for three-quarters of a century; and *Changing Times*, which received a major facelift and is now called *Kiplinger's Personal Finance Magazine*. Following along this same path, *U.S. News & World Report* has strengthened its business coverage, as *Time* and *Newsweek* did earlier. At some of these publications, the prescription for betterment has been influenced by the snappy style of *USA Today* or by the *Institutional Investor*. This has generally meant livelier writing, more arresting headlines and brighter graphics.

To be sure, not all of these attempts to improve represent earthshaking progress. They haven't completely erased the old castor oil image. However, they're substantive as well as cosmetic. In the main they are positive steps that have been well received. They've turned out better than most coincident efforts in television, and they are part of a trend that emerges as one of the more noteworthy developments in journalism during the final half of this century.

NOTES

1. In 1985 Lee became assistant managing editor of the *Times* and Andrews succeeded him as business editor. Seven years later Andrews was succeeded by William Stockton, who had edited the Sunday business section.

2. *The New York Times*, August 19, 1991. This article was written by Floyd Norris.

3. *The New York Times*, April 8, 1992. The GM story was written by Steve Lohr.

4. *The New York Times*, April 26, 1992.

5. Silk, a former *Business Week* editor, told the author he believes that while the general level of sophistication in economics reporting has improved through the years, there is still a "shortage of first-class economic journalists." "It's encouraging that one finds fewer egregious errors than in the past," he said. "The press can be faulted for not going deep enough to satisfy those who want to know what's really happening in the economy. But of course it can't go beyond the economics profession, which hasn't always done a particularly good job of explaining what's happening either." Silk has authored several books interpreting economic affairs, including *Economics in the Real World* and *Economics in Plain English* (both of which were published by Simon & Schuster, in 1984 and 1986, respectively).

6. Nichols said that when he took over the *Los Angeles Times* business section, he was not very familiar with corporate news or the securities markets, although he had some business and economics writing experience. "When I was in the business section at *Time*," he recalled, "one of the stories I wrote was about William McChesney Martin's appointment to the Federal Reserve in 1951, but it was a story I only dimly understood."

$

16 Color the Journal Gray

While other periodicals have been beefing up their business coverage, the publication that sets the standard by which all tend to be judged — *The Wall Street Journal* — continues to make changes while retaining the stoic look of yesteryear. It has enlarged its staff, added more sections, widened its editorial horizons and improved its writing, while paying little or no attention to the dictates of television or the snappier styles of more contemporary publications. Edward Scharff has written:

> In the age of video, it seems a little strange that the most popular newspaper in the country is a pictureless sheet of unrelieved gray, a visual throwback to the nineteenth century that has little news of sport, criminal mayhem, or most other subjects that are regular fare for most mass media. *The Wall Street Journal* is nothing less than a modern com-

munications miracle, by far the greatest publishing success of the postwar era.[1]

Lindley Clark, Jr., who worked for the *Journal* as a reporter, editorial page editor and columnist during most of that era, offers this assessment of what has been happening at the paper since the late 1940s:

"As the field of business and financial journalism has expanded, the *Journal* has gradually repositioned itself. It has been a long, evolutionary process that started after the Second World War, when Barney Kilgore set out to take what was primarily a financial newspaper and convert it into a paper that could appeal to a wider audience, not just people interested in stocks and bonds.

"In the 1950s we did things like abolish the Saturday edition, along with a European column that was never very good. The guys who wrote it used to go through the Sunday edition of *The New York Times* looking for items that could help flesh it out. So we got rid of that, too. We were trying to clean up our act and give readers a more appealing newspaper.

"Since then, the *Journal*'s focus has been broadened considerably. Some of the old-timers around here feel it has broadened too much, but I'm not so sure. I get a little concerned when I see commuters on the train throw away the rest of the paper and keep only the back section, where they can read about the financial markets. However, I think most of the decisions that have been taken have been pretty wise. I doubt if our circulation would have risen into the two-million range if we had kept our focus narrow."

Vermont Royster, whose *Journal* career dates back to the 1930s, played an instrumental role in widening the paper's focus and improving its writing. Like Clark, Royster began as a reporter and became an editor. Here are his thoughts on the shift in policy that set the paper on a path toward greater prosperity:

"Somewhere along the line it dawned on us that our readers were reasonably intelligent people who were interested in other things besides stocks. So we began doing more with politics and stories about the theatre and ballet and books and sports. Some of those were the forerunners of the Arts and Leisure section you see in the *Journal* today. We tried not to give our readers anything they could get in their local papers. For example, we felt we'd be crazy if we tried to keep up with which basketball teams won last night. So we emphasized columns and commentaries and reviews.

"There's no doubt that expanding our coverage contributed to the rise in our circulation and helped us attract more advertising. It got to where we couldn't accommodate all of our would-be advertisers, so the number of sections had to be increased. I confess to having mixed feelings about that. On the one hand, you have to keep the company prosperous. On the other hand, you have to keep the reader in mind. There has to be a point of diminishing returns when it comes to the size of a newspaper, any paper. It can't keep getting bigger forever."[2]

The *Journal* has long since reached a size where it contains more information than most of us can digest. Reading it is like sitting down at Thanksgiving dinner five days a week. It is well organized and indexed, allowing one to pick and choose and skip over the applesauce, and its menu is much more varied than in the past. The *Journal* ranges farther afield and pokes its nose into many more subjects. Under Norman Pearlstine, its focus widened further in the 1980s, resulting in some front-page stories that would never have appeared in the paper a couple of decades ago. Here are two examples:

For a Lurid Look
At D.C.'s Sleaze,
Just Hop Aboard

———

The Latest From the Capital
Is the Scandal Bus Tour;
Remembrances of Fanne

The writer, *Journal* staffer David Shribman, had some fun with this one.

WASHINGTON—We welcome you this morning to Sin City.

In the next 75 minutes you will be visiting the lurid side of the nation's capital. You will see the building where the Watergate scandal began and the townhouse where the Gary Hart presidential campaign ended. You will see where Oliver North shredded documents and where exotic dancer Fanne Foxe plunged into the tidal basin.

In short, this is Washington, D.C., as you know it from your morning paper.

All aboard the Scandal Tour bus. It's the tour of the sites where enormous prices were paid in reputations lost, careers ruined and families fractured — but it's yours for only $20.[3]

As this next example suggests, the *Journal* doesn't mind using its wider focus occasionally to look at some of the flapdoodle and imponderabilia on television:

Blurred Lines
**TV Network News
Is making Re-Creation
A form of Recreation**

———

*Enacting of Recent Events
Raises Credibility Issue;
Who Plays Connie Chung?*

———

Abbie Hoffman's Last Words

This article, by Kevin Goldman, reported on experiments underway at the major broadcast networks in the late 1980s to reconstruct news events using actors to represent real people. Goldman's lack of enthusiasm for the technique was evident in the opening paragraphs of his story:

These are the last words Abbie Hoffman ever uttered, more or less, before he killed himself. And You Are There, sort of:
ABBIE: "I'm OK, Jack. I'm OK (listening) "Yeah, I'm out of bed. I got my feet on the floor. Yeah. Two feet. I'll see you Wednesday? . . Thursday."
He listens impassively.
ABBIE: (con't): "I'll always be with you, Jack. Don't worry."
Abbie lies back and leaves the frame empty.

Of course that wasn't the *actual* conversation the late anti-war activist, protest leader and founder of the Yippies ever had with his brother. It's a script pieced together from interviews by CBS News for a reenactment, a dramatic rendering by an actor of Mr. Hoffman's ultimately unsuccessful struggle with depression.
The segment will soon be broadcast on the CBS News series "Saturday Night With Connie Chung," thus further

blurring the distinction between fiction and reality in TV news. It is the New Journalism come to television.[4]

Craig Horowitz considers the modern-day *Journal* "the quirkiest and most unpredictable show in serious journalism." In *New York* magazine he has written:

> While most newspapers have gone to flashy graphics, color photographs and shorter stories, the *Journal*, by comparison, looks almost quaint. It is as steadfastly gray and picture-free as it was 50 years ago. . . . Though the paper continues to run page after page of dry company news that couldn't be of much interest to anyone except shareholders and hard-core corporate groupies, it is also home to extraordinary writing, in-depth analysis and investigative reporting.[5]

Under Pearlstine, who took over as managing editor in 1983, the *Journal's* editorial staff was increased by more than 100 people and the Money and Investing section was added. Reporters and editors were encouraged to dig deeper into subjects such as the media and small business that had commanded comparatively little attention in the past, and they did. They also were encourged to write books, and they did. Some of what they wrote also appeared in the paper, and it was very good. In fact, a few of the people who were writing it got so good at what they were doing that they ended up signing lucrative publishing contracts and leaving the *Journal*. At one point in the late '80s more than a dozen staff members were churning out books. Those in that group who left include Susan Faludi, author of *Backlash*, a best seller about feminism, James Stewart (*Den of Thieves*, a book about Milken); and Bryan Burrough (*Barbarians at the Gate*, a tale about the

RJR-Nabisco takeover written with John Heyler, another *Journal* reporter).[6]

This isn't exactly the outcome that was intended when the policy of encouraging book-writing was instigated, but it's the way things turned out. Eventually Pearlstine quit too and was succeeded by Paul Steiger, who is less of an editorial free swinger and a more traditional business journalist. Steiger worked for the *Journal* as a reporter in San Francisco in the 1960s and was involved in the refurbishing of the *Los Angeles Times* business section in the 1970s.

While the *Journal*'s main competition is Business Day in the *Times*, since 1984 *Investor's Business Daily* has been nipping at its heels. This publication (originally known as *Investor's Daily*) stresses financial data and was created by William O'Neil, who heads a Los Angeles investment research firm. His thoughts on the start-up of his paper in competition with the *Journal* are recounted in some detail in Chapter 24. *Investor's Business Daily* has a much smaller army of reporters than the *Journal* and its page-one stories are shorter, less comprehensive and more predictably pro-business than *Journal* leaders. But its news section is nicely focused on events in Washington, and over time the paper has gradually become more substantial. O'Neil deserves a lot of credit for having had the nerve to challenge the *Journal*. What he did is not unlike starting a new football team and deciding to take on the Green Bay Packers of the Vince Lombardi era. The *Journal* is awesome. Although it still has the somber gray look of old, it has come far since the days when it toadied to the "big men." As the following examples suggest, it runs some very hard-hitting stories:

Hidden Treasures
**Dead S&Ls' Bad Loans
Prove To Be Bonanzas
For Big, Rich Players**

———

*They Buy the Debt Cheaply,
Then Foreclose or Devise
Solution With Borrowers*

———

Why Bottom-Fishing Pays[7]

This article, which appeared after the clean-up of the savings and loan industry was underway, posed the question: "How do you wring money out of a dead thrift institution's bad loans?" Paulette Thomas, who reported and wrote the story, went on to explain the answer: "Wealthy players" who have the clout to "swat away the small fry" buy up large packages of troubled loans at a large discount for resale at a nifty profit. The players, it turns out, are a tight little group that includes some of the same folks who were part of the S&L problem in the first place.

The *Journal*'s willingness to ruffle a few feathers also can be seen in this headline and lead:

Expensive Suits
**How a Small Company
Fell Deeply Into Debt
To Its Own Law Firm**

———

*Cost of Defending Pesticide
Zoomed as More Lawyers
And Experts Joined Case*

———

'Genghis Khan on the Steppes'

Reporter Milo Geyelin's lead-in was not designed to win friends in the legal profession:

> Jack and Margie Roberts know all about killing ants, cleaning toilets and wiping out pesky household odors. But they're still learning about lawyers.[8]

Geyelin's story concerned a family-owned chemical firm that ran up a legal bill of nearly half a million dollars battling government regulators on a product safety issue, and then wound up losing the case and battling its own law firm in the courts.

In this next article, the *Journal* tackled a sensitive issue in its own industry:

All the News?

**Many Journalists See
A Growing Reluctance
To Criticize Advertisers**

*They Say Some Newspapers,
Suffering Tough Times,
Are Softening Coverage*

To Others, the Issue is Fairness

Many journalists, who are paid to see trends, think they see an alarming one in their own industry.

With newspapers facing tough times financially, they see an increase in the tendency of newspapers to cater to advertisers or pull their punches when it comes to criticizing advertisers in print.[9]

G. Pascal Zachary's story went on to cite instances of catering and punch-pulling at various papers around the country, mostly in reaction to protests from car dealers, realtors or other local business people who seemed to harbor the notion that all business news should be positive. There were no instances mentioned at the largest papers, including the *Journal*. The piece contained quotes from several editors who said they try to be fair and responsive to advertiser complaints. One of those quoted was Steiger, who said, "At the *Journal* we try to hear out any reader who has a complaint about our coverage, whether or not that reader is an advertiser."

The willingness to tackle tough topics that others would rather not see discussed in print is what separates the best from the rest in newspaper reporting of the money world. More than anything else — more than the number of people in the business section, or the size of the news-hold — this is what sets the *Journal* and the top metropolitan dailies apart from the rest of the pack. Naturally, the freedom to rub the fur the wrong way can result in unfairness and inaccuracies unless it is backed up by superior reporting and careful editing — and that can be a problem even in the most prestigious shops. It gets to be a problem when stories are left in the hands of reporters who mishandle the numbers and don't fully understand the subjects they're covering, or who set out to make a name for themselves by savaging companies with articles that are unsubstantiated. And it becomes problematic whenever other goals interfere with the pursuit of editorial excellence, or when reporters and editors who are zealots at heart use their publications to promote their favorite causes day after day, while trashing or ignoring all other points of view.

One can find examples of each of these foibles in every periodical, including the *Journal*. They are always a source of concern. The majority of the time, however, on its front page the nation's leading financial daily exercises the privilege of tweaking noses responsibly. And it does so in stories that run longer than many of today's magazine articles. When he was the paper's page one editor, James Stewart observed:

"The premise of the (*Journal's*) front page is that people need to know what's happening now and they need to know about some things in depth. It's a formula that's become more sound as the in-depth part of journalism has been abandoned by many of our competitors because of money, reader demands, or because they are trying, more and more, to compete with television. We don't compete with television."[10]

NOTES

1. From *Worldly Power* (see Notes to chapter 4).

2. Readers will find additional comments by Clark and Royster about business journalism in chapter 24, along with the recollections of Don K. White, who was one of the *Journal's* foot soldiers on the West Coast when Kilgore was the paper's principal editor.

3. *The Wall Street Journal*, May 11, 1989.

4. *The Wall Street Journal*, October 30, 1989.

5. From "How Now Dow Jones?: The Nation's Hottest Newspaper Ponders Some Cold Realties" (*New York*, October 12, 1992). In this article, Horowitz noted that the *Journal* has gone through some slow years and questioned whether it can continue to shine. He described the paper as a place which at one time "attracted mostly eco-nerds in brown pants and bad ties whose idea of a good time was a quarterly earnings report."

6. *Backlash* (New York: Crown, 1991); *Den of Thieves* (New York: Simon & Schuster, 1992); *Barbarians at the Gate*: (New York, Harper & Row, 1990). An illustration of the use of book material in the *Journal* was Stewart's "Scenes From a Scandal: The Secret World of Michael Milken and Ivan Boesky." The article ran more than 4,000 words and filled much of the second section on October 2, 1991; it was adapted from *Den of Thieves*. After leaving the *Journal*, the Pulitzer Prize-winning Stewart turned out another exhaustive, investigative piece on the erstwhile king of junk in the March 1, 1993, issue of *The New Yorker*. It was entitled "Annals of Law: Michael Milken's Biggest Deal."

7. *The Wall Street Journal*, November 9, 1992.

8. *The Wall Street Journal*, October 8, 1991.

9. *The Wall Street Journal*, February 6, 1992.

10. From "How Now Dow Jones?" (see above).

$

17 The Critical Path

Two other periodicals that have left their supplicant ways and toadying days far behind are *Barron's*, the *Journal's* sister publication, and *Forbes*. Both are leathery and aimed at investors, and both began regenerating themselves in the 1960s.

Barron's, which was lifeless and stone-faced for several decades, started coming alive with the introduction of "Up and Down Wall Street," a front-page column that Alan Abelson began writing in 1966 at the suggestion of his editor, Robert Bleiberg. From the outset, the column hooked in readers with barbed commentary about topics other than finance, and it has continued to do so. On one occasion, for example, it chided the *Journal* for having the audacity to poll people on the question of who had been the best and worst presidential appointees during the

Reagan years. With characteristic impishness, Abelson penned his answer:

> As any dispassionate observer of Mr. Reagan's two Administrations can attest, there were no "best" appointees. There were bad and worse. Or, to stretch the very limits of charity, bad and not as bad.[1]

When United Airlines' parent company, in a costly mistake, renamed itself Allegis and then abandoned its new name after a short while, "Up and Down Wall Street" offered this sardonic comment:

> . . . we pledge Allegis that we shall never again waver in our esteem for American business. For Allegis has restored our faith in the ingenuity and generosity of this nation. Only in America would a company have the resolve and dedication to spend a year and $7 million in search of a new name. The Japanese would have bought themselves three Os and one A, wrapped them around any old consonants they happened to have in the shop and been perfectly happy.[2]

After the market crashed in October 1987, Abelson admonished the "purring pundits" and "smiling savants" who appeared on TV newscasts and talk shows reassuring viewers not to worry about the collapse of stock prices. His column began this way:

> Stick your head in the sand!
>
> That helpful advice was given free of charge to any flighty investors who might have been twittered by October the 13th, the stock market.
>
> The exhortation to the masses that they adopt this unprepossessing posture came from a sally of sages, whose visages and wisdom poured out of television screens the nation over on the weekend following the Big Skid.[3]

191

A little later, Abelson upbraided Wall Streeters who had voiced displeasure with a presidential commission's recommendations for reforms aimed at preventing a repeat of the Big Skid. He suggested wryly that the proposals might have been unpopular because they were "patently a threat to freedom of manipulation." That same column closed with a discussion of the market and a warning that even after a steep decline, certain stocks were still priced too high. Abelson told his readers:

> Whether sent into the wild blue yonder by virtue of a short squeeze or the adroit exertions of the longs, unsupported by fundamentals, stocks don't stay aloft forever. That is all ye know on earth, and all ye need to know.[4]

As these excerpts suggest, Abelson's writing has a sharp edge to it, and at times he has drawn reproof for his stern judgments and for seeming to be sympathetic to the bearish point of view. He has been accused of being too close to Wall Street's short-sellers, specialists who try to make money off bad news by selling borrowed stock at a high price and then replacing the shares after the news has driven the stock lower. Abelson dismisses those accusations as nonsense, and they have never held up in court. More often than not, his column has punctured balloons that deserved puncturing. It has a loyal following and whether or not one heeds its investment advice or agrees with its philosphical arguments, "Up and Down Wall Street" has always been fun to read. Let's take a moment to review the first portion of a column that's typical of the relentless pounding Abelson has delivered over the years to the nation's most deliberative political body:

Everybody likes to pick on Congress. It's the new American pastime, and its popularity is growing like mad. No surprise, either, since it's a lot cheaper and just as much fun tossing a calumny at a Congressman as coughing up a small fortune to spring for 18 holes or the privilege of seeing Michael Jordan or Dan Marino raise a sweat. To the average working, taxpaying stiff, on scale of 1 to 10, with 10 being great and 1 being the pits, Congress rates a solid minus 20.

And, gosh knows, we've aimed our share of brickbats at the wretches, and, frankly, we feel not the slightest twinge of regret. Still, we have to confess that every now and then, we find our impulse to indulge in a spot of Congress-bashing stayed by the realization that no matter how crooked and corrupt and greedy the representative, chances are he can lay claim to a mother. In other words, regardless of the number of checks he's bounced or postage stamps he's stolen or meals he's bummed, he's probably a human being.

Besides, even that miserable collection of wastrels and wantons, of scoundrels and spongers, of windbags and mountebanks can once in a blue moon come up with an idea so ingenious as to take your breath away and make you stand back in awestruck admiration. Just such an idea was conceived in the very twilight of the latest and unlamentedest session of Congress. The inspiration was the most profound of all, the fear that the angry electorate might decide to make the solons earn an honest living.

Specifically, a bipartisan group of lawmakers formed a "Congressional Home Appliance Caucus." Ostensibly, what impelled the founders is that they came from districts with appliance manufacturing facilities and should get together to discuss ways and means to help their common constituency. Didn't fool us for a moment, though: The true purpose of this new caucus is to enable the two-dozen-odd congressmen who have created it to run for re-election as stoves, dishwashers, driers, can openers — homey objects, in short, that evoke kindly emotions among ordinary folk rather than the wrath their actual persons would be sure to provoke. Even so, the participants in the caucus realized they had to be careful in selecting an appropriate appliance as a disguise; were they, say, to run as a garbage disposal or a vacuum, they'd be instantly identified.[5]

The acerbic tone of "Up and Down Wall Street" is a reflection of Abelson's apprenticeship at the *New York Journal American*, where, starting in the 1950s, his mentor and editor, Leslie Gould, impressed upon him the virtues of skepticism. Abelson learned his lessons well and carried them with him not only to *Barron's* but also to NBC, where for eight years he did commentary in the pre-dawn darkness on that network's earliest morning newscast. Although given only scant seconds to speak — and confronted by questions from anchors who may not have always comprehended the subject at hand — Abelson somehow managed to make critical points succinctly most mornings. He thus belongs in that small cadre of practised print journalists whose careers at some point have included creditable work on TV.

Abelson reflected on the beginnings of his column and the state of business journalism in a conversation with the author. Here is a portion of that discussion:

How did "Up and Down Wall Street" get started?

"It began at a time when the market was booming and investors were lapping up information about stocks and companies. That was in the '60s, when there wasn't any consistently skeptical voice on the financial scene. You could find stories that took a dim view of one thing or another, but they ran sporadically. We struck a chord because people were looking for a counterbalance to all the bullshit that was coming out of the brokerage houses and the companies and industries with their hordes of PR people trying to mislead the press."

And you felt that the press was, and maybe still is, being too obliging and reverential?

"Sure. The coverage tended to be reverential when I started as a reporter, and to a certain extent it still is, although over the years some of us — not only *Barron's* but *Forbes* and others, too — have stuck out our tongues a little more. However, the basic situation isn't much different now. Too many reporters still seem to think that just because a company says something, it's true. They don't realize that there is no truth unless they find it.

This inclination to be deferential seems to have deep roots. Why?

"It's understandable, in a way. After all, we live in the consummate capitalist society, where power comes from the dollar. Businessmen give at least the aura of being capable of generating monetary power. Journalists all too often are impressed by that and they're easily snowed when they interview some corporate ass who rambles on about things he doesn't fully understand himself."

There are many more specialized journalists around today, with good educational backgrounds — people with accounting or law degrees, for example, covering those fields. Isn't this a positive trend that should produce better, more perceptive reporting?

"Some editors think it has, but I don't. You find lots of reporters now who seem to know more about the difference between a convertible debenture and a non-convertible than they do about what is and what isn't a good story. They may be well educated, but in a sense they've become almost informational extensions of the industries they cover.

"I think you have to encourage every reporter, including those with advanced degrees, to follow basic journalistic techniques and treat business like any other story. You do your homework first. Then you do your digging and your interrogation, and you put it together, all the while maintaining a skeptical view, which I think is absolutely essential."

And if the skepticism turns to bitterness — which it sometimes does — what then?

"It's always possible that's going to happen, but I don't think it's the worst thing in the world. Reporters have a particular role to play. They need to learn to lean against the wind, to deflate the inflated and inflate the deflated. If they get a little bitter occasionally there's nothing wrong with that."

For more than a decade, Abelson was *Barron's* editor as well as its lead columnist. In 1993, at the age of 67, he passed the job of editor along to his compatriot, James Meagher (who had been managing editor), and agreed to continue as a columnist. Under Abelson's editorship, *Barron's*, like the *Journal*, ignored the dictates of television and the trend toward brevity and concentrated on thorough pieces, most of which ran longer — in some cases much longer — than the average *Journal* leader. A good example is "Fallen Prophet," a 10,000-word profile of Joe Granville, perhaps the most celebrated and colorful market sage of all time. It's a story that required extra length and would have lost much of its richness if it had been condensed. A portion of "Fallen Prophet" is reprinted in the Appendix.[6]

As editor, Abelson infused the entire publication with a nippier tone, drawing on the talents of in-house writers and editors such as Meagher, Kathryn Welling and Eric Savitz as well as outside contributors like Benjamin Stein, a Los Angeles lawyer and writer who has never been hesitant to load and fire. Under Abelson, the typical *Barron's* article became more pungent, though never quite as cantankerous as the most spirited Abelsonianisms in "Up and Down Wall Street."[7]

Savitz, in addition to writing articles, has done some of the legwork for Abelson's column, gathering facts and figures and conducting interviews. Both men rank among the Corporate Assassins, *TFJR Business News Reporter's* elite group of hard-nosed journalists. Abelson, in fact, has to be considered the dean of the group. When he retires from journalism, that appellation may well pass to Allan Sloan, a syndicated newspaper columnist at *Newsday*. Sloan concentrates on errant companies and bumptious financial operators. His writing style is less sportive than Abelson's but he too is feisty and iconoclastic. Neither of them mince words when they skewer their victims, and both do it in a manner reminiscent of the professional hangman who traveled the country during the antebellum years, visiting jailhouses and stringing up the condemned. Word has it that those who stood around afterwards, admiring his workmanship, could only shake their heads and say, "When he hangs 'em, they stays hanged."

Forbes, like *Barron's*, has moved along the critical path in business journalism and achieved greater success as a commercial enterprise. Its circulation is more than three times as large as the circulation of *Barron's*. After floundering during the Depression years, *Forbes* picked itself up off the mat following World War II and began to prosper in a big way under the stewardship of James Michaels, who cut his journalistic teeth as a wire service correspondent in India and covered the assassination of Mahatma Gandhi in 1948. Michaels joined *Forbes* a few years later and succeeded Byron David Mack as editor in 1961.

For a long while Michaels performed in the shadow of Malcomb Forbes, Sr., the magazine's editor-in-chief and the son of Bertie Charles. Malcomb, who died in 1991, was a very public person. While he was throwing grand parties, sailing around in balloons and attracting the attention of advertisers and the world at large, Michaels was molding *Forbes* into an interesting magazine that contains provocative insights into publicly traded companies. Malcomb had a hand in shaping its editorial approach, but it was Michaels who perfected the snappy little company story, written from the investor's viewpoint, that enabled *Forbes* to make its mark.

As the magazine has grown more popular with advertisers, it has added more pages. To help fill them, it has run articles that are somewhat longer as well as broader in nature. A case in point is "What do we get for our school dollars?" a 4,000-word cover story by Janet Novack that was highly critical of certain trends and policies in our educational system. Here is one of her conclusions:

> The school day is short and the school year remains limited (178 days on average in the U.S.). Increasingly, these

schools are struggling to squeeze more and more into this limited span. They must accommodate new politically correct fads, such as teaching self-esteem, alongside old extracurricular favorites such as band and orchestra and choir. Inevitably, accommodating the new fads squeezes the time available for teaching reading, writing and arithmetic. There are simply not enough hours in the day, and it's the basics that seem to be suffering.[8]

Novack's article mentioned a high school in Ohio that dropped a 20-minute spelling period each day but managed to find room in its curriculum for a course called Dress for Success. It wasn't the kind of piece you'd ordinarily expect to find in a financial magazine. Handled another way — without the accent on how school dollars are spent — it could easily have been a non-financial story in the education section of a newspaper or in a general interest magazine. The money angle gave it legitimacy as a *Forbes* story.

Another example of the magazine's broader reach is "Reading redux," by John Merwin. It tracked the bittersweet transformation of a Pennsylvania factory town (that once served as a model for novelist John Updike's portrayal of a fictitious community called Brewer) from palmier days to a time when the textile plants have been replaced by discount stores, making Reading "the factory outlet shopping capital of America."[9]

Still another example, perhaps the best of all, was *Forbes'* 75th anniversary issue, which addressed the nagging fear that the American Dream is slipping away. Many publications have run articles on this, usually profiles of families who feel they don't have it as good as their parents did, college dropouts who say their living standards aren't rising, or others who for one reason or another

think the dream is dying and the country is going to hell.
It's a subject that has been addressed in various ways by
numerous magazines and newspapers.

Forbes chose to deal with it by inviting 11 authors and
scholars to weigh in with essays. The 11 included Updike,
whose piece was entitled "Where is the space to chase
rainbows?" and Peggy Noonan, a former scriptwriter for
Dan Rather and speechwriter for Ronald Reagan and
George Bush. While Updike's essay and several of the
others supported the notion that Americans are less well
off today, Noonan's piece suggested that the idea is mostly
a bunch of foolishness cooked up by the chronically dis-
gruntled. In his introduction to the special issue — "Oh,
Our Aching Angst" — Michaels made it clear he sides with
Noonan. He wrote that the main source of the notion that
today's middle-class Americans have it tougher is

> writers and academicians who have a low opinion of cap-
> italism and of American popular culture. The media ma-
> chine turns this highbrow griping into sound bites and data
> bites and feeds them to the masses.

According to Michaels, the media machine also sees to it
that

> we are punished hourly with mindless keening about dis-
> tribution of wealth, the greed of the rich and the rights and
> wrongs suffered by this minority and that allegedly op-
> pressed group.[10]

While *Forbes* has widened its reach with caustic and
sometimes controversial treatment of major themes and
trends, it also has added more columns of practical investment advice, including several on stocks and one on
bonds written by Ben Weberman, who has reported on

the fixed-income markets for more than 30 years. A prototypical Weberman column, written in 1991, guided investors searching for higher yields through the arcane world of Planned Amortization Class Collateralized Mortgage Obligations (PACCMOs) along with other esoteric mortgage-backed securities. The column contained a warning that while such securities paid returns higher than one could earn in a money market account, they also carried certain risks. It was a good example of personal finance reporting that sounds an appropriate cautionary note and offers sensible advice rather than hot tips on how to get rich.[11]

Meantime, short, corky stories on publicly-traded companies and their chief executives remain *Forbes'* stock-in-trade. These articles, which can be found in every issue, read quickly and reach firm conclusions, not all of them favorable. While some of these pieces are filled with praise, those for which the magazine is probably better known deliver scathing indictments such as the one that began with this headline:

What's Hawaiian for rotten management?

Written by Mark Beauchamp, this article blasted the leadership of Hawaiian Airlines for running the air carrier "almost into the ground." Beauchamp began by posing this question: "How do you flirt with bankruptcy in a business that is indispensable during an unprecedented economic boom?" He then gave his answer:

You get swell-headed, expand stupidly, manage poorly, neglect maintenance, delay and cancel flights and then plunge into a ruinous price war trying to gain market share.[12]

Another example of Forbesian stricture appeared during a period when it looked as if Donald Trump might be down to his last million. *Forbes* posed the key question:

Can Donald pay his hotel bill?

This story revealed that although Trump's bankers were allowing him to continue to own and run Manhattan's prestigious Plaza Hotel, the hotel had lost $100 million over a two-year period and wasn't paying full interest on its debt. After noting that Trump had borrowed extensively to buy the place, the authors of the piece, Richard Stern and Tatiana Pouschine, went on to address another question:

> Why is the Plaza doing so badly? The hotel itself is as popular as ever. Last year it had a positive cash flow of nearly $21 million before interest expense. It is very much a going concern. Trump simply paid too much and his obliging bankers lent him too much.[13]

With help from an audited financial statement they managed to obtain, Stern and Pouschine documented Trump's interest burden and showed skepticism toward his proposal to raise cash by converting half of the hotel into condominiums and selling them for hefty prices amounting to $1,500 or more a square foot.

Sometimes *Forbes'* doubting, critical approach produces negative articles about financial operators and companies (usually medium-size or small firms) that stir the blood in executive suites. One can find business people who feel the magazine reaches pretty far on occasion in its quest for strong conclusions. Its assertive style reflects a belief that readers prefer journalism that is "didactic and entertaining," to quote one of Michaels' favorite phrases. It's a creed which holds that articles should take a firm position rather than laying out the pros and cons and letting the reader judge their merits. We get more on this now from James Flanigan, who wrote and edited at *Forbes* under Michaels before becoming a columnist at the *Los Angeles Times*:[14]

"*Forbes* has always been a place where new writers learn very quickly that they can't do stories which say 'on the one hand this and on the other hand that.' Any hint that your piece might be going in that direction would automatically get you an audience with Michaels. Jim would tell you that you're 'belaboring the fucking obvious' — which is exactly how he liked to put it — and he would remind you that articles should have a point of view or they're a waste of the reader's time and they don't belong in the magazine.

"Naturally, the writers have to back up their conclusions. They can't just say a company is badly run without providing some documentation. That has never been acceptable. However, at *Forbes* the attitude has always been 'if you end up getting it wrong it isn't the end of the world. You can always come back and do another article later and revise your opinion.' It is a style of financial journalism that I gloried in and reveled in for a long while. It's *Forbes'* style, very distinct and very popular with readers."

Its creator and curator, Michaels, was still editing copy and admonishing his writers to avoid belaboring the obvious when he turned 70 in 1992. His act, like Abelson's, will be an extremely hard one to follow.

NOTES

1. *Barron's,* April 11, 1988.

2. *Barron's,* June 15, 1987.

3. *Barron's,* October 23, 1987.

4. *Barron's,* January 11, 1988.

5. *Barron's,* October 26, 1992. Another passage from a similarly derisive Abelson column is reprinted in the Appendix.

6. "Fallen *Prophet,*" written by Rhonda Brammer, ran in the August 24, 1992, issue. Along with a lengthy extract from this article, the reader will find in the Appendix the Foreward from the first issue of *Barron's* in 1921.

7. Other writers who adhered to a doubting style at *Barron's* and went on to employ that approach elsewhere with favorable results include Floyd Norris of *The New York Times* and James Grant, editor of *Grant's Interest Rate Observer* and author of *Money of the Mind: Borrowing and Lending in America from the Civil War to Michael Milken* (New York: Farrar, Straus, Giroux, 1992). Under James Meagher and managing editor Edwin Finn, *Barron's* format is being revised in an attempt to increase circulation and attract more advertising, but the publication's editorial tone remains essentially unchanged.

8. *Forbes,* October 12, 1992.

9. *Forbes,* March 9, 1987.

10. The 75th anniversary issue was dated September 14, 1992. A longer excerpt from Michaels' introductory piece appears in the Appendix.

11. From a Weberman column entitled "Good yield, market risk" — *Forbes,* October 21, 1991.

12. *Forbes,* June 26, 1989.

13. *Forbes,* July 8, 1991.

14. Flanigan began his career at the *New York Herald Tribune* before gravitating to *Forbes.* He then moved back and forth three times between *Forbes* and the *Los Angeles Times* before settling in at the *Times* as a columnist in 1986.

$

18 Less Zip, More Relevance

The *Institutional Investor* continued to set a brisk pace for a long while after Jerry Goodman left it and turned his attention to television. By making notables of the unheralded, by running thorough articles written with verve, and by illustrating them with irreverent graphics, *II* served as a springhead for others who were striving to invigorate their editorial products. No other magazine born in the final half of this century has done more to demonstrate that financial journalism doesn't have to be dull.[1]

It is only recently that the *Institutional Investor* has lost some of its zip, like a showgirl who has danced front and center in the chorus line for a good many years. That analogy might, in fact, provide an appropriate visual for a story on the maturing of *II*. It's less paradigmatic now, gentler, fatter and very prosperous. A specialized trade publication, it circulates among the heavy hitters in the

205

money world who can afford its $265 annual subscription. The company that publishes it has become part of Capital Cities/ABC, which bought it for some $70 million in 1984. That deal allowed Gil Kaplan, *II*'s founder, to divide his time between overseeing the magazine for his new bosses as its publisher and editor-in-chief and pursuing his favorite avocation, traveling around the world conducting symphony orchestras. Nine years later, Kaplan bowed out of *II* altogether. His name remains on the masthead as editor emeritus.[2]

Kaplan was in his 20s and the *wunderkind* of financial publishing when he started *II* in 1967. His special afflatus back then was in identifying an unfilled niche in the coverage of investment management and hiring Goodman and others to help him fill it. After reading a few "Adam Smith" articles in *New York* magazine, Kaplan called Goodman, acknowledged that he was young, that he was starting a magazine, and that he wanted to fill it with lively journalism. He made Goodman a shareholder in his new publishing company and gave him the title of editor along with a salary of $10,000 a year. By then Goodman was a card-carrying Wall Streeter as well as a writer, and he knew enough about business to know he wanted to participate in the new publishing enterprise primarily as a part owner. He applied himself energetically to the task of making *II* a winner, as did Kaplan and everyone else, and the magazine caught on immediately. Wall Streeters read and talked about it, and it was an overnight success. Looking back on its genetic years, Peter Landau recalls:

"If you stop and analyze why the magazine took off, you come to the realization that there really wasn't anything all that mysterious about it. We listened to what people on the Street were saying and who they were talking about. We wrote long takes (lengthy articles) and dressed them up."

That's essentially right. *II* was a simple concept, well executed, though there is a little more to it than that. One Sunday night many moons ago, while returning to New York by train from a weekend on Long Island, Kaplan and I were ruminating about various reasons why the magazine was off to a good start. We touched on some of the more apparent ones, including the dramatizing of events and the skills of people like Goodman, Landau, Chris Welles and Fred Bleakley, along with their counterparts in advertising and other departments.[3] Gil then mentioned another, less obvious reason that hadn't crossed my mind. "When you look at us closely," he said, "you can see that sometimes we're able to make stories seem more relevant than they really are."

Today, nearly all magazines ballyhoo the relevance of articles to one degree or another. While the methods for doing it can be overused and carried to the point where the effort backfires, there is nothing sinister about the techniques themselves. They include reinforcing each headline with a "deck" or short statement underscoring a story's significance. This message is often reiterated on the contents page and driven home again in the article itself, in the opening paragraphs, which address two questions: Why should readers pay attention to the story, and why should they read it now?[4]

II didn't invent these techniques, but it refined them and became very adept at using them, and it still uses them. With its deeper editorial bench and a bigger supply of manuscripts, it no longer has to make snowballs out of compost every month or strain as hard for pertinence. But that wasn't always the case when the magazine was starting out and still inchoate. Its staff was stretched thin, and there was no reserve of decent articles available for use when a manuscript that was scheduled to run proved odorous or weak. Nearly everything that was assigned ran, even if it had to be given a quick, superficial scrubbing and made to seem stronger or handsomer than it was. There were occasions when the reinforcing and reiterating were pushed hard, sometimes harder than necessary, though seldom to the point where they endangered the magazine's authenticity. As the years rolled by and the *II*'s pool of freelance and staff writers grew, the task of filling each issue with material that didn't have to be scrubbed, fumigated and flogged became easier. It was aided by the fact that for a long while each issue of *II* contained less than a half-dozen articles, or about a third as many as the magazine runs today.

Let's take a brief look at the line-up of stories in a typical issue from two decades ago — June 1973 — when *II* was still young and kittenish. The cover piece — "What Makes Danny Run?" — profiled Dan Dorfman, who was starting to gain prominence as the author of the *Journal*'s "Heard on the Street" column. Dorfman is practically a household name now, but he wasn't then. The story had a sense of discovery to it and was based on the premise that institutional investors were becoming aware of Dorfman and wondering what to make of him. Written in an entertaining style by John DeMott, it described how Dorfman gathered tips about stocks and examined criticism that he was pushy and negatively-oriented. It ran more than 4,000 words and was accompanied by a table showing what had happened to the prices of various securities after they were mentioned in his column. The cover photo showed Dorfman looking puckish and leaning on a typewriter.

The cover line read: "The controversial power of Dan Dorfman." On the contents page, *II* said:

> Not many in the business have met the man whose likeness appears on this month's cover, but almost everyone is aware of his presence. . . . This story describes how Dorfman wields his considerable journalistic muscle and why he does what he does.

On page 40, the deck preceding the article pounded the drum a little harder, advising investment managers that the piece should be read without delay because "it's just possible that he (Dorfman) could wreak havoc with your portfolio tomorrow morning."

That same issue featured another long article that was less entertaining than the Dorfman profile but probably even more germane. Entitled "How Wall Street is Learning to Deal," it was written by Fred Bleakley and examined a trend among brokerage firms toward dealing in stocks instead of merely placing buy and sell orders for clients. This was a development Bleakley and *II* had spotted at an early stage, and one which subscribers were ready to hear more about. The contents page said that

> the trend toward more risk-taking on the part of brokers is growing inexorably, as more and more firms across the country make markets. This story poses some hard questions. Will a broker have to be a market maker to get orders? How will exchange specialists be able to cope with strong upstairs markets in their best stocks? And what will all this mean to the very existence of the auction market?

Bleakley's article contained Wall Street jargon that most *II* readers understood and was illustrated with a drawing of an investment manager sticking his head into a bear's mouth. The caption read: "More and more firms are let-

ting it be known that they are 'at risk.'" The deck further
underscored the story's importance by explaining that it
was based on dozens of interviews, and that

> it discloses what appears to be an inexorable movement
> toward more risk-taking on the part of brokers, and offers
> some suggestions about where it all could lead.

The June issue also carried an article by Charles Maxwell, a Wall Street oil analyst, about the investment impli-
cations of the 1970s energy crisis. It was timely but a slow
read. Entitled "Energy: Forget the crisis, what will the
solutions mean?" Maxwell's report was touted on the contents page as one that "looks beyond the immediate crisis
and suggests that many energy stocks should be more
than able to hold their own." This theme was summarized
again in the deck and, for good measure, once more in the
lead to the article. Even readers scanning the magazine
while they were half asleep couldn't possibly fail to get the
message.

The June issue included two other profiles in addition
to the Dorfman story. One of them was linked to
Bleakley's article and entitled "Salem Lewis: The big bear
at Bear, Stearns." It described Lewis as a pioneer in the
buying and selling of large quantities of stock. In the
language of the Street, he was a "block trader," one of
the first. As such he was someone many *II* readers dealt
with or were interested in, so this piece required very
little hype on the contents page and was not accompanied
by a deck.

The other profile in that issue — "Mr. Bucher goes to
Washington" — had some built-in appeal but still needed
a push. It introduced the reader to Jeff Bucher, the first
bank trust official to become a member of the Federal Re-

serve Board. This story, which I wrote, gave readers a glimpse of the Federal Reserve's operations. While refraining from offering up Bucher as an instant expert on monetary policy, it included tips from him on the art of analyzing the actions of the Fed. The deck made the point that

> Fed-watching is an exercise most money managers practice at one time or another, so Institutional Investor asked Bucher for his views now on what to look for and how his experience as an insider of the body that determines the nation's monetary policy differed from his preconceptions of it.

As a counterweight to this demure discourse we decorated the article with an impious photo of Bucher the banker jogging in a sweatsuit on the mall across from the Federal Reserve building, with the Washington monument in the background.

It is that impiety that's missing to some extent in the more ripened *II* of the '90s. While it's still very sound editorially, it is no longer a hot, frisky magazine that has everyone talking. As far as I know, no one ever posted a sign in its editorial office declaring that henceforth *II* would become less rambunctious, but at some point things began drifting that way. My first inkling of this came in 1983, when I spent some time in Thailand freelancing a story on the investment situation in that country. Entitled "Backs to the Wall in Bangkok," it led off with a reference to Genghis Khan, the warlord who had stormed through Thailand a few centuries before I got there.[5] The mention of old Genghis created an analogy that lent itself to some pleasantly provocative visual possibilities, which was why I put it in the lead. However, when the story appeared in print, it came packaged in a plain vanilla layout that was indistinguishable from the treatment afforded investment stories in other, more utilitarian magazines.

Another illustration of the drift away from impiety appeared in *II* during the days when the junk bond market was flying high. The excesses which occurred in that lightly supervised financial frolic damaged countless lives and several large enterprises, including First Executive Corp., a California insurance holding company with affiliates that were investing in junk, or securities which pay high yields and are issued by companies that cannot get a top-notch credit rating.

First Executive's major domo was Fred Carr, a veteran investor who was operating aggressively in the stock market when I first met him during the go-go period in the 1960s. Back then he was called a "gunslinger" — a money manager who concentrated on small, relatively unknown growth companies, some of which entailed risks that weren't ideally suited for the faint of heart. Carr hated the "gunslinger" sobriquet, which he acquired as a successful mutual fund manager. In its best year, 1967, his Enterprise Fund recorded a huge total return of 115%, largely because it was invested in a number of hot growth stocks that became even hotter after Carr found them. His achievements at Enterprise made him a bonafide financial celebrity. In the *Institutional Investor* and elsewhere, he was portrayed with maximum pageantry as a mutual fund maestro, one of the true dramatis personae of his time.

One of the things that struck me about Carr back then was the way he fretted about his investments and about the uncertainty of what might lie ahead. He came across as a serious risk taker, but also as a serious worrier. Although he enjoyed jetting around the world and throwing grand parties, when it came to business he was nobody's fool. If he felt it was time to punt, his instincts were usually pretty good. He was not, I might add, among those who were surprised when the go-go period which brought him to prominence eventually went. By then, he had left the company that ran the Enterprise Fund.

Thus it was of some interest to find an *II* article on First Executive in 1986 entitled "Fred Carr is Still Living Dangerously."[6] Visually, the piece was unimaginative. Instead of playing on the theme of dangerous living, which could have triggered some clever graphics, *II* ran an unexciting photo of Carr and several subordinates in an office. It was a dreary shot and a lifeless layout. The article itself was similarly solemn but competently reported and timely. There was no question of its relevance. It disclosed that First Executive and its affiliates were "taking the insurance industry by storm" with a scheme of pouring money into high-yielding junk bonds and paying "lofty rates" on policies. And it said that Carr was uneasy about the future. Written by Hilary Rosenberg, it mentioned his fear of the unknown. "Carr may do the unconventional," she reported, "but he is also one to be wary of pitfalls." She said he "worries a lot" and does so "with good reason."

Her story mentioned that the government had just launched an investigation into Drexel Burnham Lambert, the junk bond factory that later blew up, and into Drexel's relationship with Ivan Boesky. The piece explained that both Boesky and Drexel had ties to Carr and that some investors and regulators were becoming "skittish" about debt deals and his organization's liberal use of junk bonds. Carr's past accomplishments were recounted in detail along with his efforts (which obviously proved inadequate) to safeguard his firm against a major disaster in junk bonds. The story did not predict such a disaster, but anyone who read it could hardly have been surprised later when the market for junk tumbled and took First Executive with it.

Although the *Institutional Investor* isn't quite the high stepper it once was, it continues to wear some war paint. Its contents page is colorful, and occasionally the cover art has flashes of the old irreverence: a cartoon of former Amex chairman James Robinson in the altogether; a story on wild trading in the foreign currency jungle dressed up with grinning lions and other denizens of the jungle. Even in its post-pubescent years, the magazine has shown that once in a great while it can still kick up its heels and put on a startling show for its readers. It managed to do that in the autumn of 1987, just after the Big Skid, weighing in with a story as adventurous as anything Goodman and his cohorts had cooked up during the magazine's salad days. While other periodicals were printing competent though not particularly daring articles on the '87 crash, *II* ran a cover piece entitled "Apocalypse Now?" It conveyed the disquieting news that a few men of affluence were stockpiling machine guns and canned food and preparing for an economic and financial collapse that could trigger rioting and social chaos.[7]

Decorated with grim photos from the Great Depression, the piece acknowledged that these hoarders were "a little extreme." But it chronicled the prevailing unease without the snickering tone that frequently accompanies discussion of apocalyptic scenarios. It reported that such scenarios often follow a pattern, singling out an abundance of debt as a key reason for concern and also citing other dangers such as shaky financial institutions, the threat of protectionism and the influence of foreign lenders who hold large amounts of U.S. Treasury securities. The story said an "economic day of reckoning" might be drawing near. This, it was suggested, could take the form of another depression, social upheaval, runaway inflation or some other calamity, if not right away, then in the not too distant future.

"Apocalypse Now?" generated hearty discussion within the *II* organization — not everyone felt that putting it on the cover was a swell idea — and it was sufficiently alarming to irritate some readers. One peeved corporate PR executive fired off a letter to the editors complaining that the article had a "sick twist." "It is very disturbing," he wrote, "to see a responsible publication like yours reverting to sensationalism." There was other negative response as well, which should hardly be surprising and isn't necessarily all bad, especially if it comes from those who can be counted on to routinely dismiss any suggestion that our economic system is flawed.

Looking back, it's clear that the article — like the rich and the nervous with their firearms at the ready — represented an overreaction to the conditions at the time. The October crash was a humdinger, knocking 508 points off the Dow Jones Industrials in a single day. But Wall Street and the country calmed down afterwards instead of coming apart. Angry hordes did not storm the stock exchange in the wake of the selloff, and, as far as I know, no brokers were found barricaded in their offices eating canned tunafish or brandishing an Uzi.

Even so, "Apocalypse Now?" was worth reading. It marked one of *II*'s infrequent forays outside the confines of finance and into the broader realm of socio-economics. Written by Cary Reich, *II*'s executive editor at the time, it

215

went well beyond the ordinary fare one finds in a trade journal.[8] By abandoning safe ground and risking disapprobation, it explored issues that seldom get addressed in a publication of that sort, notably the proposition that one of these days something more serious than a lower Dow might be in the offing.

NOTES

1. A good illustration of the *Institutional Investor's* knack for turning the unheralded into notables has been its All-America Research Team, financial analysts chosen for their acumen who are dressed up each year on *II*'s cover as football players.

2. Along with the magazine, Capital Cities/ABC acquired a series of investment conferences plus a few other specialized publications operating under the *II* umbrella, including the *Wall Street Letter*. When Kaplan stepped down, the flagship magazine's circulation had grown to about 150,000 subscribers in more than 100 countries.

3. Welles later taught financial journalism at Columbia University, wrote for the *Los Angeles Times* and other publications, and joined *Business Week's* senior editorial staff when *BW* was making the transition from dull to readable in the 1980s. Bleakley went from *II* to *The New York Times* and from there to *The Wall Street Journal*. *II*'s advertising effort in the late '60s and '70s was spearheaded by Mark Yarry and Fred Rubenstein. The two people chiefly responsible for making the magazine a slick production were Herb Rosenthal and Bruce Ward. As an indication of the ambitiousness of their operation, it may be worth noting that Ward and Rosenthal combined their talents at one point to create a life-size pull-out of a British investment manager who was featured in a sister publication that I was editing at the time.

4. Even the casually observant reader will recognize that the technique of including a deck or subtitle is also used on the covers or jackets of many books, including this one.

5. *II*, August 1983. Of all the articles I wrote for *II* from 1969 to '83 as a member of the staff or as a freelancer, "Backs to the Wall in Bangkok" was the most challenging and the last one. The most enjoyable was "Benjamin Graham: The grandfather of investment value is still concerned," a long profile of Graham that ran in the April 1974 issue.

6. *II*, December 1986. First Executive began running into trouble in 1987 and filed for bankruptcy in 1991.

7. *II*, November 1987.

8. Reich, the author of "Apocalypse *Now?*" is also the author of *Financier — The Biography of Andre Meyer: a story of money, power, and the reshaping of American business* (New York: William Morrow, 1983). This book traced the career of Meyer, a refugee from World War II who became a domineering Wall Streeter and served as a consultant to the rich and the mighty for three decades.

$

19 *Galbraith Banks Cordtz Weaver & Loeb*

With the passage of time, *Fortune* has slipped from the position of prominence it once enjoyed. Like the *Institutional Investor* — though to a greater extent and for a much longer period — it was the most talked about periodical in its field. For roughly four decades after it began in 1930, *Fortune* bestrode the money world like a colossus. It educated and entertained. It offered exhaustive evaluations of corporate strategy and public policy. It was elegant, smartly illustrated, often poetical, and in a class by itself.

Fortune's reign as *primus inter pares* ended gradually over the past quarter-century. Here are five views of its decline and its glory years:

J.K. Galbraith was a member of the editorial staff off and on for five years before returning to Harvard in 1948. In chapter 5 he described his first writing assignment for the magazine during World War II. Here are some of his thoughts about *Fortune* then and now:

"When I was at the magazine, we regarded what we were doing with a good deal of detached humor. There was a tradition of approaching stories that way, which had been established by people like Dwight Macdonald and Archie MacLeish in the 1930s, and it continued. We found ourselves constantly reacting to what we saw as some of the absurdities of the American business system.

"I recall one story, which I worked on with Wilder Hobson, about proper executive dress. We classified businessmen around the country by their attire, with categories such as Anglo-Park Avenue Dash and Southern Comfort, illustrated with photographs. Dress is a topic that many businessmen take seriously and one which could have been addressed in a serious manner, but our piece was done entirely tongue-in-check.

"Today, most of the writing in *Fortune* lacks the element of wry amusement. It tends to treat business and the issues of the day with solemnity, and that has to affect the quality of the writing. The magazine's economic forecasts are invariably serious and often contradictory. In my day, we would have accepted the reality that economists make forecasts not because they know but because they are asked.

"I was given a lifetime subscription when I left, so I still look at the magazine. What I have sensed for some time is a more sycophantic commitment to the established business point of view. I suspect this change must have played some role in what has happened to *Fortune* over the years."

Louis Banks was managing editor from 1965 to 1970.[1] By then *Fortune* was featuring more stories about management, and its tone was more earnest. It continued to feature capacious articles and sterling graphics. Its circulation and advertising revenue were starting to grow more slowly, and its rivals were showing signs of energizing themselves. On the whole, though, *Fortune* remained the front runner during that time. Here are some of Banks' recollections:

"We were still living in a charmed situation when I was editing the magazine. It was a monthly with a deep staff and a large format, and it still had a kind of intellectual monopoly on business journalism. *Business Week* was going along in its groove. At *Forbes*, Jim Michaels was only starting to hit his stride. *The Wall Street Journal* was getting better, but it hadn't yet gotten up a full head of steam. That was a very good time for *Fortune*, and it was wonderful to have been part of it.

"However, it was inevitable that things would change. Our competitors began to catch up. They started doing more definitive corporation stories and profiles as well as more analytical science and technology pieces. What happened to *Fortune* was that it lost its monopoly in those areas."

Dan Cordtz was an associate editor hired by Banks in 1966. Before coming to *Fortune*, he had worked for *The Wall Street Journal*. Cordtz left *Fortune* for ABC in 1974: He remembers:

"When I was on the *Journal*, *Fortune* was considered mecca for a business writer. Most of us aspired to work there. At the *Journal*, we all wanted to write the big front-page leaders instead of those crappy little pieces on the inside of the paper, and a *Fortune* story looked to us to be the equivalent of about three *Journal* leaders. It was monumental. It contained everything you ever wanted to tell a reader about the subject.

"The magazine wasn't as literary or philosophical then as it had been during the days when people like Galbraith and MacLeish were writing for it, but all things considered it was still very good. It was topical and thorough. I can remember the first piece I did for it, on the battle for control of the Rock Island Railroad. I discovered somewhat to my astonishment that nearly everyone I interviewed was willing to open up and talk about the intrigue and the details of the battle. I was able to put together a long story that read almost like a book.

"One of the things that happened to change the course of events at *Fortune* was that senior executives at Time-Life decided they wanted the magazine to be more of a financial success. The first thing they did was reduce the size, figuring that a smaller format would appeal to more people, and that if more people read it, more advertisers would go for it and it would become more profitable. I was such a traditionalist that I thought even that change was terrible, but as it turned out it didn't really affect the content very much.

"Then the rest of the stuff started, although that was after I left. The frequency was increased to twice a month, and many of the articles were shortened. One of the concerns with the old *Fortune* was that people were no longer taking the time to read the long stories, which was a legitimate concern and a consequence of the growing popularity of television. The trouble with switching to very short stories, however, is that you rarely learn enough from them to make reading them worthwhile."

Paul Weaver was an assistant managing editor in the late 1970s an early '80s. After leaving *Fortune*, he started his own magazine, the *Fed Fortnightly*, which reported on the Federal Reserve; it survived for a while but eventually went out of business. His thoughts about *Fortune*:

"As part of the rethinking and tinkering that was going on during the transition to the new *Fortune*, many of our stories became very brief, maybe too brief. I think that reached an extreme along about 1982 or '83. Subsequently there was a shift back toward a few longer pieces, perhaps one or two in each issue.

"Keep in mind that a couple of other things were taking place then which also were important. The audience for business news, and for information in general, was becoming much more fragmented. The trend was and still is toward special interest publications. General interest magazines such as *Look* and *Colliers* felt the impact of this years ago, and of course we're seeing it now in television, where general interest programs are having to compete for viewers with programs on cable and public broadcasting that cater to the special interests of certain audiences.

"For a general business magazine, this trend has made it harder to find a range of topics that correspond to the real interests of a large number of readers. When I was at *Fortune*, deciding what those topics were was especially difficult because traditional thinking about what should be in the magazine wasn't always in sync with the results of reader surveys.

"I remember one survey in 1982 which showed that our readers didn't care all that much for corporation stories and wanted more information about other subjects such as the economy and which way government was steering the economy. That survey was largely ignored, but it shouldn't have been. It reflected not only prevailing economic conditions at the time but also a gradual loss of belief in the idea that there is a group of enlightened and cultured professional corporate managers in this country who have great vision and are worth reading about. That idea was a cornerstone of *Fortune* for a very long while."

Prior to becoming *Fortune*'s managing editor in 1984, Marshall Loeb held that same position at *Money*, where he turned what had been a marginally profitable magazine into a huge success. Soon after he replaced William Rukeyser (Lou's brother) as m/e at *Fortune*, its vital statistics, including newsstand sales, began improving. Drawing on what had worked well at *Money*, Loeb expanded *Fortune*'s coverage of personal finance, and he created cover stories with sweeping, largely upbeat themes. Here are four examples from 1989:

THE YEAR'S 25 MOST FASCINATING BUSINESS PEOPLE

AMERICA'S MOST ADMIRED CORPORATIONS

HOW TO GET CUSTOMERS TO LOVE YOU

WILL YOU BE ABLE TO RETIRE?[2]

These days *Fortune* cover lines are often supported by a deck or subtitle. This represents another departure from olden times, when such devices were used inside the magazine but seldom on the cover. Some examples from the Loeb era:

TALK ABOUT BIG PAY!

Spreading fast from boss to
blue-collar worker, incentive
pay promises richer — but
riskier — rewards.
— December 19, 1988

SPEED

Beating competitors to
market is today's hottest
strategy. Here's why — and
how to do it.
— February 13, 1989

MADE IN THE U.S.A.

Manufacturers Start To
Do It Right
— May 21, 1990

IS YOUR CAREER ON TRACK?

Competition is fierce,
and the route to the top
is changing. Here's how to
measure your progress.
— July 2, 1990

NEW IDEAS FOR THE '90s

America's Best Business
Thinkers Explain the Keys
to Future Success
— February 8, 1993

As a fortnightly, *Fortune* is not as timely as *Business Week*, nor as definitive as it was in the past. In terms of prestige, it's not the same colossus it once was; but it is alive and kicking, thanks in no small measure to Loeb's efforts, which began during a difficult period for the Time-Life organization. It was going through a trying merger with Warner Communications,[3] cutting costs at all of its publications (including *Fortune*) and struggling with a new venture, a combination listings guide and magazine that the company launched unsuccessfully at great cost in 1983.[4] Nearly all of Loeb's career has been spent at Time-Life, and over the years he has been involved in numerous developments there concerning business journalism.[5] Here is his assessment of the modern *Fortune* compared with the original version:

"The magazine was a startling success when it first began in 1930 because it was innovative and audacious. It had the confident nerve to charge a dollar a copy during the Depression. It was the best looking magazine in the country without question and enormously influential. It continued along that path for quite a while until it began encountering more competition. Its staple had been the long in-depth story. However, a lot of other business journals came along and started doing those stories. *Fortune* could do them in more depth, but it no longer had that game exclusively to itself.

"Its competitors — notably *Business Week* and *Forbes*, and *The Wall Street Journal* with its front-page leaders — became significantly better. *Fortune* was still doing pretty well, but there was some stalling of growth, and things reached a point in the '70s when it was felt that changes had to be made. As a result, *Fortune* is not the same magazine it was 30 or 40 years ago, but I believe it does reflect the interests and habits of today's readers."

"Some of the changes were made before I came to the magazine, and others took place afterwards. We began doing a fair number of non-corporate stories after I arrived, and we began running both longer pieces — including some of the longest that have ever appeared in the magazine — and others that were a bit brisker. We tried to put more emphasis on stories about entrepreneurial business, individuals who make a difference and management styles that are fascinating or instructive, as well as on personal finance."

Much of the editorial fare in today's *Fortune* is lighter and less explosive than the heavy bombs that were dropped on companies like U.S. Steel, and on arms manufacturers and government policymakers, in the 1930s and '40s. Old-timers from that epoch say that Roosevelt Administration officials used to tremble in anticipation of what might be written about them in the magazine. They also say, proudly, that *Fortune* caused companies to overhaul their business strategies, and that it virtually dictated the choice of the Republican presidential nominee, Wendell Wilkie, in 1940. Maybe the magazine did have that kind of clout then, but it doesn't any longer. Loeb's thoughts on the subject of its diminished influence:

"I'd love to see *Fortune* have a greater influence. But I'm also realistic enough to acknowledge that there are many more good publications out there now than there were in the '30s and '40s, when a cover story in *Fortune* could shake the world. Today, you do what you can to influence public policy and make the world a better place, and that's all you can do."

On Loeb's watch, *Fortune* has reflected his belief that

business journalism should not strive to be overly pugnacious or critical:

"I think it's wrong and dangerous to go into a story with a mindset that you're going to find out what's wrong with Mother Teresa, or that there has to be a skeleton in every closet. It's dangerous to go into a story trying to prove that the CEO of a company is a dirty guy. I think you go in with all the best information you can get. You come well prepared. And you then tell the story fully and fairly.

"One of the difficulties is that a writer may do a terrific article revealing some wrongdoing or nefarious act, and everyone will commend him for it. Then the question becomes 'okay, what are you going to do for an encore?' That's when you often start to see the stretching and the reaching for shocking or negative angles. Sure, there's a role for advocacy journalism, for investigative journalism and for revelatory journalism, but journalism has many more facets to it than just those.

"You often hear business people complain that they don't get a fair shake, that some reporters are looking for a 'when did you stop beating your wife' story, that they're not knowledgeable, or that they take quotes out of context, and so forth. In some instances those complaints are justified. It doubtless is correct that some people in the press have an axe to grind against business, or that they come to a story ill prepared or are not given enough time to delve into a subject properly. When those things happen — and they do happen — I often think of a comment made by Lou Banks. He said it very well when he said 'there are times when business and business journalists deserve one another.'"

NOTES

1. *Fortune*'s managing editors between the late 1960s and early '90s were (in order) Louis Banks, Robert Lubar, William Rukeyser and Marshall Loeb.

2. These cover stories ran on January 2, January 30, March 13 and July 31. Updated versions of "America's Most Admired Corporations" have appeared in the magazine since 1989.

3. The merger with Warner was unpopular with a number of Time-Life staffers and alumni. It drew sharp criticism from Richard Clurman, former chief of correspondents, in *To the End of Time: the seduction and conquest of a media empire* (New York: Simon & Schuster, 1992). It also was rapped by former *Time* correspondent Robert Sam Anson in an article entitled "Greed and Ego in Gotham City: How self-centered executives are destroying the greatest magazine empire the world has known." That piece ran in the August 1989 issue of *Manhattan, inc.*, a 1980s start-up that was eventually folded into *M* magazine. Clay Felker, an editor with an excellent feel for cat-and-doggish business stories like the Warner merger, was involved in the birth of those two magazines as well as the launching of *New York*.

4. For more on this ill-fated venture, *TV-Cable Week*, the reader is referred to *The Fanciest Dive* (New York: W.W. Norton, 1986) by former Time-Life writer Christopher Byron, now a business columnist at *New York*. His book recounts in detail the sad but silly saga of *TV-Cable Week*'s demise. The author wishes to acknowledge that he is a shareholder of Time Warner, and not a particularly happy one as regards the talent and money ($40 million or so) wasted on that fiasco. As a measure of how desperate its plight must have been from the very beginning, *TV-Cable Week* approached me about becoming its first West Coast bureau chief, and then thought better of the idea. Managing editor Richard Burgheim said he decided to spare me the grief of asking me to take on that assignment. At the time I didn't realize how grateful I should feel, but I did after reading Byron's book.

5. Loeb — whose books include *Marshall Loeb's Money Guide* (published by Little Brown) — played a major role in the expansion of *Time*'s Business section, which he edited for several years. He also had a hand in the start-up of an Economy section in response to heightened interest in economic news following Nixon's imposition of wage-price controls in 1971. The author worked with Loeb on both of those sections before Loeb went to *Money* (where he succeeded Bill Rukeyser, just as he did later at *Fortune*). At all three magazines, Loeb's success

can be traced in part to his tireless nature. On nights when issues of *Time* were closing, he could be found bouncing around the editorial offices at 3 a.m. bright-eyed and bushy-tailed, cheerfully asking questions, polishing stories and rewriting headlines while those on the staff who were mere mortals struggled to stay awake.

$

20 Postscript: Fortune and the Chipmunks

My own tour of duty at *Fortune* took place before Marshall Loeb arrived, not long after Cordtz and Banks had departed, and nearly three decades after Galbraith had left. It occurred while Paul Weaver was there and during the managing editorships of Bob Lubar and Bill Rukeyser.

From a distance, I witnessed the erosion of the magazine's position of eminence from 1977 to 1981. I may even have contributed to it, for all I know, though if so I hope the contribution was modest, as was my role at the magazine. During that period, I gave up my post as *Time*'s West Coast business correspondent and agreed to open a California bureau for *Fortune* as an associate editor. The idea was to scout around for stories in the West which might not be readily spotted by those who were peering out across the country from their conning tower in New York.

The pioneering aspect of the assignment appealed to me, along with the challenge of soloing on projects requiring extensive reporting. Until the late '70s, most *Fortune* stories had been assembled by teams consisting of a writer and a researcher who immersed themselves in the reporting, sometimes for many weeks. The gathering of quotes and facts went on and on until it reached the stage where, having interviewed everyone they could think of, they understood the subject about as well as some of the people they were interviewing — at which point it was time to stop asking questions and start writing. After that, revisions took place, and this process too went on and on, only to be followed by another lengthy procedure involving fact-checking and final tinkering until at last a magnum opus of many thousands of words was finally ready for public viewing.

The system was deliberative — maddeningly so for anyone accustomed to the stimulative pace of daily or even weekly journalism. But it produced splendid articles and helped *Fortune* set a high standard for quality. By the time I arrived, the system had been modified as part of a general effort to trim expenses. Writers were being encouraged to do more of their own interviewing, and those researchers who were available to assist were being paired mostly with my counterparts in New York. This meant that a majority of the reporting on my projects had to be done without research help, and in almost the same amount of time that a team of two would be given to complete the same job.

The Los Angeles experiment presented another challenge as well. Since those who whiled away their days in the New York office evaluating story ideas suffered from East Coast myopia and were under the influence of New York-based writers who were following the same companies and industries that I was, the best hope for gaining approval for the articles I favored was to work directly with the managing editor, the ultimate decider on story ideas at all Time-Life magazines. The m/e at *Fortune* when I began, Lubar, was a gracious gentleman in the twilight of his career who was overseeing the conversion to a fortnightly. A couple of years earlier, I had been mentioned as a possible participant in a task force that was making advance preparations for the changeover. However, my overseers at *Time* declined to free me up for that duty, and by the time I finally switched magazines the fortnightly operation had already begun.

At that point one of the more pressing needs was to provide an antidote to the dreaded myopia and direct Lubar's attention toward happenings in the West. To that end I urged him to fly out and spend a few days looking around and talking with some of the movers and shakers in finance and industry as well as with labor leaders and others. Lubar listened politely to my entreaties about the importance of such a trip, but that's as far as it went. On one occasion, after I had been on the staff for several months, on one of my journeys back to the editorial offices in New York I ran into a confirmed myopic who asked how things were going in San Francisco, whereupon I explained that the magazine's new West Coast operation was located some 400 miles south of there. I then proceeded to corral Lubar and push the trip idea again. This time I pitched it with a reminder that it had the supplicatory endorsement of the magazine's Los Angeles advertising representatives, two amiable chaps who had their own motives for wanting him to fly out and shake hands with local business leaders.

All of these petitions were politely rebuffed. Lubar vowed that one day he would pay an official visit to California, but he never did. Nonetheless, we communicated about story ideas often enough by phone so that in my second full year on the staff, 1979, I managed to complete eight articles, which equaled the high on the magazine.[1] However, those eight did not represent an especially memorable achievement. A couple of them were respectable enough, including a long, moderately irreverent profile of David Murdoch, one of the West's more stylish tycoons.[2] Some of the others, however, fell short of the mark. In the interest of timeliness and efficiency — goals which took on increasing importance as the new fortnightly came into being — the articles were allowed to reach the completion stage prematurely.

A good example was a piece on the European operations of a California building materials company, Wickes, which I finished without ever taking the time to visit those operations to see first-hand how things were going. Instead of packing my bags and flying off to do additional reporting, I decided to write the story with help from Time-Life correspondents in Europe and bounce on to the next project, which as I recall had a certain expeditiousness to it. Had I gone to Europe for a closer look, with the benefit of hindsight I can say that the Wickes article would have been stronger and had a different tone.[3] The blame for acquiescing in such expediencies, of course, rested solely with me. By permitting myself to get caught up in the drive to boost productivity, streamline the editorial process and make *Fortune* more timely, I participated in the retreat from

233

comprehensiveness that was taking place bit by bit all over the magazine.

Not long after he succeeded Lubar as managing editor, Bill Rukeyser decided to come to California, and for a short while I had visions of touring around with him and resuscitating some of my grander ideas — the ones I felt might be more saleable after an on-site inspection and a briefing, such as an update on working conditions in California's vineyards. As it turned out, when he did come west Rukeyser checked into the Hotel Bel Air and spent much of his time with our advertising representatives and their corporate contacts.

During his tenure as managing editor, *Fortune* continued to do some good work. A few of its top-notch veterans such as Carol Loomis kept turning out splendid in-depth pieces without getting swept up in the fortnightly Zeitgeist. However, the drift toward more concise corporate stories was underway, and that represented a drawback from my standpoint since those projects held little fascination for me. In keeping with an old tradition at the magazine I ended up compromising and working on several of them. A few proved mildly interesting, while others had themes that seemed slightly contrived. One of the shortcomings of this type of piece is that it sometimes springs from the notion that a company has a cohesive, well-thought-out strategy when in reality management is simply winging it from one year to the next and hoping things will work out so the hefty paychecks and the perks can continue.

As time passed, many of my story suggestions — which were non-corporate for the most part and not always upbeat — were shunted aside, and I found myself manning the journalistic equivalent of a foreign legion outpost. After Rukeyser's California trip, I continued to man it for about another year, part of which was spent talking to myself. During that time I completed four or five articles of no great consequence, and one that proved highly satisfying. Done in the old style, it required dozens of interviews, took eight weeks to finish and was my final piece for the magazine. The reporting for it took me to Los Alamos and the Pentagon, though its origins were in some scraps of information I had picked up on a visit to northern California's Silicon Valley. It was a lengthy story about plans for a multibillion-dollar defense project that would later become known as Star Wars.[4] The piece was crafted to appeal to the knowledgeable reader as well as the lay person. Both could learn something from it, which is a test *Fortune* articles had met with a greater degree of regularity in earlier days.

Since I was domiciled in an outpost instead of New York, my perspective on *Fortune*'s loss of eminence isn't a typical insider's view. I would add only one or two comments to those made by others in chapter 19. From my vantage point it appeared that the process of compromising with definitiveness played a role in the descent from magnificence, as did the constant cost cutting and an inclination to accept rather than snigger at business values and the pronouncements of executives. When I was breaking in as a reporter on the *Herald Tribune*, Vartanig G. Vartan, one of its savviest journalists, admonished me to always keep in mind that CEOs put their underwear on one leg at a time like everyone else. That notion was not part of the general trend of thought during *Fortune*'s most troubled years.

The magazine treated business a bit too dutifully then, and it took itself very seriously, to the point where delusions of nobility began developing on the staff. This, too, proved mildly pernicious. Basking in the glow of past glories, some editors and writers seemed to regard themselves as the aristocracy of business journalism. Invitations to black-tie dinners or private off-the-record meetings with big shots and other marginal activities took on more importance than they deserved, and the end product suffered for that, as it usually does when reporters begin losing sight of who they are and become overly impressed by their titles or their surroundings.

Fortune has always been somewhat aloof. It became less so after Loeb's arrival. Under his editorship it has reflected his political-economic sentiments, which are more egalitarian than those of most of his peers, though they're not as liberal as they were when he was writing speeches for Hubert Humphrey in the 1960s. Before Loeb took over, the magazine's tone was more elitist, and the elitism was slightly insidious. An example of it appeared in a story on a company headquartered in what the magazine called an "unglamorous" Midwestern town: Wooster, Ohio.[5] To be sure, Wooster isn't the big time, but it's a pleasant community tucked away in America's heartland, the kind of place that may not always be fully appreciated when viewed from the upper floors of the Time-Life building in midtown Manhattan. With help from an unnamed securities analyst, Wooster was sneered at in *Fortune* as "the kind of two-story town where all the men serve on the bank board and their wives on the committee to save chipmunks."

Harrumph.

NOTES

1. That same year, one other member of the staff, Don Holt, also wrote eight articles. A former *Newsweek* writer, Holt later became *Fortune*'s international editor. Another productive staffer, Roy Rowan, turned out seven stories. Both he and Holt were based in New York. Juan Cameron in Washington and Robert Ball in London each wrote six that year.

2. "The Man who Collects Companies" (*Fortune*, March 26, 1979). An acquisitive and successful businessman who became influential in California Republican politics, David Murdoch was not enamored of the press and threatened to fire any employe who talked to reporters, a fact which was duly noted in my story. It chronicled his rise from shoe salesman to tycoon and quoted, by name, a former associate who felicitously described himself and Murdoch as "two skunks in a whirlwind" during a period in their careers when they were rushing from one clever deal to another. A mutual acquaintance later told me that Murdoch was unimpressed by the article.

3. "Wickes Corp.'s Retailing Triumph in Europe" (*Fortune*, August 13, 1979).

4. "Washington's New Push for Anti-Missiles" (*Fortune*, October 19, 1981).

5. "You Can Go Home Again" (*Fortune*, June 16, 1981). This story, by Peter Nulty, cast the spotlight on Stanley Gault, who left General Electric to become chief executive of Rubbermaid, headquartered in Wooster, Gault's home town. (He later became CEO at Goodyear.) The June 16 issue led off with a piece about a perceived trend in business toward "working smarter." The issue also featured a directory of the Second 500 Largest Industrial Corporations. Rubbermaid was number 594. In that same issue, at New York's request, I batted out a short article of no particular distinction about company number 805, Brush Wellman, a producer of a lightweight material called beryllium.

$

V
OTHER
PERSPECTIVES

Economists who have been quoted frequently in the papers — and who have contributed articles to the print media and appeared on TV — tend to have definite opinions about news coverage of the world of money. So do many reporters, correspondents and editors. In this section — which is based on interviews that took place in the late 1980s and early '90s — we get the views of 19 economists, journalists and others who are or were involved with the money world.

21 *Milton Friedman*
Lester Thurow
Robert Samuelson

Milton Friedman

Friedman's distinguished career covers more than a half-century. A Nobel prize winner, a monetarist and a prodigious writer, he has authored or co-authored more than 20 books along with numerous articles and op-ed page pieces. Friedman is a Senior Research Fellow at the Hoover Institution.

"The impression most people have is that when you get two economists together, you end up with at least three different opinions. The fact of the matter is, there is general agreement on the established principles of economics, and with respect to a wide range of issues there is almost complete unanimity among professional economists. For example, you can hardly find anyone who has a good word to say about protective tariffs or minimum wages or job-creating programs or the effects of a prolonged period of wage-and-price controls. Where we sometimes differ, or appear to differ, is in the area of short-term policy prescriptions and in situations where economists advising on political campaigns tend to stress whatever sounds favorable to their candidate.

"However, you would never know there was any broad agreement from reading the typical economic story or hearing it reported on the air. Like many other economists, I have had the experience of being interviewed and then having the writer express my views in ways that make it appear as if they're in direct conflict with the views of others, when in fact the differences are subtle. And I've been on television shows where the line of questioning was aimed entirely at the differences between my statements and those of the other people on the program.

"The press tends to draw sharp contrasts, and to some extent that's understandable. After all, it doesn't make for a very exciting story to say that 'A' and 'B' mostly agree. It's more interesting to be able to say they disagree."

Friedman points to what he sees as another, more serious criticism of economics coverage:

"Journalists tend to look at the immediate effects of an event or trend and rarely go beyond that to analyze the indirect and less obvious effects. One illustration of this is the effect of the exchange rate for the dollar. When the rate was high we all read many times that this resulted in a loss of jobs. It's easy to see that one of the immediate effects is to make it harder for Ford to sell U.S.-made cars overseas. The entire auto industry, in fact, may experience layoffs. It's not as easy to see the benefits over a longer term of increased foreign investment and spending in the U.S., or the fact that American consumers benefit by being able to buy foreign-made mechandise at lower prices."

Friedman's thoughts on the issue of an anti-business sentiment among journalists:

"Without doubt the press has a left-wing ideological bias, but it is less apparent in business reporting, and I think one needs to be careful in making judgments. If a major company does something bad after many years of doing good things, that makes the front page because it's newsworthy, not necessarily because the reporter or editor is biased against business.

"When it comes to economics coverage, it's usually a case of ignorance rather than bias. The reporter doesn't fully understand what he's writing about; or the story — and this happens often in economics and finance — is framed in terms that make accurate reporting almost impossible. Take as an example a report on why the stock market goes up or down on a particular day. Who the hell knows why? One day the reason given for a rise is the expectation of lower interest rates. The next day the decline is supposedly caused by profit taking. It's all blah."

For 16 years, from 1968 to 1984, Friedman penned a regular economics column for *Newsweek*. His reflections on that experience:

"It was quite an innovation at the time. Originally I was to be part of a triumverate, with Paul Samuelson at the other end of the spectrum and Henry Wallich, who was supposed to be in the middle. Then Henry went to the Federal Reserve and Samuelson was replaced by Lester Thurow.

"At the outset, my greatest worry was that I would run out of topics, but that never happened. The discipline of having to write to a certain length was very useful. *Newsweek* provided editorial assistance and made suggestions, but they never tried to affect the content of what I wrote.

"All in all it was a favorable experience, and it persuaded me that it's possible to write sophisticated economics in language that's understandable to the ordinary person. Some people say it can't be done because you have to use too much jargon or you have to write down to your audience. I don't believe that.

"When *Newsweek* decided to close down both Thurow and myself in '84, they said they were doing it because they wanted more reporting of economics and less editorializing. And to some extent it's true that the fellow they took on afterwards, Robert Samuelson (no relation to Paul), meets that requirement, although he certainly does a fair amount of editorializing. The other person they took on was Jane Bryant Quinn, who has moved them more in the direction of personal finance. Both of those columns are well written, and they are both an outgrowth of our original effort."

$

Lester Thurow

Thurow, who was Friedman's co-conspirator on the *Newsweek* columns, is dean of MIT's Sloan School of Management. A former member of the editorial board at *The New York Times*, he has done television commentary and written numerous articles as well as several books on economics, including *Head to Head*:

the coming economic battles among Japan, Europe and America (New York: Morrow, 1992).

"I'm sure when you look back at our *Newsweek* columns they'll stand out as as a milestone of sorts in newsmagazine coverage of economics. Nothing like that had been attempted before. My own thoughts about the experience are mixed. When I started writing for *Newsweek*, I had just finished a year (1979) on the editorial board of the *Times*, where there was plenty of discussion about what would be said in print. I was edited fairly heavily and I enjoyed that and learned a lot. At *Newsweek* I naturally expected that what I was doing would be an integral part of what the business section of the magazine was covering that week. But it wasn't like that at all. It was do your own thing. I had total journalistic freedom and I really wanted less freedom.

"I don't have particularly fond memories of being shut down along with Milton when they decided to try something else, but there were positive aspects to the *Newsweek* experience. It provided an unusually good opportunity to educate a broad audience, and I believe I was able to break some new ground with explanatory pieces, particularly in the area of international economics. It was difficult, because by the time you got through explaining what all the terms meant there wasn't a whole lot of space left in which to make your points.

"Another problem was that the format of those columns was set up to create the appearance of conflict — and this is something you find all the time in journalism. One guy on the left, one guy on the right. I can understand why editors feel a need to do this, but it tends to be confusing for the reader because it makes the disagreements seem sharper than they really are.

"On television, this is an even worse problem. You tape an interview that runs 20 minutes and that evening you see that it's been boiled down to a few seconds on the air. They ask, do you believe the end of the world economy has come? One economist basically says yes. Another says no, and that's it. Over and out. What's the viewer supposed to think?"

Thurow has mixed feelings about the overall quality of business and financial coverage.

"There's no doubt that the day-to-day coverage in newspapers has gotten better. The increased size of the business sections is one indication. But it's not only the quantity — the quality has improved, too. That's true whether you look at *The Wall Street Journal*, *The New York Times* or any number of local metropolitan papers. I confess to being a newspaper junkie. I read a lot and I can sense that the improvement has been across the board.

"However, if we can believe the polls which show that more and more people are abandoning newspapers and relying on television, then, overall, the economics reporting that the average American is exposed to each day has deteriorated. Television believes that the human attention span is 90 seconds. Well, if all we're shown night after night is one report after another that's 90 seconds long, or 30 seconds in some cases, then pretty soon that really does become our attention span."

Thurow is especially critical of television's choice of subject matter when it does try to cover the money world.

"If much of what we're given on the evening business report deals with what happened on Wall Street that day, then pretty soon we begin to believe that what goes on down there each day really is important, when in most cases it isn't.

"In this country more so than in continental Europe, when we talk about business reporting, we actually mean financial reporting. Giving primacy to financial markets is part of our Anglo-Saxon tradition. Newspapers are guilty of this, too. They devote page after page to stock quotations, and TV emphasizes stock market programs. This is unfortunate because that space and that time could be put to better use. What is happening in finance is much less important for our long-term well-being than what's happening in industry."

$

Robert Samuelson

Prior to becoming an economics columnist at *Newsweek* in 1984, Samuelson was a freelance writer. In the 1960s he majored in government at Harvard and worked on the *Crimson*. His first reporting job after graduation in 1967 was in Bart Rowen's revitalized business section at *The Washington Post*.

"I got into journalism at a time when many newspapers were hiring and starting to do more with business news. By the time I got to the *Post*, Bart's section had grown to about a half-dozen people, so it was still relatively small. I was able to work on many different kinds of stories, including some corporate pieces. In the four years I was there the two biggest stories I did were the Penn Central bankruptcy and the problems at Lockheed.

From the *Post*, Samuelson moved to the *National Journal* in 1973 and wrote a weekly column that appeared in several papers, including the *Post* and the *Los Angeles Times*.

"Business journalism in the late '60s and early '70s was considered a very specialized area. I felt that there was a wider audience for it, and that the ordinary news format was too restricting. That's why I wanted to do a column. I wanted to write about economic life, a concept that embraces lifestyles and family concerns as well as traditional business and economic news.

"At the time, there was a clear distinction between business coverage and economics coverage — between corporate and industry news on the one hand, and, on the other, macroeconomic stories which dealt with things like government policy for manipulating aggregate demand. The division between those two started becoming less rigid after wage-and-price controls and our energy and trade problems in the '70s focused attention on specific industries and projected them into the mainstream of policymaking.

"Meanwhile, the utopian idea that we could fine tune the economy to maintain prosperity began to fade, and we started to sense that our unquestioned confidence in the everlasting superiority of American business might be misplaced. This led to attempts to relate what was happening in various companies and industries to the broader picture, and since then we have seen a further blurring of the line between economic and business stories."

When Samuelson began writing for *Newsweek*, he tried to structure his column in a way that would allow him maximum freedom to deal with the issues.

"Whether we're talking about Keynesian policy, monetary policy, energy, tariffs, debt accumulation, the cost of health care, day care or whatever, the choices that are made and their long-term consequences are usually more complicated than you can explain in a daily news story. They need to be discussed, however, and in a column they can be. I can write about them even if public officials don't happen to be speaking out about them at the moment. I still consider myself a reporter, but it's easier for me now to deal with topics that aren't necessarily making the headlines or the nightly news.

"Mostly, my goal is to elucidate and clarify how the world works or how it ought to work. I would like to think that occasionally I can influence policy by the force of my arguments, but I don't delude myself into thinking that if I write a column calling for action, the next week the Congress of the United States is going to act. When government does things that I consider stupid, I have the normal journalistic juices and I react. I write a column that says they're stupid. I try to explain what's going on, what the choices are, and what I think ought to be done. But I don't expect to have an enormous impact.

"I regard the power of the press as vastly exaggerated, expecially in economic matters. That's because pocketbook issues touch everyone, and as a result you get policies that are driven mainly by events and by public opinion. If inflation heats up and we get a new anti-inflation policy — as we did at the end of the '70s — that doesn't happen because journalists call for a new policy. It happens because the Federal Reserve responds to the damage that rising prices are doing to the economy."

$

22

Sylvia Porter
William Wolman
Barry Bosworth
Paul Erdman

Sylvia Porter

Few journalists have done more to put financial news on the map than Sylvia Porter, and none has done more to advance the cause of women in this area of journalism. During her lifetime, she wrote more than a half-dozen books on personal finance along with a newsletter and a column that was syndicated in over 400 newspapers. These comments were made in a conversation that took place three years before her death in 1991.

"I was an English major in school and after I graduated (cum laude, from Hunter College in 1932), I reviewed books for newspapers and earned about $5 for each review. That wasn't much, but this was during the Depression and $5 was better than nothing. Of course, I read all kinds of books, but the ones that interested me the most were about finance.

"My mother, who was a widow by then, had lost everything in the '29 crash. As you can imagine, the experience of watching that money disappear had an impact on me. I felt that I wanted to learn more about what was happening and I wanted to write about it."

After doing graduate work at New York University, in 1934 Porter started writing a column on government securities in the *American Banker*; the following year she started reporting for *The New York Post*.

"Economics reporting was in a primitive stage then. Those of us who were getting into it used to wonder where it would lead. One of the few people in the field who understood what he was writing about was Elliott Bell of *Business Week*. He helped me a lot, and I loved him for it. And there were others who had some grasp of the subject, too, but not very many, which is remarkable when you stop to think about it. After all, the economy was the big story of the day."

Porter often wrote critically about policy issues, at one point accusing the Roosevelt Administration of "obstinacy, stupidity or sheer ill advice" in its handling of government bond operations. For a long while, her editors masked the fact that she was a woman by running her material under the byline "S.F. Porter." That ended after they realized she was doing a better job than most of her male competitors.

"Many of the reporters who covered events like the daily fixing of the price of gold would go marching into the

White House every morning and jot down whatever they were told, and then they'd go off and write their stories. And they did that, day after day, with no clear idea of the international effects of the news they were reporting. To them, it was just another story.

"I didn't have a very clear idea at first either, but I tried to learn. And the more I learned, the more I began to realize that the gold fixing and some of the other things I was dealing with had important consequences for the future of the country and the world. This had the effect of making me more cautious in my reporting."

That experience during the New Deal helped shape Porter's view of a major inadequacy in economics reporting that has never totally disappeared.

"Throughout my career, I always kept studying and reading and trying to learn more. But even then I found that I still didn't have enough knowledge to do many of the stories I wrote. Some journalists in this field might not make that admission. They would rather bluff it, but if they do they're only bluffing themselves.

"This isn't as much of a problem with a column as it is if you're covering breaking news, but it can still be a problem. I would say that probably the biggest single failing in our business is the fact that journalists on deadline are constantly forced to report on complicated matters they don't fully understand. It happens all the time, every day, in the newspapers, at the wire services and on radio and television. For that reason you could say we're still in a somewhat primitive stage, though obviously there has been a lot of progress since the '30s."

Porter became well known for her ability to translate what she called the "bafflegab" of the money world into plain English. After her baptism in economics reporting during the Depression, she began writing about personal finance as well as macroeconomics.

"One of the things that turned me in the direction of personal finance was remembering how my ma and pa had lost money in Liberty Bonds by selling them at the wrong time, which is what a lot of people did after the First World War. Of course most of the Wall Street crowd knew what it was doing and sold the bonds when prices were higher.

"I wrote about that as the Second World War was coming closer, and also about what the war might mean for the economy. After Pearl Harbor, (Treasury Secretary) Henry Morgenthau traced me to Florida, where I was vacationing, and summoned me to Washington to talk about the government's plans for issuing some type of savings bond to help pay for the war. I was impressed, especially because he reached me on a Sunday and I was in my summer clothes. He arranged for a department store to open its doors and sell me a winter dress. I thought to myself, what power!

"Morgenthau and I met and talked about the new bonds. I gave him some advice about how to make the program safer for the public, and he took it. I'm proud of that. I told him the bonds should be non-marketable, otherwise many people might be inclined to sell at the wrong time. This would be bad not only for them, I said, but also for the entire country. He accepted that."

In her writing, Porter was often on the mark in predicting the prices at which Treasury bond issues were about to be sold. Her explanation was that during their interviews the sometimes indecisive and elderly Morgenthau (he was born in 1856) would ask her what she thought the price should be and why; the advice she gave him frequently proved identical to the numbers that were announced later by the Treasury.

"It has been suggested that I had inside information on the Treasury's offerings, but I did not. What I wrote was simply my judgment based on my understanding of the bond market."

One of the more memorable moments of Porter's career came in the 1950s, when she wrote several columns probing Walter Winchell's radio broadcasts. Winchell (as we noted in Chapter 11) was in the habit of touting low-priced stocks on the air, and there were allegations that those who knew which stocks he was about to recommend were buying them in advance and selling them after his broadcasts had pushed them up in price. Porter's reporting job put a severe damper on his stock advisory activities.

"Winchell never forgave me for writing about that. We had a sharp exchange of words about it one time when we ran into each other at the Stork Club. I was outraged by what he was doing on the air, and I felt that people ought to be told about the situation."

$

William Wolman

Wolman earned a Ph.D. in economics at Stanford and taught economics at Washington State University.

That background has influenced both his perspective on business news and the content of *Business Week*, where he held the title of editor for several years before becoming the magazine's chief economist.

"When I was at Washington State — it's called that now, though it wasn't then — I mostly read *Fortune*, which was held in high regard among economists in those days. That was in the '50s.

"My colleagues on the faculty, however, kept urging me to take a look at this grubby little magazine called *Business Week*. So I did, and while it carried no bylines it was obvious to me that someone with considerable understanding of economics was writing for it, mainly about the near-term outlook. That someone turned out to be Leonard Silk, who was economics editor at the time.

"Through a referral from Tilford Gaines of the Federal Reserve Bank of New York, who knew that I wanted to write, I eventually ended up interviewing with Silk and going to work for *Business Week*. It proved to be a good move for me, because whatever I've been as a journalist I would have been even worse as an academic."

After Silk moved to *The New York Times*, Wolman began overseeing *Business Week*'s economics coverage.

"One of the things we did — and this really started before Len left the magazine — was to cover economics as a profession and treat what economists said as news. That was unusual at the time. The other thing that was unusual was that Elliott Bell, our editor, actually printed what we wrote even though some of it was pretty rarefied stuff by conventional journalistic standards.

"Then other magazines began doing somewhat the

same thing, and as time went by the pronouncements of economists became less exciting and less newsworthy. Because of that, starting sometime in the late 1970s we altered our approach and tried to use our economic expertise in other ways. We began looking at business journalistically as an economist would look at it."

That shift in tactics occurred at a time when *Business Week*, under managing editor Lew Young, was doing more with technological coverage. This led *BW* into areas such as the link between hi-tech and prosperity and into territory that had belonged largely to *Fortune*. Wolman played a hand in developing several cover stories with sweeping themes and an economic flavor, including "The Reindustrialization of America" and "The Hollow Corporation." (Short excerpts from both appear in the Appendix.)

"Reindustrialization" was one of the most famous stories I ever worked on. It involved the whole magazine. Basically, it warned that American industry was slipping and called for a coordinated policy, involving government and business, to correct that. The piece appeared in the summer of 1980. Reagan's election in November blew the idea of that kind of policy right out of the water.

"In 1986 we came up with another big cover story — 'The Hollow Corporation' — which was really 'Son of Reindustrialization.' That one wasn't a conventional economics piece, either. It described the weakened condition many companies had gotten themselves into and analyzed the consequences of our not having pursued an industrial policy earlier.

"All you can do is keep analyzing a situation like this and waiting for it to change. You can't really influence policy all that much. In this day and age, business magazines and news magazines have a lot less clout than they once did."

$

Barry Bosworth

Bosworth served on the White House Council of Economic Advisers in the late 1960s and, in the late '70s, as Jimmy Carter's specialist on inflation, a job where he had extensive contact with the press. He is a Senior Fellow at the Brookings Institution and the author of *Critical Choices*, published by Brookings in 1989.

"When I was in the Carter Administration, I thought about inflation all day long, every day. There was no way a reporter could come up with a question I hadn't thought of. I knew what the questions would be. I knew what my answers were going to be. I perfected them. I could do the whole thing in my sleep.

"I got into a lot of trouble with White House people over things I was quoted on in the newspapers about the problem of inflation and the task of combating it. But the truth was, I was not misquoted. The coverage in the papers was pretty accurate."

That accuracy did not extend to network television reporting, according to Bosworth.

"After a while, the White House decided that I should start going on television and talking about economic policy. That was a disaster. The reporters were bored by the issues. They were not interested in learning about them. They seemed more interested in learning how to conduct themselves in front of the camera. They tended to cast their stories in terms of which White House adviser was on the rise or on the decline, or whatever — anything but the issues.

"There were a few exceptions such as Steve Aug of ABC who came prepared and knew what to ask. With those people I could keep my answers short because I had confidence that the interviewer would come back with the follow-up questions that were necessary to flesh out the point. However, with the majority of interviewers my answers had to be longer because I felt I had to cover everything in one response.

"Then, when I would turn on the TV at night I'd find that what I was saying was being snipped up in the editing process and taken out of context. The interviews were constantly messed up. It was a horrendous experience."

Bosworth gives the printed press favorable marks for its analysis of the political environment in which economic policy was being shaped during the Carter years.

"This is one area where the reporters on the better newspapers and magazines seem to get interested and do pretty well. From my vantage point, I would say they did a fairly good job of sniffing out the different viewpoints and figuring out what was going inside the Carter Administration.

"Remember, this was a time when many people still thought we could ease down the inflation rate without going through a recession. You had the head of the Department of Labor articulating a deep belief in the need for a job-creating program. You had the chairman of the Council of Economic Advisers pushing for a general tax cut. You had the head of the Treasury urging that the tax cut be concentrated on business. It was a very ideological debate.

"Each participant, each department, had a staff of economists constantly generating figures to support their side of the argument. In a situation like that, economists can become prostitutes and massage the numbers to please their bosses. There was so much of that going on that the economic analysis was neutralizing itself. The political people didn't have the ability to weigh the conflicting analyses, and they were saying that if the economists couldn't agree among themselves then the decisions would be made on political grounds.

"When he was elected, Carter had been told that economic policy was important and complicated and that he should get some experts in the field. He did. He brought in about five different experts who gave him five different points of view. To his credit, he tried to reconcile the differences. But he was not good at doing that in an environment where things were being leaked and some of the debate was being conducted in the press.

"By nature Carter was an incrementalist on economic policy, a marginal change here, a marginal change there. However, he was never able to articulate any particular point of view publicly, and I think the press understood that. The commentaries we were reading contained some good insights into the situation."

According to Bosworth, there was much less open discussion of economic policy when he was in the

White House in the '60s than there was during the Carter years.

"If Carter had been able to operate in the environment of the '60s, he would have been more effective. From the standpoint of having to explain difficult economic policy options to the press, he was President at the wrong time.

"In the late '60s, there wasn't much talk in the papers about what policy should be. With a few exceptions, the reporters were pretty much lost when it came to figuring out what the options were, or the trade-offs. They might ask about the outlook for the economy, or something equally simple, but that's about all.

"As a result, we were able to put through a tax increase without having everyone involved argue the issue to death in the newspapers. There was debate, but it was mainly hidden from public view. It took place inside government before a judge — the President — who handed down his decision. After that, we went public with the policy and an agreed-upon explanation.

"On balance, I still believe it's healthy to have a more open discussion of these matters. But it places heavy responsibility on the press to explain the situation accurately and fairly.

"I don't worry so much about *The New York Times* or *The Wall Street Journal* or *The Washington Post* or the *Los Angeles Times*. But I worry a lot about television, which unfortunately is where most people get most of their information about economic policy."

$

Paul Erdman

He is best known as a novelist (*The Silver Bears, The Billion-Dollar Sure Thing*). Erdman is also a former banker who was jailed in Switzerland during a financial scandal a quarter-century ago. He has drawn on his knowledge of finance and economics to write nonfiction books and contributed to magazines and newspapers in the U.S. and abroad.

"I had written reports on markets and done product studies for Stanford Research Institute in the late 1950s, and my doctoral thesis at the University of Basel was in economics. Then, I started pursuing economic themes in my writing when I was in jail. That's where I began writing novels, and the fiction led to the nonfiction.

"I slid over into journalism from there, though it wasn't deliberate. I filled in as a talk show host on KGO radio in San Francisco on a program that was supposed to be about personal finance. When I took it over I redid the format and gave a ten-minute spiel on the world economy and threw the thing open to questions. That might sound dull to some people, but it wasn't a boring show. Listeners called in. They were interested.

"After that, Clay Felker at *Manhattan, inc.* asked me to write some predictive pieces for him, so I did, and one day I looked at the masthead and discovered that I was listed as a contributing editor. I've done some things for other publications, too, but not a lot. I don't consider myself basically a journalist."

Erdman's novels such as *The Crash of '79, The Crash of '89* and *The Last Days of America* usually contain cheerless economic themes. So does some of his nonfiction.

"The inclination to be upbeat is a chronic weakness of most economics writing. Anyone who knows anything about economics has to be acquainted with business cycle theory and knows that the economy goes down as well as up. It's an undeniable part of our system.

"Yet if you look back at what many business economists have said over the years, you'll find them writing and talking as if that isn't so — and journalists tend to parrot what they say. So what the public hears is that recession is hardly ever on the horizon. When it hits, as it always does sooner or later, the question is posed: Is this really a recession? If the business economists conclude reluctantly that it is, they'll declare that it's going to be short and shallow. If it turns out to be more severe instead, as sometimes happens, then they start wondering what went wrong.

"It's un-American to be realistic about the business cycle. You become categorized as a gloom and doomer. I'm categorized that way, but I don't care. I've coined a comparable term to describe the other guys. I call them the onward and upward crowd. In the long run, they're going to be right, but in the near or medium term, which counts for a lot, they're frequently wrong.

"I'm sure my outlook is influenced by my having lived in Switzerland for so long. The Swiss tend to look down on the rest of the world from their neutral pinnacle. Their country is unimportant in the greater scheme of things, so they're always making judgments, mostly negative ones, about the economies of other countries. Some of that rubbed off on me."

In his writing, Erdman has never hesitated to offer forecasts that are not only downbeat but also unusual in that they are almost never hedged.

"The hedging that appears in a lot of economics writing serves no one's interests except the guy who writes the stuff. If I was an economist at a brokerage house writing about the economic outlook, I'd probably feel some pressure to include positive things in whatever I wrote. If I was on the staff of a magazine, I might feel I had to hedge a little to avoid being dead wrong and jeopardizing my job. But those things don't concern me because I don't have a job to protect. I'm a self-employed writer. It's fun to not have to hedge, although it is risky."

Erdman's overall assessment of economics coverage:

"It's getting better, but then it couldn't get much worse than it was 25 years ago. Back then, *The Wall Street Journal* used to run lots of puffy stories about business on the front page. Now they go after incompetent managements and crooks and give it to them right in the chops. And they often write the stuff in a dramatic style, which appeals to me. *Forbes* and *Barron's* do a lot of that, too. *Fortune* seems to have drifted the other way since its left-wing days, when it was socking it to U.S. Steel and some other big companies pretty hard."

$

23   *Andrew Brimmer*
Arthur Burns
Joseph Coyne
Paul Craig Roberts

Andrew Brimmer

Brimmer earned his Ph.D. in economics at Harvard and was the first Afro-American appointed to the Federal Reserve Board. He served as a governor of the nation's central bank from 1966 to 1974. A director of the Gannett Company for many years, he has long kept a watchful eye on newspaper coverage of the economy.

"When I first came to Washington in the early '60s, it was rare for any kind of story relating to economics to appear on the front page of a major metropolitan daily. So it was unusual when my appointment to the Federal Reserve Board in '66 made page one of *The New York Times*. The year I left the Federal Reserve, 1974, I wrote a letter to

President Ford suggesting a rebate of income taxes to help check the recession. That story, too, made page one of the *Times*. By then it was somewhat less of a rarity. We had just experienced several big economic developments that dominated the news such as the end of fixed exchange rates along with the imposition of wage-and-price controls, and the oil embargo. But it still wasn't commonplace for economic stories to appear on page one.

"Today, of course, it happens all the time. Economic articles appear regularly on the front page and throughout the general news sections of daily papers, and the business sections have expanded further into areas other than the financial markets."

Brimmer's opinion of press coverage of the Federal Reserve:

"When I was at the Fed, I felt that those few reporters who paid attention to our activities did a reasonably good job of covering us. They were mostly specialists working for the major publications. People like Ed Dale at the *Times* and Bart Rowen at the *Post*. Nowadays, there are more journalists interested in the Fed's activities, but many of them are not specialists who know their subject inside and out, and they often seem to be in need of guidance.

"On the whole, however, press coverage of economic policymaking has improved. If I had to pick a starting point, I would say the improvement probably began during the 1960 presidential campaign, when economic policy was debated vigorously. JFK's basic strategy was to portray the Republicans as having been insensitive to economic problems during the Eisenhower years. Kennedy organized a large-scale mobilization of economists for the campaign and drew on their expertise in developing an economic program. That program was imbedded in the party platform in a way that's common for both major parties today, but it wasn't then. This created a situation where all of a sudden the press found itself having to report economic policy information and cover some of the people such as Walter Heller who were behind the programs. That was a milestone."

Brimmer points to a few other key developments in newspaper coverage of the economy since the Kennedy era.

"Looking back at what's happened over the past three decades, I would say that what Rowen accomplished at the *Post* certainly stands out. He was a leader in improving the general level of economics coverage. At *The New York Times*, the creation of Business Day was, of course, a major breakthrough. Pulling that section together so it could stand alone as a separate newspaper was a first. *USA Today* copied the idea with its Money section, which also can stand alone. It offers a telescopic presentation of economic affairs, condensed and not as penetrating, but the range of topics covered in the section is very wide.

"At *The Wall Street Journal*, if I had to single out one innovation from the many that have taken place there, it would be the redesign of the back page of the front section ('Politics & Policy'). That page offers the reader in-depth coverage of the interface between the political arena and the economy, which is a critical area that has always needed more attention. It's a unique page. The caliber of the analysis is very high, the reporting is thorough, and the writing is usually superb."

$

Arthur Burns

Burns was chairman of the Council of Economic Advisers during the Eisenhower Administration, a White House counselor at the start of Nixon's first term, and chairman of the Federal Reserve from 1970 to 1978. From 1981 to 1985 he was ambassador to West Germany. The interview in which he made these comments took place about a year before his death in 1988.

"There was a more pronounced leftist bias during the Eisenhower years than there has been in recent times among reporters covering the economy. They exaggerated the intensity of the ups and downs — especially the downs — and didn't pay enough attention to the fact that the decade of the '50s was one of substantial economic stability and remarkable prosperity.

"However, we made a mistake in not trying to educate the members of the press and win them over. We hid our virtues. At the Council of Economic Advisers, my approach was a very timid one. I wanted to have as little to do with reporters as possible. I didn't quite trust them. I brought to my job at the CEA academic habits along with Republican attitudes of suspiciousness.

"I didn't want to have anything to do with Congress either, but I had to deal with them, and I did it reluctantly. I insisted on testifying about economic affairs in executive session, with no reporters present and no transcript or record of what I said. I felt that if I had to testify, I did not want to have to couch my statements in careful language for public consumption. Without the protection of an executive session I was afraid I might say something that would appear in print and embarrass the President.

"Looking back, it's clear that my attitude was naive and stupid. While I'm not trying to make excuses for it, bear in mind that when I came to the CEA in 1953, it was a discredited institution. It had gotten involved in partisan politics. There had been bickering in public among CEA members about policy and much press coverage of the bickering. In that atmosphere, we established a policy of no talking to reporters. I wanted a thoroughly professional staff. I reminded everyone that our job was to assist Mr. Eisenhower in developing economic policy, and that we were going to stick to business. I was determined that we would not compromise our efforts by getting quoted and perhaps misquoted in the press. However, I carried things to an extreme."

Years later, in the Nixon White House and at the Federal Reserve, Burns tried to pursue what he considered a less wary and more open approach toward the media.

"By the time I joined the Nixon Administration I think I had acquired a somewhat more enlightened view. And at first, for a short while, we did have better relations, not only with reporters covering the economy but with the press corps in general. I played a hand in developing those relations, though I didn't do so overtly.

"However, along about the latter part of 1969 there was an incident where some documents leaked, and soon after that edicts started coming down that no one was to deal with journalists unless they notified Mr. Nixon's press secretary. Well, that irritated the reporters as well as a lot of people within the administration. It got to a point where I didn't get involved or try to straighten the situation out. I gave up. Bad elements were taking control at the White House. I was going to the Federal Reserve and I said to hell with it.

"As Chairman of the Fed, I made an attempt to build a dialogue with the press through background briefings, and I have no complaints about how that turned out. I got as good a press as I deserved, perhaps better. During that period I came to realize that whatever biases they may have, journalists are basically professionals. Their views on politics and economics are not likely to totally dominate their reporting. They compete with each other and try to achieve excellence and favorable status within their field. Give them a chance at a good story and as likely as not they're going to report it."

If he had been presented with an opportunity to do it all over again, Burns acknowledged that he would have opened the door to the press even wider at the Federal Reserve.

"As I look back, I would say the Fed could and probably should conduct more seminars. It ought to be done on a fairly small scale, perhaps a dozen members of the staff meeting with 15 or 20 reporters. We did a little of that, but not as much as we should have. You must remember that people at the Fed are not always the best expositors. They're not Ronald Reagans when it comes to communicating, and they fear that if they expose themselves to the press, they might look bad or they might make some indiscreet comments about monetary policy.

"My feeling is that regular and properly conducted seminars could explain how the Fed operates and provide a general feel for the economic parameters in which it's operating at the moment. That would be helpful to the less experienced reporters and it could have value for the older hands, too. Of course, the sessions would have to be conducted without conveying any privileged information about policy decisions, but I believe that could be done."

Burns expressed the belief that the Council of Economic Advisers also could open its doors wider, even though its members cannot always be candid.

"With the CEA, it's more delicate. Members of the Council could be a little more helpful to the press, but they must be extremely careful to avoid putting themselves in the position of being seen as opposed to the President's economic policies. That means they have to keep quiet on some subjects, and if they feel so strongly that they can't remain quiet, then they ought to resign.

"Marty Feldstein's problems with Mr. Reagan were an illustration of that. Marty is a first-rate economist, but when he was head of the Council he made speeches and gave interviews which created the impression that he was arguing against the President's program. He didn't keep quiet and he didn't resign. Things got so bad at the White House that Mr. Reagan was thinking of abolishing the CEA. When I was ambassador to Bonn, I made a special trip back to urge him not to do it, and I'd like to think I had something to do with his decision to keep the Council."

$

Joseph Coyne

A former Associated Press reporter, Joe Coyne became chief of the Federal Reserve's public information office in 1973. His responsibilities there include fielding inquiries from reporters and counseling Fed officials on how to deal with the press.

"We try to do background briefing sessions for reporters, but we don't have many on-the-record news conferences around here. That's partly my doing and it's partly the nature of the institution. The Federal Reserve doesn't seek publicity, and I don't feel we should call a news conference unless we have something important to announce. That isn't often. But when it does happen, we pull out all the stops.

"In August of 1979 Paul Volcker held his first news conference here shortly after he came to the Fed. That was the one where he announced a major change in policy aimed at fighting inflation, which was real news. The decision on the new policy was approved on a Saturday, and that afternoon I asked him if we could call in the reporters immediately. By doing it right away, I felt we could minimize the chance of leaks over the weekend and the possibilitiy of stories containing inaccurate interpretations of what we were doing.

"Volcker agreed. We decided to hold the news conference at 6 p.m. and started calling the reporters. Some of them didn't even get two hours notice. Along with the newspapers, magazines and wire services, we called the TV networks. One of the bureau chiefs said he didn't understand anything about this monetary stuff and what was it all about? He said he only had one camera crew available and it was assigned to the Pope, who was in Washington that weekend. I knew I couldn't possibly explain monetary policy to the guy quickly over the phone, so I just said to him, 'long after the Pope is gone, this story will be remembered.' He diverted the camera crew from his Papal Excellency to cover our news conference, and he told me later he wasn't sorry."

The policy announced at that news conference broke the back of inflation but put the economy through a brutal recession for a couple of years. During that time the Fed received surprisingly gentle treatment in the media. Coyne belives there were two reasons for that.

"One reason was that Congress sat still while we were fighting inflation. The other was that the White House stood behind us. As a result, reporters were not going around to either of those two places and scrounging up countless stories about opposition to the Fed's anti-inflation policy. That made a big difference.

"On any issue, the press tends to report and reflect back the views of opinion makers, but in this instance there wasn't much of a contrary view to reflect. There was criticism, but generally our policy was accepted because inflation had gotten out of control. By 1982 the measures Volcker announced in '79 were succeeding, and that success has since had the effect of raising our visibility. Everyone has heard of us now. It's nice in some respects, but it's bad in the sense that a lot of people think the Fed somehow ought to be able to solve any economic problem that arises, and it can't."

Coyne has identified three areas where news coverage of the Fed and economic policymaking are cause for concern:

"One area that troubles me is the reporting of Fed activities by specialists who service the financial markets rather than the news media. Some of those specialists tend to act like the markets they serve. To them, every rumor is a new story. They get drawn into the psychology of the marketplace, and that can produce some very irresponsible reporting.

"Another thing that concerns me from time to time is the habit of trying to draw out members of our Board of Governors in ways that are designed to manufacture a conflict over monetary policy. Typically the reporter pins down governor A in a certain position, and then places governor B, very precisely, in a different position. Having been a reporter myself I can understand why they want to do that. It makes for a story and it's an old journalistic technique. But when they use it in covering the Fed, most of the time they stretch it too far and get things wrong.

"The Board of Governors is mainly a collegial group. They discuss and debate, and while they have differences, usually those differences are less sharp than the press imagines. Often the members end up voting with a consensus. But reporters don't always understand this. Possibly that's because they're accustomed to covering Congress, which is a confrontational group by nature rather than a collegial one.

"The other major complaint I have concerns the herd instinct. One reporter in Washington blows the whistle and everyone follows. It seems as if no one can get an exclusive story anymore without everyone else feeling that they have to match it or beat it. This leads to some extraordinary reaching. It's a problem that isn't confined to coverage of the Fed, but we feel it, and it has gotten worse over the years."

$

Paul Craig Roberts

An advocate of supply-side economics, which stresses low taxes as incentives, Roberts was an editor at *The Wall Street Journal* from 1978 to 1980. He is a columnist for *Business Week*, Chairman of the Institute for Political Economy and the author of *The Supply-Side Revolution* (Cambridge: Harvard University Press, 1984).

"One of the biggest problems with reporting economic policy is that it's hard for anyone to write anything radically different from what the herd is writing. In that respect, economic journalists are a little like economic forecasters. They echo each other.

"The way it works, people in government leak stories and develop symbiotic relationships, giving certain reporters bits of inside information about economic policy. In return, they expect the reporter to go along with whatever spin the leaker has put on the story.

"This means that whoever starts out feeding a certain line to the press tends to control what's written. The line he puts out becomes the dominant view. Even those who are not being fed the line, and who are suspicious of it, find it's risky to take a position that's totally different."

In support of his argument, Roberts cites his own experience in government. After leaving the *Journal*, he was assistant secretary for economic policy at the Treasury in 1981–82.

"I briefed reporters countless times about supply-side economics, but they almost never reported my positions. I discovered that those in the White House who opposed my point of view had been quick to put out their party line, a series of lines actually, which became the orthodox view in the press.

"First, everyone wrote that tax cuts were going to cause an upsurge of inflation. When that didn't happen, the party line was changed and the herd wrote that tax cuts were going to prevent interest rates from falling. When that didn't happen, the line was changed again and the herd started writing that deficits resulting from tax cuts would prevent an economic recovery.

"When the recovery came anyway the herd wrote that it would be lopsided, with Treasury borrowings crowding out private borrowers and hurting interest-sensitive industries. When that didn't materialize, the herd started writing that the recovery wouldn't last. But of course it did. It lasted longer than any peacetime recovery in history.

"At every stage, the press parroted whatever the party line was at that particular moment. Article after article reflected the same set of beliefs, and those of us who supported supply-side policies were consistently portrayed as fools."

As Roberts sees it, on matters of economic policy many reporters can be manipulated fairly easily.

"I have worked in the media and I'm not anxious to be critical. But I think it's important to offer some insights into how the system operates. The press is manipulable in this area because there isn't a whole lot of original thinking going on out there among reporters assigned to the economics beat.

"Whoever in government is the most manipulative is likely to set the agenda. If you're assigned to the beat and a senior White House official offers you an exclusive story on policy, if you don't take it he'll give it to someone else. And if that happens too often your editor is going to start wondering why you're not getting the exclusives. The alternative to letting yourself be used is to let yourself get scooped and see the story snapped up by the competition. Reporters know they have to survive, so they're forced into playing the game.

"One reason they didn't pay much attention when I was trying to brief them on what I felt were good stories was that an assistant secretary of the Treasury isn't as high a source as someone in the White House who is close to the President. With me, they had a source who was less highly placed to begin with, and a very different theme.

"At virtually every phase of the policymaking process, before final decisions were made I found that those who were against supply-side proposals were taking the issue to the press and working to influence the coverage, and they were succeeding. Out of sheer frustration, I finally took to writing pieces with the supply-side point-of-view under my own name on the op-ed page of the *Journal*."

Roberts contends that the system he describes is unhealthy and does not serve the public's best interests.

"In the typical situation in any administration, different policies are being considered. Before they can all be presented to the President for his decision, one side or the other usually attempts to preempt the decision by trying to get a reporter to do a job on the opposition in return for being fed some inside dope. If that happens often enough, it becomes hard for the President to make a decision in an even-handed manner because the issue has been leaked to the media in a way that forces his hand, leaving him in a position where he feels he has to choose A over B. Things have been twisted around to where he is made to look as if he's against motherhood, the flag and common sense if he chooses B.

"All of this may seem like it's just part of the normal democratic process of airing a debate over policy. But if what's really happening is that clever leaks and manipulation are helping clinch the debate, then I'm not sure how much of a positive development that is. Under those circumstances, you have to ask yourself who really has control of policy?"

$

24   *Vermont Royster*
Lindley Clark
Donald K. White
William O'Neil

Vermont Royster

During *The Wall Street Journal*'s rise to prominence, Royster figured heavily in many of the improvements that were made throughout the paper. From 1958 to 1971, he held the title of editor.

"When I started with the *Journal* in the 1930s, the staff was small and I could freewheel and write about different subjects and reach out and do stories before anyone else got to them. That situation continued into the 1950s, and it gave me an advantage and a wider perspective than most people get when they go into journalism today.

"There was less competition then. I was in Washington, covering the Federal Reserve along with the SEC and several other agencies. Those places were good sources of business news, but hardly anyone paid attention to them. They were just beginning to be covered by a few of the other newspapers.

"I didn't concern myself much with the magazines. The best of them, *Fortune*, was basically a feature magazine that didn't contain much hard business news. It was a classy publication with graceful writing, but I didn't look at it to see if I'd been scooped.

"I used to freelance an occasional feature for *Barron's*, but I had trouble finding enough pieces to make that a reliable source of income. *Barron's* was highly specialized then, and totally Wall Street oriented. It paid much less attention than it does now to the Washington scene. When I did come up with a feature for them, they used to pay me the magnificent sum of $50 for it."

That was long before *Barron's* began probing the political world, and before the *Journal* began competing with *Fortune* by carrying interpretive page-one features that were similar to *Fortune* articles. It also was before the advent of specialization in business reporting.

"There certainly weren't many specialists back then. Now, you have people with law degrees covering the courts. When I was assigned to cover the Supreme Court in the '30s, I bought a book on the history of the U.S. Constitution and started studying it religiously. I carried it around with me all the time. The book had a good index that I referred to over and over when I wrote my stories, including my second-day pieces that interpreted what had been decided by the court the day before.

"When I got out of college in '35, it never occurred to me that I might not have all the knowledge I needed to cover certain topics for the paper. But I managed, and I have long since reached a conclusion that I've mentioned several times in talks and at a seminar I did at the journalism school in Chapel Hill (the University of North Carolina).

"Anyone who goes into journalism is going to encounter subjects for which he has no formal educational background. It's bound to happen. It always has and always will. The world changes, and as it does journalists have to change with it. We can't possibly foresee all of the topics we'll be asked to write about tomorrow.

"When Walter Cronkite went to Cape Canaveral to cover the first space shots, he had to bone up on the subject of rockets and outer space just like every other reporter who was there, including me. I had to bone up on that stuff too — the terminology, the technology, the issues and the costs. Of course no one paid any attention to me because I wasn't on TV and I wasn't famous.

"My point is that the best education is to learn how to learn. When journalists come up against new things, in business or in any other field, they need to know how and where to acquire the information that can help them write a good story."

$

Lindley H. Clark, Jr.

The longtime author of the *Journal*'s "Speaking of Business" column, Clark earned both his masters and his undergraduate degree in economics at the University of Chicago.

"When I came out of college in 1949, I started working in journalism, and I never left. I thought about going with *The Journal of Commerce* in Chicago, but instead I went with *The Wall Street Journal*, which wound up buying The *Journal of Commerce*'s Chicago operation and making it the Midwest edition.

"There were very few people then who were doing a decent job of writing about the economy, and very few newspapers that were doing a decent job of covering it. I remember thinking as I finished school that I was getting into a field that was wide open."

For more than 40 years, Clark served as a jack-of-all-trades at the *Journal* in New York.

"I did a little bit of everything. I wrote editorials for 10 years (from 1961 to 1972). I was economics news editor for a while. I started 'Speaking of Business' in the '60s, at a time when the paper was having difficulty commenting on business and economics. Although it may sound odd, back then there were many who felt we didn't know enough about business to lecture businessmen. It occurred to me that we could do it in a signed column. Sometime in the '80s things progressed to where the column had served its purpose to a certain extent. By then our editorial page had become less timid about giving advice and commenting on business."

Clark's writings have always reflected the monetarist views that are a hallmark of his alma mater. Interestingly, after Robert Bartley took over the *Journal*'s editorial page in the 1970s, Clark found himself somewhat at odds with the supply-side thinking that began to dominate the page he had once edited.

"My principal professor at the University of Chicago was Milton Friedman, and we remained friends after I left school. My views are similar to his. And I guess you'd say they're similar to those of Thomas Jefferson, who said the best government is the government that governs least. Government is not unnecessary, but intervention in the economy should be held to a minimum.

"That's one place where I totally agree with Bob Bartley. Our disagreements have been in areas like whether cutting the marginal tax rates would result in a great upsurge in economic activity and bring in so much revenue that there wouldn't be large budget deficits. I'm concerned about deficits. Bob, of course, feels that I worry too much about them."

Clark's thoughts on the role of newspapers as an influence on economic policymaking:

"The first function of any paper has always been to inform. The *Journal* thinks of its typical reader as a person who didn't major in economics but who can understand reasonably complex concepts if they're explained in clear language. The thing I've enjoyed most about my job is taking those complex subjects and trying to simplify them for readers.

"Persuading on policy issues is a lower priority. Lots of people get an inflated impression of what's possible on that score. I've always tried not to. Sure, when I was writing editorials I used to attempt to persuade policymakers to change their errant ways, and sometimes I would try to persuade voters to throw the rascals out. However, I noticed over the years that those efforts had very little effect, and I think this is generally true of most journalistic attempts to guide policy.

"Bartley's operation has been an exception to the rule — and not just Bob's writing, but also that of Craig Roberts, Jude Wanniski and others who have written on the same theme on the editorial pages. The *Journal* gave supply-side economics a respectability that it otherwise would not have had. For better or worse, we contributed to the prominence of that approach to economic policy."

Clark's perspective on the genesis of the *Journal's* expanded editorial page:

"When we became the largest circulation paper in the country during the '70s, we realized that some of our readers were buying the *Journal* not as a second paper but as their only paper. We felt that our responsibilities were changing and that we should offer a broader range of opinions. So the editorial and op-ed pages were expanded, and today they contain a diversity of views that has become one of the paper's strengths."

$

Donald K. White

A columnist and financial editor in his native San Francisco for many years, White began his newspaper career as a sports writer and general assignment reporter in Texas. His first job in business journalism was on *The Wall Street Journal* in the mid-1940s.

"After the usual out-of-town tryouts, I was ready to come back home, so I wandered into the San Francisco office of the *Journal* one day and said I was looking for a reporting job but I didn't know anything about business. The editor who interviewed me said, 'that's good. We're looking for people just like you. You can start work on Monday.'

"I joined a reporting staff of about five, none of whom had formal training in business or economics. We were each given several big, nationally prominent outfits like Chevron and Bank of America to keep an eye on. They weren't divided up by industry, which was great because that gave us a look at a lot of different businesses. Of course, it also made it harder for us to become highly knowledgeable about any one business, so we weren't as accurate with some of our analysis, and from the reader's standpoint the end product wasn't as penetrating."

White's indoctrination as a *Journal* reporter took place at the time that Barney Kilgore, Royster and others were setting out to broaden the paper's appeal.

"Being new to the game, I figured it would be smart to try to imitate some business jargon in my stories, and that got me into trouble. My editors would get after me and say, 'don't use those words. Say it in plain English. That's what we're trying to do around here. That's why we hired you.'

"The idea of taking pains to make everything under-standable was part of the effort to make the paper more readable for people who didn't care about stocks. Kilgore, of course, was the main driving force behind that effort. He had become the man at the top of the mountain by then. He came through San Francisco to greet the troops twice while I was on the staff, and I got to shake hands with him."

White's recollections of his tour of duty in the *Journal*'s infantry provide a glimpse of the work routine at the paper's West Coast operation during the late '40s.

"The West Coast edition was smaller and had less advertising, but the front page was identical to the national editon. The so-called western news, which was what I worked on, was crammed into the last few pages. If what we were writing about was worth more than seven or eight paragraphs, we wrote it for the front end of the paper. Otherwise, it ran in the back.

"The job was interesting and fun. The humor level on the staff was high and the camaraderie was good. We took what we were doing seriously enough, but none of us were serious investors. We didn't have any money to invest.

"Once a month or so we were expected to come up with a story for the front page of the national edition, usually an A-head, the light feature that appears in the middle of the page. Naturally, you wanted to do that if you had any kind of ego. A byline on page one was better than a story with no byline on page 12.

"Every day, all of our copy was sent east by teletype for editing and then shipped back to San Francisco, where we had two or three copy editors who did mostly proofreading. As you can imagine, we got a lot of advice and counseling from New York, along with endless requests to contribute to round-up stories on topics like the nationwide outlook for car sales.

"Whenever I'd draw that assignment, I'd get out my trusty list of 10 or 20 Northern California auto dealers — the usual suspects — and call some of them. I'd create a file out what they told me and send it off. Then I'd see the finished story, written in New York, which would make a general statement like 'auto sales are weak in the West' or whatever — backed up by quotes from dealers, including a few of the ones I had interviewed."

Those nationwide round-ups were similar to stories *Time* had started doing during the Depression. Later, *Newsweek* and *Business Week* began doing them, too. White points out, however, that in the 1940s those publications were not regarded by most *Journal* staffers as formidable competitors.

"In the truest *Journal* tradition, we didn't feel we had any serious competition, and we really didn't have much. *Business Week* was very drab. *Time* and *Newsweek* devoted some space but not a lot to the type of news we were covering. The monthly magazines didn't count because they didn't try to go after breaking stories.

"The local papers did try to go after them, but they had very tiny staffs and small business sections. *The New York Times* and *Herald Tribune* had pretty good sections but very little circulation in the West, and the *Los Angeles Times'* business coverage was pathetic. There wasn't any *USA Today* or *Investor's Daily*. Radio didn't do much of anything with business news, and of course there wasn't any television."

$

William O'Neil

O'Neil started his own institutional research firm in Los Angeles in 1964. Twenty years later he launched

Investor's Daily (later renamed *Investor's Business Daily*) in direct competition with *The Wall Street Journal*.

"Before we started the paper, we went through the *Journal* page by page identifying areas where we felt we could provide information that they didn't offer. Although we never thought of ourselves as competing with *The New York Times* to any great extent, we did the same with them. We found that their coverage was generally more sophisticated than the *Journal*'s. We also took a look at the *Los Angeles Times* and found that its coverage had improved and was fairly accurate.

"The important thing, however, is that we saw right away that we could come up with comprehensive statistical material and tables that most newspaper readers had never had an opportunitity to see before. We spent a year and tons of money designing our paper and getting that material and the tables ready for publication."

O'Neil acknowledges that there were those who felt it was naive for him to take on the Goliath of financial newspapers.

"We had one big advantage in that our sister company, which does investment research, had built a huge data base on stocks and the economy over the years. We drew heavily on that right from the start. We felt going in that we knew the market and the economy very well.

"However, we had a big disadvantage in that we didn't know the publishing business. We had to learn it from the ground up, and we made mistakes. We didn't have any experience at building circulation, and we didn't realize how difficult it would be to get the paper delivered everywhere at the same time.

"We didn't have a staff of hundreds of reporters, so we knew we couldn't stand up to the *Journal* editorially at the start. And of course we didn't have the aura. In the eyes of some people, we were the upstarts from California challenging the Holy Bible."

In O'Neil's opinion, *Investor's Business Daily* turned out even better than he had expected.

"After we started publishing, we got quite a few favorable letters from readers. One said, 'I love your paper even more than chocolate cake.' Another woman wrote that while some men have mistresses, her husband has our newspaper. She said, 'I don't see him as much any more, but hopefully as he does better in the market things will work out for the best for both of us.'

"We have heard from professional investors who say they find data in the tables in our paper that can't be found anywhere else. Another thing some of our readers like is the fact that we follow Washington more closely than we follow Wall Street. That's because what happens in Washington has more impact on the markets and on the economy. Not everyone in the financial press understands this."

After its first half-decade, O'Neil summed up the status of his publishing venture this way:

"We believe our readers are generally satisfied with our product. However, we're constantly tinkering with it and making little changes in the editorial content to try to improve it. We feel we can do that without upsetting the reader because we're a data base-oriented paper — our tables and our statistical material are our anchor.

"As time goes by we want to do more with editorials,

which are the heart and soul of any newspaper. We've done a few things that turned out well and others that were rather mediocre. We've taken some positions editorially that have been totally different from those taken in the *Journal* and other financial publications. We're not right all of the time, but when we weigh in on an issue, we think we know what we're talking about."

O'Neil regards the day-to-day competition between *Investor's Business Daily* and *The Wall Street Journal* as a healthy development.

"It's good for the country to have another voice speaking out on business and finance every day. And it's particularly good to have that voice coming from some place other than New York, where the publications and the networks tend to think pretty much the same thoughts and say pretty much the same things.

"On balance, we're good for the *Journal*, even though we've taken readers away from them. We've forced them to try to improve their product. When they added a third section on the financial markets, to my way of thinking that was a direct response to our paper."

$

25 *William German*
Will Hearst
Joe Livingston
Herbert Stein

William German

German became executive editor of the *San Francisco Chronicle* in 1982. He has presided over changes in business coverage that are both similar to and in some ways different from those taking place at other papers around the country.

"For a long while, the *Chronicle* went along barely doing its duty on business and financial news. Like many other papers, it honored its obligation to publish the stock market numbers, plus about one page of news and a column written by the business editor every day — and that was it.

"Gradually we became aware that there was growing interest in business news. We sensed it from looking at what others were doing, including *The New York Times* and the *Los Angeles Times*. We sensed it, too, from the increasing popularity of syndicated business and financial columns, from reader comments and from our polls and research.

"One of the things our research found back in 1980 and '81 was a strong correlation between readership of the business section and the sports section, with about equal interest in each. That suggested to us that strengthening our business page would have the effect of increasing readership of our sports page, and probably vice versa."

The *Chronicle* began adding a few columns of business news in 1981 but didn't give business a cleared-front section until 1984, and at first it was only done once a week, on Mondays.

"We probably would have engineered the improvement sooner, but we had production problems. The only way we could add pages was to print the paper in what's called the collect mode, where you're really printing on two press units set up in identical fashion. This meant that the business and sports sections had to have the same number of pages. Not only that, they also had to print on the same color paper — green, which was the traditional color of our sports section.

"This gets complicated, but the gist of it is that both sections had to grow simultaneously, which created a dilemma when we decided to start a Business Monday section with more pages in it. Our temporary solution was to split the classified advertising and run some of it on green paper behind sports. That set off an understandable howl among advertisers. If you're selling real estate, for example, you want your ads to appear where the rest of the real estate ads appear, and on white paper.

"We got away with this for a while, but only with the explanation that we were seeking a better answer. And that answer turned out to be an expanded sports section on Mondays, with more coverage of outdoor activities like hiking. The moral of the story is, there's a solution to everything; but we only found it in this case by moving slowly and taking things one step at a time."

Since then, new press equipment has been added, allowing greater flexibility. The *Chronicle*'s business section has been given a cleared front on a daily basis together with a regular column of commentary by Herb Greenberg. Readers of the sports section have learned to settle for a stripe of green ink each morning instead of their beloved green paper. Meanwhile, according to German, the *Chronicle* also took one other important step:

"Our editor and publisher, Dick Thieriot, became convinced that newspapers don't pay enough attention to the economic and business aspects of local news. He came up with the notion that we should have economics specialists on the general city staff. So we pinned the badge of economics editor on one of our reporters and assigned two other people as assistants, and those three started doing different types of stories, always emphasizing an economic or business angle.

"It has never been completely clear what the boundary line is between the work they do and what the business section covers. At first we worried about that, but we don't any longer. Since this arrangement started in '82 we've had some good people in the cityside economics editor's spot, including Dan Rosenheim (who became the *Chronicle*'s city editor), and the system has produced some very good stories. What began as a 'what the heck, let's try it' experiment has become standard procedure."

$

Will Hearst

Hearst has been editor and publisher of the San Francisco's afternoon daily, the *Examiner*, since 1984. He is the son of William Randolph Hearst, Jr., and the grandson of the founder of the Hearst publishing empire.

"The evolution taking place in business and financial news is reflected in many newspapers around the country, including our own. There was a time when the *Examiner* ran a small, out-of-the-way business section. The presumption was that the general reader had no interest in that type of news. It was thought to appeal to only a very specialized readership. I call that the Shipping Tables era. You printed the Shipping Tables along with other esoteric stuff, figuring there must be someone out there who wanted that information. If you had a reporter who couldn't cut it on other parts of the paper, you shifted him over to Business, figuring it didn't matter since hardly anyone saw that section anyway.

"Then, we began discovering that people were interested in stories about the economy and personal finance and investigative pieces exposing the soft underside of business. We started to realize that the business world could be a fascinating place to write about. The better magazines in the field, and authors like Tom Peters and 'Adam Smith,' demonstrated that well-written stuff about the movers and shakers in business and finance could be useful and entertaining.

"As part of the evolution, the expectations of our readers began to change. They looked to us to write about business in a more interesting and credible way. Reporters started taking this type of news more seriously. Today, there's a sense among them that business and finance can produce some very good pieces that ought to be reported as thoroughly as any other kind of story."

Hearst feels that newspaper business sections have come a long way since the days when they were a dumping ground for mediocre reporters. He points out that today they are attracting a new breed of journalist.

"We're seeing job applicants in their 20s who've already had some experience reporting business news. They're not interested in working on metro or some other part of the paper. Their attitude is, I'm a business journalist. This is my profession. They have pride of authorship. By nature they tend to be investigative — I suppose that's partly the influence of Woodward and Bernstein — but on the whole I don't think they're any more suspicious of business than they are of law or medicine or politics. They have a somewhat skeptical attitude toward all of those subjects."

With business magazines and national newspapers offering more coverage of the money world, metropolitan dailies such as the *Examiner* find themselves in a tough competitive situation.

"Our readers have access to the information in the national media, so we have to recognize that we don't own that turf. We can learn some things from those publications, such as how to write more interpretively. At the same time, it's important to remember that, in one area at least, we and other metropolitan dailies have an advantage. We're able to emphasize local business news that our readers rarely find in the national press. We have done a lot of that and we've found that our readership is even more interested in the local picture than we had thought. That's true throughout the paper."

Hearst concedes that, for some readers, the business section of a metropolitan daily such as the *Examiner* has become supplementary reading to *The Wall Street Journal* and Business Day in *The New York Times*.

"A lot depends on your focus. If you're the president of a local firm whose fortunes depend heavily on what happens in local government or in the local economy, then I believe we can do a better job of covering what's important to you than the *Journal* or the *Times* can. On the other hand, if you're the president of a local firm and you're interested in a particular bill under consideration in Washington, then the *Journal* or the *Times* probably can give you a better overview of the legislative situation than we can. And if you're the president of a firm that's totally global in its orientation, then you won't find as comprehensive a report in our paper as you will in the *Times* or the *Journal*."

In nearly every newspaper, the bulk of the agate ghetto is taken up with stock market tables, which fill page after page. In the age of up-to-the-minute computerized information, those tables are less valuable than they once were. Hearst's thoughts on the possibility that they may someday disappear:

"Whether we'll ever reach the stage where we'll drop the daily stock tables I'm not sure. If we did, that would free up several more pages for news. But every time I walk by a newsstand in the afternoon and see someone waiting for our final edition (the one with the closing stock prices) I get nervous about doing it because I can see there are loyal readers out there who still depend on us for those quotations. I have a hunch that what may happen is that 24-hour computerized trading will someday eliminate the closing stock price, and at that point we'll feel we can eliminate the tables."

In Hearst's view, newspapers should continue looking for new ways to present business news more effectively.

"Every story has a length that God wants it to have. Our task is to figure out exactly what that is and do a better job of conserving the reader's time. I'm one of those who believes we can learn a lot from *USA Today*, which is good at organizing news and condensing certain stories into three or four inches of type instead of letting them run on. By the same token, they can learn from metropolitan dailies that some articles really do need to be given more space."

Hearst has mixed feelings about the value of a signed column commenting on current events.

"If it can be done well, it's worthwhile. People are hungry for quality commentary. Otherwise, in my opinion, it shouldn't be done at all. Alan Abelson has handled it much better than anyone else. Sometimes I think about running his type of column every day — not only for business, but out on page one — a column with perspective and opinions on the major news of the day. Now, that is either a very innovative idea or it's one that's ready for the scrap heap."

$

Joe Livingston

One of the true pioneers in business journalism, Joe Livingston reported, wrote and edited for over a half-century, first for *Business Week* and later for three Philadelphia newspapers. These comment were made in a conversation more than a year before his death on Christmas Day in 1989.

"In September 1929, when I was a general reporter on the *Brooklyn Times*, I formed a pool with some friends and started buying stocks. The first one I bought was American Car and Foundry, which paid a 6% dividend. I didn't know enough then to realize that the company wasn't earning enough to cover the dividend. We took a loss on that stock along with a few others, and after the October crash I decided I had better learn something about business.

"I tried to get into the financial department at the paper, but my editor said 'For God's sake, you've finally learned how to write a decent news story, and now you want to switch to the section that nobody reads? You're crazy.' A few months later, the Depression started taking its toll on newspapers and I was let go. So I did some studying for a few years and finally I landed a job as an economics writer at *Business Week* in 1935. I stayed there for seven years and wound up writing the 'Business Outlook' columns along with some of the editorials."

In 1942 Livingston took a leave from *Business Week* to join the War Production Board and edit a publication called *War Progress*, which kept track of what American industry was producing and where it was being shipped.

"What we were doing at the Production Board had some bearing on the improvement that took place in economics reporting after the war. We gathered material from many different sources, and that material provided some fresh insights into the economy. We also found ways of presenting it so it was easier to understand.

"Quite a few of our statistics on industrial production were new. Editorially, we did some innovative things with rewriting and lead-ins and charts and headlines that represented small breakthroughs in economic journalism and were later picked up by other publications."

At *War Progress*, Livingston and his colleagues had White House authority to collect information from government agencies, but they still had to dig for many of their facts and figures.

"Not everyone opened their doors and cooperated with us, which was understandable. We were working with sensitive data. Our publication had a limited circulation of about 200, mainly senior U.S. government and military people plus the British and the French. The Russians weren't given any copies because we didn't quite trust them.

"What we wrote was for internal consumption, but there were leaks. One time I remember, *PM*, the leftist New York newspaper started by Ralph Ingersoll — one of the *Fortune* radicals from the '30s — got its hands on an issue of *War Progress* that showed a decline from one month to the next in Lend Lease shipments to the Russians. It was only a statistical aberration, but *PM* jumped on it and ran a story saying America wasn't doing enough to help Moscow fight the war. After that incident, Edward Stettinius at Lend Lease rejected all of our requests for information and refused to have anything to do with us."

Toward the end of the war, Livingston moved to the Office of War Mobilization, where he wrote about the task of keeping the U.S. economy healthy in peacetime, the same topic that J.K. Galbraith explored in *Fortune* in 1944. (Excerpts from both Livingston's treatise on reconversion and Galbraith's article are reprinted in the Appendix.)

"When the war ended, I decided I didn't care to return to *Business Week* and group journalism. New York was ceasing to be the center of the economic universe. Washington was becoming more important. So I stayed there and started writing an economics column for the *Post* and a few other papers. The column was called 'Business Outlook,' which the folks at *Business Week* didn't appreciate very much.

"One of the things I featured in the column was a semi-annual survey of ten economists who gave their forecasts for the period ahead. After a couple of years I wrote about how skilled those ten guys were. Then I went back and took a closer look at the figures and it turned out that their forecasts weren't as accurate as I had thought, so that wasn't very smart. However, I added more economists and refined the survey and it got better and became popular and eventually it was emulated by others."

Livingston went on to establish a base of operations in Philadelphia, where he continued his newspaper column and edited business news for four decades, first at the *Record* and later at the *Bulletin* and the *Inquirer*. He offered this perspective on the role of a business columnist:

"The first point I would make is that in the age of television your readers are getting a lot of their business news from the tube. It may not be very good, but that's where they're getting it. This means you have to work harder than ever to engage their interest and explain things that are not properly explained on TV, and you have to do it in ways that hold their attention.

"The other point I'd make — and this is something I learned through the years — is that column writing involves yielding to your prejudices after a hard fight. You try not to grind axes, but you often have to take a position. After interviewing several economists and hearing different points of view, you have to sit down and start writing and making choices, and those choices invariably are based on your beliefs and prejudices. You try to divorce your strongest feelings from your writing and you try to be fair, but that's the way it is."

$

Herbert Stein

Stein worked on the Committee for Economic Development (CED) after World War II and later served as chief economic adviser in the Nixon White House. A Senior Fellow at the American Enterprise Institute and a lucid writer, he has contributed frequently to magazines and newspapers and was one of the original economists in Livingston's "Business Outlook" survey.

"Joe Livingston was an innovator. He was ahead of the others with some of the things he did during the Second World War and afterwards. After I stopped writing pieces for him at *War Progress* and went into the Navy, he borrowed me back from the Navy to work with him at War Mobilization, and he kept on doing creative things while he was there.

"There weren't many journalists writing about economics at the start of the war who had any training in economics. Joe didn't have much, but he had acquired a familiarity with some of the issues. Whatever there might have been in the way of a science of economics during that period seldom got reported. Most of the coverage was about business."

According to Stein, that pattern began changing during the war.

"People began to sense that government was going to be involved in the economy in a bigger way. Before the war, reporters had looked to Wall Street for answers to their economic questions. But some of the people there had gotten themselves pretty well discredited in the '30s, and Washington was starting to become the arbiter on economic matters.

"In fact, by the end of the war it was almost as if the government had declared that it was going to do business in Latin. Therefore everyone who wanted to report on what government was doing would need to understand Latin. Government declared that it was going to do business in economics, so everyone had to start learning the language of economics. The press had a lot of catching up to do."

While conceding that progress has been made since then, Stein still finds reporting of economic affairs in the daily media less than satisfactory.

"Typically, reporters who have an economics story to do call up every economist they can think of and ask for a few words about the latest government statistic. They tend to call people with political connections because they view economics as a branch of politics. Those aren't always the best economists to talk to, but I suppose it's better than if the reporters just talked to each other or didn't talk to anyone.

"When I was in the Nixon Administration the shallowness and the tendency to harp on things were particularly agitating. Unemployment for the month would go down, but in some category it would still be up, and that would get emphasized. The good news would end up being bad news, and the reporters would charge off after that part of the story like hounds running after a rabbit.

"Another thing that has always been irritating to me and to others is the proclivity for manufacturing a controversy instead of trying to clarify the issues. Television is the worst offender there. Even the best programs such as

MacNeil/Lehrer seem to be looking for a fight most of the time when they try to cover economic policy. It's pretty hard to find much on TV that sheds light rather than heat on this subject."

Stein has been writing books since the late 1960s. On two of them he collaborated with his son Ben. In his 1984 best seller *Presidential Economics* (New York: Simon & Schuster, 1984), Herb described the process of politicizing economic policymaking in Washington. He believes the press has helped foster that process.

"The main element in the politicization is short-sightedness, and the daily press is very short-sighted. It concentrates on what happened today or this week or this month, and its habit of focusing on the short run encourages politicians to do the same.

"We got away from that for a while after the war. We paid more serious attention to the longer term then, mainly because of fear that if we didn't get our policies right we might return to the Depression. But there is less inclination now to take the longer view. What we need is calm, moderate analysis and discussion of fundamental issues, but I'm afraid that isn't the press's bag."

$

APPENDIX

Excerpts from Articles

"The Chronicle"
The Commercial & Financial Chronicle
July 1, 1865
(unsigned)

The end of the war, through which the country has just passed, inaugurates an era of peace and prosperity which only needs wise legislation to find encouragement; and with such a stimulus, natural recuperative energies will soon be at work, to heal the wounds our civil strife has made, and to lead us once more into the paths of industry and affluence.

At no time in our history has the knowledge and diffusion of commercial truths, and the advocacy of the well defined principles which govern the economy of wealth, been so needed as now. During the war we have seen one false theory after another exploded, and all the wild schemes for producing wealth, faster than the measured action of industrial laws will permit, come to naught, until all are convinced that value only resides in labor and time. Weary, then, of a constant succession of dearly bought experiences, do we now turn to the teachings of the great leaders in political economy for wisdom and guidance.

311

The country has bravely survived the restrictions which a fatal industrial system once placed upon its energies. It has also with crippled powers survived those forms of restriction which unwise legislation has at times imposed. Let the vast improvements which will be sure to follow the gradual removal of the latter, prove to the partisans of both that the country has hitherto been prosperous in spite of them, and not as some think by reason of them.

To secure this great end, to attain the prosperity which thus lies within our reach, and to open wide the gates of our vast natural resources to the toiling masses, who now contend against oppression and poverty in less favored lands, it is necessary that the policy of the country should be based wholly upon her industrial and commercial interests. These have ever pointed the right way, and will yet lead us from difficulty and doubt to success and certainty.

It is not overstating the plain truth to aver that these great interests have never yet found a fitting exponent in the newspaper press of this country. The pursuits of industry have been looked upon too exclusively in their money making aspects — too little in their social and political ones. The great influence which they have always exercised upon the fortunes of our country and which they must always continue to exercise, have been forgotten in the strifes of petty politicians, and in the heat of personal discussion. No comprehensive paper devoted wholly to the great mercantile and commercial interests, has yet appeared. Taking the entire press of the country together we shall find that these interests have to a certain extent obtained public recognition; but in no single journal have they received undivided attention.

It is to fill this place in the ranks of the public press, and supply this want, that *The Commercial & Financial Chronicle* aspires. Nor will it stop with the advocacy of correct principles; but will be in every essential sense a newspaper. All that the economist, the merchant, the banker, the manufacturer, the agriculturist, the shipper, the insurer, and the speculator, may need to know in the course of his daily pursuits, will be found duly chronicled in its columns.

To this great purpose we apply ourselves. Let the public in due time answer whether or not we have successfully accomplished it.

"The Pacific Railroad"
ibid.

The navigators of the fifteenth century, whose adventurous spirit first lifted the veil of geographical ignorance, were inspired to their vast and wonderfully successful explorations chiefly by the intense desire of the commercial communities of Europe to discover an ocean channel for the trade of India. The transportation of the rich commodities of the East across the Isthmus of Suez, or by the tedious and dangerous journeys of caravans, to the Mediterranean, involved such an outlay of labor, time and money, that even the limited experience of Christendom awakening from the lethargy of Medieval darkness, appreciated the benefits to be derived from the opening of a safer and less expensive route to the great fountain of affluence. To that object was devoted the energy of Vasco de Gama and the courage, zeal and perseverance of Columbus. When Captain Diaz doubled the extreme point of Africa, and in obedience to his instinct of seamanship, named it the Stormy Cape, the sagacious King of Portugal, forseeing the realization of the hope of the commercial world, gave it the more significant appellation of Good Hope. So when the Genoese mariner, six years later, anchored his bark off the wild shores of Guanahani, and

313

beheld the dusky natives crowding in awe and wonder to gaze upon his little fleet, he hesitated not to call them Indians, in the belief that he had accomplished the object of his mission.

Three centuries and a half have passed, and the science of navigation has kept pace with the advance of enlightment, perhaps has led the van in the march of progress; but the paramount desideratum of the commercial world has not yet been attained. Almost every region of the habitable globe has been made a mart for enterprise. Swift steamers glide across the sea where the small galleys of Gama and Columbus plowed their uncertain way. The geographical construction of the earth, a mystery to the profound students of the middle age, is now familiar to every school boy within the area of civilization. We know where to go for the fruits and fabrics that are essential to our luxury or comfort, but we have not yet opened the nearest, surest and cheapest route to the lands where the richest freights and the most profitable investments invite us. The straight road to the Indies, suggesting itself to every observant mind, is still untraveled. A tithe of the enterprise of Columbus, a particle of the hopeful nature of Isabella, assisted by the boundless resources of modern skill and science, would have opened the channel ten years ago, may open it within the next half decade. But our heavily laden East Indiamen still follow the track of Gama and his contemporaries around the stormbeaten headlands of Good Hope, or struggle with the baffling winds that sweep about Cape Horn, or undergo the costly process of twice breaking bulk, at Panama and Aspinwall, without a corresponding advantage in the shortening of ocean transit. It is true that the attention of Europe is now earnestly occupied with the completion of the ship canal across the Isthmus of Suez; but the consummation of this valuable work, illustrating the importance that the master minds of the old world attach to the improvement of the facilities for intercourse with India, should be a spur to American enterprise in the same direction.

We have chosen this form of introduction to the subject of the Pacific Railroad, because is presents one of the results of that undertaking not heretofore sufficiently considered. The commerce of Asia is about to be developed beyond its former proportions, and there is no reason why this Republic should not be made the world's thoroughfare, through which the wealth of the East shall roll from coast to coast, paying tribute, as it passes, into the coffers of our people. The internal dissensions that for years have disturbed the industrial system of China are now at an end. The spirit of exclusiveness that has hidden the greater portion of the riches of Japan as in a sealed casket guarded by jealousy and prejudice, is yielding slowly but surely to the persistent advances of a higher order of civilization. The unhappy strife in our own country that for four years has shut out the world from commerce in the great staple of the South, has occasioned research and experiment in regard to the cotton growing facilities of the East, and the production of that commodity in India under the energetic and skillful management of Europeans will greatly enhance the Indian trade. Let us see, now, whether we cannot compel the merchants of Europe, by the never failing law of advantage to themselves, to make us the carriers and our country the viaduct of that immense trade.

Let us suppose the Pacific Railroad constructed and in active operation, with sufficient rolling stock for the transportation of Eastern merchandise at remunerative rates. By swift steamers from the farthermost ports of Asia the average voyage would be twenty days. By railroad, from the Pacific to the Atlantic coast would be, over a good road, with powerful engines, eight days. From the Atlantic to the European port would be twelve days. Allowing five days for incidental delays, breaking bulk, etc., the merchant at Liverpool could receive his goods in forty-five days from the date of their dispatch from Hong Kong, Calcutta, or other Asiatic port. The machinery of commercial speculation renders it impossible for business men to ignore the avenue that is the speediest means of communication with the marts at which they traffic. If the American merchant could send a cargo of tea from China to Liverpool in forty-five days, the English merchant would be compelled to accept the same facilities or to relinquish competition. The inevitable result of the completion of the Pacific Railroad would be the transfer of the principal part of the trade of the Indies from its present channels to the great thoroughfare of nations that would be established in this Republic.

Do our people appreciate the magnificent future that would thus be opened to them? Do they realize that opportunity to pay the National debt? Venice in her days of glory owed her grandeur and prosperity to the circumstance that the commerce of India passed by her threshold, paying toll to her on its way to market. Let it not be said that American enterprise hesitated and faltered in the path of such a splendid destiny.

But not only in that respect does this magnificent project appeal to the interests and to the national pride of the American people. In the far West millions of acres of fertile land wait to be redeemed from waste and unproductiveness. The Pacific Railroad would drag immigration along its iron course. Wherever the speeding engine would pause in its rapid career, to be fed with wood and water, there would a house be built, and then a hamlet, and then a town, and then great, populous and busy inland cities, each one the centre of an area of thriving settlements, each one a link in the quick forged chain of civilization from ocean to ocean, from the teeming marts on the Atlantic border to the golden placers and rich valleys of Oregon and California. Thus would a wilderness be made a garden, as if by the touch of a magician's wand; and vast tracts of public lands that are now unsalable, because isolated from the arteries of trade, would become at once a source of boundless revenue to the Republic.

What is there to prevent the present realization of this vision? Are we too poor, despite our boasted affluence, to pay our way to this mine of gold, that will repay a hundred fold?

During the past four years the attention of the government and people has been concentrated upon the task of preserving the integrity of the Union, and the construction of public works not connected with the duty of the time, has necessarily languished. But the return of peace is the signal for redoubled energy in the development of the resources of the Republic; and the great burden of debt and taxation that oppresses the country makes the obligation greater to apply capital and labor without stint towards the perfection of the instruments of recuperation. Among these, none are so potent as the enhancement of facilities for domestic trade and foreign commerce, and the completion of the Pacific Railroad would be a giant stride towards resuscitation from the fearful effects of civil strife, placing us in the sphere of traffic beyond the competition of the world. The next Congress will be vested with great responsibilities, in purifying the political atmosphere from the lingering taint of discord and convulsion; but however arduous and complicated their duties may be, it is to be hoped that early in the session, they will find or make an opportunity to give the impulse of national legislation to this great enterprise; and no means will prove so effectual to communicate this impulse as throwing open the task, and awarding its advantages to whomsoever will carry it forward to completion.

$

"Foreward"
Barron's
May 9, 1921
unsigned (C.W. Barron)

Trade was plain sailing when the Tyrians based the beginnings of world commerce on man's desire for a splendid purple dye. Finance was readily grasped when Venice propounded mercantile decisions over the arching Rialto. When shrewd Dutchmen smoked in terms of golden thalers on the dyke at Amsterdam, when shippers and shipmen foregathered under the dusty charts at Lloyds', matters of capital and investment, commodities and their prices, statistics and probabilities were not yet very deeply involved. Even later, in the days when weathered merchants sauntered along the Battery at New York or through Merchants' Row at Boston, the question of money and its uses was comparatively simple.

Today it presents complexities partly the result of natural progress, growth and expansion, partly superinduced by the seismic shock of a world-war and by its subsequent rifts, eddies and tremors.

With clear appreciation of difficulties to be met and close and confident attention to the best means of meeting them, we submit to those who read for profit a new financial publication having for its motto "the application of money to practical ends."

Elementary yet sufficient, the phrase is the adequate definition of "finance." The word "finance" is so freely used throughout the world of business and relation spheres that one would think its definition thoroughly understood and appreciated, yet it must be admitted that there are all to many influences in our modern money matters which tend to obscure and nullify the clear-cut description "application of money to practical ends."

Though avowedly a financial weekly, we feel that our efforts would be unduly circumscribed were we to limit ourselves strictly to a periodic exposition of finance in its ordinary acceptation. By engaging to furnish a modest, careful and comprehensive weekly review of "the application of money to practical ends," we feel that we are working from a new viewpoint, have secured an effective post of vantage, and will consistently supply a novel fulcrum on which the thoughtful investor may plan to get a purchase with his dollar level in a worth-while effort to budge the world of wealth.

We believe the time singularly right for the launching of a fresh effort in the journalism of commerce, industry and broader moneyed endeavor. Ask the producer of raw materials what is wanted for business and he will say "confidence among the manufacturers." Ask the manufacturers and they will say "confidence among wholesalers and retailers." Ask them and they will complain of a lack of confidence on the part of the consumer. Ask the consumer, ask the wage earner, and the assurance will be given that more confidence among those higher up, manufacturers, builders, employers in general would do much to solve the problem.

What we want is confidence.

A fresh financial publication based on sound sources of information and policy should be a helpful factor in assuring return of confidence in the world of business.

Neither the financial journal nor the financier it properly serves, neither projector nor investor in moneyed enterprise, neither special interest nor general public, neither capital nor labor, producer, middleman nor consumer can fail to gain inspiration, encouragement and effective assistance from a studied, consistent and countrywide "application of money to practical ends."

$

"Economic Possibilities for Our Grandchildren"
The Saturday Evening Post
October 11, 1930
by John Maynard Keynes

The purposive man is always trying to secure a spurious and delusive immortality for his acts by pushing his interest in them forward into time. He does not love his cat, but his cat's kittens; nor, in truth, the kittens, but only the kittens' kittens, and so on forward forever to the end of catdom. For him jam is not jam, unless it is a case of jam tomorrow and never jam today. Thus by pushing his jam always forward into the future, he strives to secure for his act of boiling it an immortality.

Let me remind you of the professor in Sylvie and Bruno.

"Only the tailor, sir, with your little bill," said a meek voice outside the door.

"Ah, well, I can soon settle his business," the professor said to the children, "if you'll just wait a minute. How much is it, this year, my man?" The tailor had come in while he was speaking.

"Well, it's been a-doubling so many years, you see," the tailor replied, a little gruffly, "and I think I'd like the money now. It's £2000, it is!"

"Oh, that's nothing!" the professor carelessly remarked, feeling in his pocket, as if he always carried at least that amount about with him. "But wouldn't you like to wait just another year, and make it £4000? Just think how rich you'd be! Why, you might be a king, if you liked!"

"I don't know as I'd care about being a king," the man said thoughtfully. "But it dew sound a powerful sight o' money! Well, I think I'll wait ———"

"Of course you will!" said the professor. "There's good sense in you, I see. Good day to you, my man!"

"Will you ever have to pay him that £4000?" Sylvie asked as the door closed on the departing creditor.

"Never, my child!" the professor replied emphatically. "He'll go on doubling it, till he dies. You see, it's always worth while waiting another year, to get twice as much money!"

Perhaps it is not an accident that the race which did most to bring the promise of immortality into the heart and essence of our religions has also done most for the principle of compound interest and particularly loves this most purposive of human institutions.

I see us free, therefore, to return to some of the most sure and certain principles of religion and traditional virtue — that avarice is a vice, that the exaction of usury is a misdemeanor and the love of money detestable, that those walk most truly in the paths of virtue and sane wisdom who take least thought for the morrow. We shall once more value ends above means and prefer the good to useful. We shall honor those who can teach us how to pluck the hour and the day virtuously and well, the delightful people who are capable of taking direct enjoyment in things, the lilies of the field which toil not, neither do they spin.

But beware! The time for all this is not yet. For at least another hundred years we must pretend to ourselves and to everyone that fair is foul and foul is fair: for foul is useful and fair is not. Avarice and usury and precaution must be our gods for a little longer still. For only they can lead us out of the tunnel of economic necessity into daylight.

$

"Vanished Billions"
The Saturday Evening Post
February 13, 1932
by Edwin LeFèvre

It would have meant money and comfort to millions of Americans if they had followed advice given three thousand years ago: "In the day of prosperity be joyful, but in the day of adversity consider!" Translated from the King James version into stock-market jargon, it is: "In a bear market be sure you do what you didn't do in the bull market!" When you deal with states of mind you learn that men have always been what they are today, ticker or no ticker.

The reason why the stock market must necessarily remain the same is that speculators don't change; they can't. They could see no top early in 1929 and they could see no bottom late in 1931. Shrewd business men who wouldn't sell absurdly overpriced securities would not buy, two years later, underpriced stocks and bonds. The same blindness to actual values was there, only that while the heavy black bandage was greed in the bull market, it was fear in the bear market. Reckless fools lost first because they deserved to lose, and careful wise men lost later because a world-wide earthquake doesn't ask for personal references. Nevertheless, there is a general belief that the wise rich escaped punishment — as usual. You incessantly hear about the huge losses of the unlucky multitude, though there has not been any destruction of actual wealth or tangible property, as happens in war.

The financial reviews at the end of the year that dwelt on the extent of the losses did not remind the losers that the first to go were the dream dollars. Everybody who looked for easy money in 1928 or 1929 lost both dreams and cash in 1929 or 1930. In 1931 nobody was spared.

The powerful millionaires accumulated minus signs then, when owners and former owners of stocks and bonds consisted of poor, poorer and paupers. Poverty, like riches, is relative. A poor man finds this hard to believe because he thinks in superlatives: Himself and his hardships. The great social equalizer is the common need to live on less than a man has been accustomed to spending; and everybody has had to do that lately. Nevertheless, delusions persist: The delusion that the world, so wonderful during the boom, is going to pot via the lost-money route; that the way to recover from hard times is to keep on hoping that somebody else will do something about it, preferably the politicians or the bankers; that cities, states and Uncle Sam can put off giving the taxpayers their money's worth as long as they try to offset deficits by increasing the taxes of the rich. This last is as great a delusion as the human mind can hold, its chief purpose being to win votes and to increase the burdens of the ultimate consumer — the deluded poor. You can pass a law that will make rich men poor, but you cannot enact one that will make poor men rich. But they tell you that the rich, having suffered less than the poor in the past, must suffer more in the future! Reduce wages, but don't touch mine! Sell your goods cheaper, but don't ask me to come down in my prices! I am playing safe by hoarding my money, but you must spend more than ever, to make work for the unemployed.

$

"What's To Become of Us?"
Fortune
December 1933
unsigned (MacLeish)

The American tradition, it need hardly be said, requires some defining. The intellectuals, particularly those now in vogue, deny its existence. And so, in their way, did the young men, young no longer, of the Mencken era. Mr. Mencken was not himself, of course, a doubter. It was merely his cheerful function to wash in public the American drawers. But the drawers, in that caustic process, shrank and tore. And by the time the launderer had retired, the shriveled garment was valuable for little more than the obscene uses to which Mr. Mencken's successors have since devoted it. The result is the series of learned volumes and academic essays in which it has been conclusively proved that American literature has no roots, American custom no vitality, and American life no past. The explanation of that illuminating theory is of course the universal explanation of all such phenomena — ignorance. Young men brought up in New York or Chicago or Philadelphia draw upon the rich and varied experience of their own indistinguishable back yards to present the picture of a continent and the image of a nation. And gentlemen immersed in the categories of European politics apply to the life of a nation they have never really seen terms which have no application and definitions which do not define.

The fact is, of course, as any traveler out of the ordinary ruts will know, that the American tradition is as distinct and peculiar as that of any country. It is however an agricultural, or rather a rural, tradition. It never existed in the great cities, for the great cities were never, in any but a geographic sense, American. It was to be found only in the small communities. And it neither had nor has any relation whatever to industrialism. From the industrial point of view it is pure anachronism. For it is a tradition of individual responsibility and its guiding principle is the principle that a man must control and direct his own life, that he must take full responsibility for the well-being of the community in which he lives, and that he cannot in decency surrender the direction of his life or of his community to any other power. It is, in other words, a tradition of individualism. But it is not the tradition of individualism which, with the spurious addition of the word "rugged," rang through the political orations of the '90's and the 1900's. Rugged individualism is a gray horse of a very different color. It is the individualism of the so called Empire Builders, the individualism of unlimited rights — and no obligations whatever. It is a degradation of individualism which has today brought the whole concept of individualism into disrepute. The individualism of the American tradition is a totally different thing: it is the individualism of duty. Its end is the freedom of life, not the accumulation of wealth. And its means are responsible and independent citizenship as that word has been understood for a hundred years in the American colonies and for a hundred and fifty years in the American states.

The American tradition so defined obviously exists only among a small minority of the population — the small minority of Americans of old stock who have lived for a great many generations directly upon the land. The family of the President is such a family. It is a quite undistinguished American family of Dutch origin which has lived in Dutchess County, seventy miles up the Hudson from New York, since the French and Indian wars. It is, and long has been, moderately wealthy. James Roosevelt, the President's father, served for a time as a Vice President of the Delaware & Hudson. Sara Delano, the President's mother, was the daughter of a China trader who had retired with a fortune to an estate across the river. But the whole background of the family is rural. It inherited the tradition of the families living in the Valley. It had a sense of the community. It had a habit of citizenship. It was part of the Republic. And that tradition the President quite naturally and inevitably inherited. He has always been interested in people as only a man living in a small community can be interested in people. He thinks in terms of people. He never makes an abstract decision but always a decision stated in terms of the probable effect upon one group or another. And his mental picture of the country, his primary assumption about American life, is the somewhat questionable assumption that America still is a collection, a congeries, of such small communities as he knows. He becomes almost oracular on the subject. He is certain that the country is just that — and that what will be good for the small communities will be good for the nation . . .

The essence of the American tradition is individual initiative. To talk therefore about the abrogation of the profit system is hysteria. Individual initiative assumes the profit system. It is based upon it. It cannot exist without it. But another fact is also clear. The new society would not be a society which existed for the sole purpose of permitting a few men in preferred positions to make all the profits they were capable of making. It would not be a society dedicated to the principle that $10,000,000 profits for Mr. Wiggin are admirable profits if Mr. Wiggin is smart enough to make them. After all the conception that society exists to be exploited by the smart is a conception which has had no place at any time in the traditions of Old America.

The upshot then is that any competent observer plotting Mr. Roosevelt's probable course would expect him to hold to individualism and the profit system but to insist that no man should be able to exploit the profit system to the injury of others. Now there is a political parallel to such a state of affairs. Its name is democracy. And it also is an essential part of the American tradition. The basic conception back of democracy is the conception that all men are free but that no man is free to injure other men. And it is the function of government to enforce the limitation as well as to guarantee the right. So far in American history that function of government has been limited to political affairs, and two kinds of society have coexisted in the country. Politically men have been one thing with one set of rights; industrially they have been another thing with another set of rights. Nothing then is more probable than that the kind of man Mr. Roosevelt is might be expected to introduce into industry the principles which, as principles at least, have long existed in politics. The result would be a democratized industry.

What would an American democratized industry be like? First of all it would be a self-governing industry. That step Mr. Roosevelt has already taken. When the codes are in full operation American industry will be organized, trade by trade, in vertical self-governing structures. Secondly it would be an industry in which labor would have full voice in the determination of its relation to society. That step Mr. Roosevelt is taking. His National Labor Board operating under the new declaration of labor rights contained in the recovery legislation has supported the claims of union labor to recognition, forced collective bargaining (but under a face-saving dodge) even upon the steel companies, and settled strikes involving hundreds of thousands of workers upon declarations of principle never before heard from official lips in this country. Thirdly democratized industry would be an industry of which the chief purpose would be the service of the consumer — which is to say the service of the nation as a whole. That step lies in the future. But the first movements have been taken. Already the principal and most vital effect of the recovery program, though scarcely noticed by the newspapers, is the successful assertion by the Administration of the principle that all industry, and not merely the public utilities, is, in the legal phrase, "affected with a public interest" and may therefore be regulated by government. The country has acquiesced unconsciously in that declaration.

So far as the consumer is concerned it is true that the practical effects of Mr. Roosevelt's program to date have been injurious rather than helpful. He has attempted to increase purchasing power by raising wages and has, in the process, raised prices to such an extent as to more than cancel the advantage to the earner of the wage. And his Rationalization of industry, combined with the removal of the restrictions of the Sherman Act, makes higher prices in the future not only more possible but actually more probable. But the entire program has not yet been carried out. And, in any event, for purposes of prophecy it is rather Mr. Roosevelt's intention than the results achieved in the first six months which signify. As to his intention there can be no doubt that his most firmly held purpose is to increase the purchasing power of the public as consumer. Which means not only temporarily to raise wages but permanently to ameliorate the condition of the consuming nation vis-a-vis its industry.

But as regards all these aspects of the new society one fundamental fact must be noticed. They can only be realized under some degree of governmental control. And the question at once rises — how much governmental control and how exercised? As to the former the answer is: the least possible. To the American tradition the best government has always been the least government. But the least control possible nevertheless means, under the conditions laid down, a great deal of control. To prevent the exploitation of society by the unprincipled means a governmental control over credit and its uses and abuses which no previous American government would ever have attempted. To prevent the exploitation of labor by employers means a continuing vigilance. And adequately to protect the nation as consumer not only against greedy price rises but against the disasters caused by selfish competition, unlimited production, and insane booms is a labor which will require the hand of government upon the very nerves of the economic order. And which will require a degree of industrial knowledge and expertness which no American, or indeed European, government has ever possessed.

It is not however regulation itself but the purposes of regulation which are important. Granted that Mr. Roosevelt, shaped as he is by nature and tradition, will preserve basic individualism qualified only by those recognitions of duty to society which have always qualified it in Old America — granted, that is, that he will attempt to preserve a profit system operating under the eye of a kind of public conscience, the regulations which he is obliged to impose to enforce that end will irk only those who are irked by any limitation upon sheer industrial banditry.

$

"The Job Before Us"
Fortune
January 1944
unsigned (Galbraith)

We have promised our fighting men and ourselves a
more productive economy in the next peace than we had
in the last. On the wisdom with which we demobilize
much of that productivity depends.

To write the story of demobilization, *Fortune* will attempt something new in business journalism. The story
will be written to fit the actual process itself. Demobilization will not consist of unconnected topical happenings. It
will be a flow of closely fused developments. Restoration
of peacetime production in one part of the economy will
depend on what is happening elsewhere in the economy.
The whole process will move together.

Furthermore, demobilization will not occur all at once.
In some industries it is already under way; in others it will
continue for years. And in the U.S. we do not manage
things in accordance with a preconceived design although
we may be influenced by some over-all design. Our system of government and our form of economy are, to some
extent, a denial that any process of master planning is
necessary. What we do in both government and business
is erect stone on stone by a process of improvisation and
short-range planning.

Business journalism is not a perfected art in the U.S.
Businessmen can count on their journalists for competent
and even brilliant treatment of individual topics — taxation, renegotiation, coal supply, and newsprint production. Their trade press keeps them admirably informed on
the news, regulations, obligations, and politics of their
own industry. But complete business reporting would require not only the competent coverage of individual topics

we have, but also good coverage of the tightly fused relationship of one development to another and to the course of business as a whole. Such journalism doesn't exist in the U.S.

Today the problem of the merchant fleet, for example, is not the time required to build a Liberty ship or even how she compares in speed with ships of our allies. Rather it is what these ships or their more efficient successors will carry tomorrow and the day after. The answer to this is only partly in our new shipyards, the hiring halls of the N.M.U., and the subsidies American-flag vessels may receive after the war. More of the story is in credits we may grant other countries with which to buy our machinery or motorcars, and in tariffs we and our neighbors build. Most of all the answer is in how prosperous we are — no tariff ever throttled ocean shipping so efficiently as a good depression. The prime fact about future cargoes is how much British woolens and whiskey Americans can afford and how freely Britishers can spend for our cotton and tobacco.

With the war we have learned the importance of weighing the impact of individual decisions on each other and especially on the total work load of a burdened economy. Likewise we have learned how important is the behavior of total output for individual decision. With these lessons have come striking advances in the measures that can be applied to the over-all performance of the economy.

Fortune proposes, with the aid of this experience and these new tools, to tackle the gap in present business journalism. They will be used during coming months in reports on the unwinding of wartime production and materials controls, distributing the first scarce supplies of materials, terminating contracts and disposing of the war plants that comprise the new public domain. Before the Emergency Price Control Act of 1942 expires next summer,

331

we shall examine the need for price fixing and rationing during demobilization. Foreign-trade and overseas-lending policies during and after demobilization will be up for examination. So will tax and expenditure policies for a stable peace. We shall look at our postwar labor force and consider the future of the ghost towns of total war. There will be a report on farms, housing, and railroads during and after conversion. From what we learn of these matters will come new estimates of the total postwar production we can expect.

We plan to keep this experiment in integrated journalism abreast of the times. Without apology we are beginning it now — before the war is won. Americans learned the cost of not planning for a war that had become inevitable. The transition to peace is now inevitable. . . . One good reason for expecting prosperity after the war is the fact that we can lay down its specifications. For this we can thank a little-observed but spectacular improvement in the statistical measures of the current output of the U.S. plant. These measures did not exist after World War I or even a decade ago. Only this war demonstrated their full usefulness.

In the winter of 1942, government statisticians pictured a national output worth $132 billion (in 1941 prices) in the twelve months ending in July, 1943. They underestimated, as did most people then, what America, fully mobilized, could do. Production exceeded the estimates by over 25 per cent. Therefore military production was higher, civilians had more; the grim companion estimates that 1943 would provide only a 1932 living standard didn't come true.

But though the estimates were not right they were right enough to give an invaluable compass bearing on war economy. Businessmen in Washington and at home knew that a $132 billion production and a growing Army spelled labor shortages. The lumber industry knew its troubles would be among the worst. The $56 billion of war expenditure, included in the estimate, meant tight control of metals. The projection of but $64 billion worth of civilian goods and services to meet war-inflated consumer demand gave the Treasury the measure, if not the solution, of its tax problem. From the same figures, Sears, Roebuck could decide that books should be added to its mail-order line. Even though there were more goods in 1943 than anyone expected, the Treasury still needed all the taxes it could get — and Sears all the merchandise it could find. . . . The most important single requirement of a good demobilization is that we be sure of a goal. We must be convinced that we are a $165 billion country, generously plus or only slightly minus. If we plan for less we shall get less.

Brave words to the contrary, many Americans (including, apparently, a lot of worried soldiers) expect to return after the war to a good old-fashioned depression. This state of mind is more than unfortunate. It is dangerous. Should a like mind control private and public planning through demobilization, then the U.S. will return to 1939.

Plan boldly and we can't.

$

"Reconversion—The Job Ahead"
War Progress
June 1944
by J. A. Livingston

The United States has but recently come through a gruesome economic experience — the depression of the 30's. The efforts to bootstrap out of it are even now, in wartime, living experiences for many of us. It took a Hitler and a war to put production and employment over the top of the 20's. No wonder people worry about the oncoming peace — and the way we prepare for it.

What it all comes down to is this: we, the people now at home, are the parents of tomorrow. Our actions will determine not only whether we shall have full employment or unemployment, high prices or low prices, a contracting market or an expanding one, but also the relations of labor and government, labor and business, business and government. They will likewise affect the relations of farmers and consumers to the other groups and the government itself . . .

Right now the volume of goods and services produced in the United States is running at the highest level in history — about $200,000,000,000. But nearly half of that — some $90,000,000,000 — represents Army, Navy, and Maritime Commission purchases. Ultimately, most of that $90,000,000,000 will drop out of the market. When it does, civilians must be in there buying — and not at prewar levels either.

Insofar as it means going back, the term "reconversion" is misleading. The war has lifted the nation's economic sights. During the 30's, President Roosevelt and others talked of a net national income of $100,000,000,000, or the equivalent of about $150,000,000,000 in total production of goods and services at today's prices. But nowadays it is accepted economic gospel that after the war the total production of goods and services will have to run to perhaps as much as $175,000,000,000 if the country is to have a reasonably satisfactory level of postwar employment. Hence when the government's $90,000,000,000 of war business drops out of a $200,000,000,000 economy, civilians must extend their purchases another $65,000,000,000. Actually, the government will continue as a buyer of peacetime goods in the form of public works, armament, etc. But civilians will have to buy far more goods and services than they have ever been able to buy in the past.

Before civilians can buy, manufacturers must first manufacture the refrigerators, automobiles, and washing machines; and builders must first build the homes the civilians will want. And wholesalers and retailers must restock their shelves. In short, the economic process must be unlimbered for peace. Some industries, of course, will carry on as usual. The railroads will merely haul automobiles and refrigerators instead of plane parts and tanks; textile mills will weave business suitings instead of khaki.

$

"The Reindustrialization of America: Revitalizing the U.S. economy"
Business Week
June 30, 1980
(unsigned)

The U.S. economy must undergo a fundamental change if it is to retain a measure of economic viability let alone leadership in the remaining 20 years of this century. The goal must be nothing less than the reindustrialization of America. A conscious effort to rebuild America's productive capacity is the only real alternative to the precipitous loss of competitiveness of the last 15 years, of which this year's wave of plant closings across the continent is only the most vivid manifestation.

Reindustrialization will require sweeping changes in basic institutions, in the framework for economic policymaking, and in the way the major actors on the economic scene — business, labor, government, and minorities —

think about what they put into the economy and what they get out of it. From these changes must come a new social contract between these groups, based on a specific recognition of what each must contribute to accelerating economic growth and what each can expect to receive.

$

"The Hollow Corporation"
Business Week
March 3, 1986

"American companies have either shifted output to low-wage countries or come to buy parts and assembled products from countries like Japan that can make quality products at low prices. The result is a hollowing of American industry. The U.S. is abandoning its status as an industrial power."

Akio Morita
Sony Corp. chairman and co-founder

While economists engage in an eerily detached debate about whether the U.S. is losing its industrial base — and even whether it matters — Sony's 64-year-old chief affirms what American business leaders have been seeing for more than a decade. In industry after industry, manufacturers are closing up shop or curtailing their operations and becoming marketing organizations for other producers, mostly foreign.

(This introductory portion of "The Hollow Corporation" was written by Norman Jonas; other *BW* staffers, including William Wolman, participated in the preparation of this special report.)

Autos, steel, machine tools, videorecorders, industrial robots, fiber optics, semiconductor chips — these are some of the markets in which the U.S. is losing dominance or has been driven out. More markets are destined to feel the bite of foreign competition.

The result is the evolution of a new kind of company: manufacturers that do little or no manufacturing and are increasingly becoming service-oriented. They may perform a host of profit-making functions — from design to distribution — but lack their own production base. In contrast to traditional manufacturers, they are hollow corporations.

(The anticipated consequences of this development were summed up by *Business Week* in the following paragraph.)

Unchecked, this trend will ultimately hurt the U.S. economy. The traditional industrial sector has long been the leader in U.S. growth in productivity, the wellspring of innovation, and the generator of a rising standard of living. The spectacular rise in employment in the fast-growing service sector will continue to offset the loss of jobs in manufacturing. But services, on average, do not measure up well against manufacturing in productivity growth or in personal income. In short, the idea that a post-industrial America can become increasingly prosperous as a service-based economy appears to be a dangerous myth.

$

"Up & Down Wall Street"
Barron's
April 20, 1992
by Alan Abelson

Every major social movement requires a human cata-
lyst, some personality that imparts energy to it, a mesmer-
izing presence that attracts recruits to proselytize and
build and sustain fervor's momentum. Civil rights, for example, had Martin Luther King, and feminism had Betty
Friedan. America-on-wheels got rolling because of Henry
Ford, and the nation's appetite for fast food was whetted
insatiably by Ray Kroc.

Now comes another gathering tide destined to wash
over this fair land, awaiting only that dynamic persona to
unleash it. We're referring to the Men's Movement, whose
slogan is Save the Male! and whose intent is to revive all
those qualities that one equated with manliness, even gen-
tlemanliness, in days of yore. (Days of yore grandpa.)

What those qualities are — beyond belching at the dinner table — remains in considerable confusion and dis-
pute, but their importance is conceded by virtually all
members of the oppressed group known as men. And
now at last comes that missing link, which can close the
circle, electrify the movement and make it a force finally to
be reckoned with. This long-awaited agent of gender re-
generation is none other than Ivan Boesky.

Ivan Boesky, you may recall, was the Michelangelo of
arbitrageurs, the man who brought that arcane art to its
apotheosis. Like other great artists before him, he inevitably evoked envy among his lessers, who conspired to
bring him down. Mr. Boesky, the victim of prosecutorial
zeal (a disease that afflicts U.S. Attorneys assigned to
cases of securities malefaction and that was first identified
by *The Wall Street Journal*), did time for his supposed sins

338

and after paying his debt to society is once more in the company of free men.

The bringing of Mr. Boesky's brilliant career to a crashing stop also, as it turned out, was the beginning of the end of an era in Wall Street. It took a few years to unravel, but its denouement was wondrously apt, as the Great Predator himself followed Mr. Boesky and several small fry to the cooler.

So it is that Ivan Boesky, trader at liberty, is now ready to lead men out of the wilderness. What qualifies him to assume this role is not a scholarly work on the decline of the human male or a treatise on the masculine mystique or even an appearance on "Larry King Live." What qualifies him, in short, is not a lot of talk but something he has actually done. Deeds, not words.

Specifically, he has sued his wife for a million bucks a year in alimony. When that news broke, members of the men's movement, across the nation, in bars, in locker rooms, in off-track betting parlors, billiard emporiums, wherever they were gathered, rose up as one and shouted, "Way to go, Ivan!" And in that moment transcendent, the men's movement found its galvanizing spirit, its leader.

On the basis of this one splendid act, we'd say Ivan's a sue-in to be the main man in the men's movement. Just as generations of French have looked back over the centuries with awe and admiration at Joan of Arc, so future liberated men will look back across the eons with esteem and gratitude at Ivan the Arb.

$

"Fallen Prophet"
Barron's
August 24, 1992
by Rhonda Brammer

It's 10 years almost to the week since the start of the greatest bull market in history.

And it's 10 years almost to the week since the start of the decline and fall of Joe Granville, a descent that transformed the world's most famous investment personality into something of a joke, a synonym for errant forecasting.

It is, unhappy as it may be for him, an anniversary worth noting. For Granville had reached an unprecedented peak of prominence — he was certainly the first and only Wall Street technician to command attention both on the 6 o'clock news and in the nonfinancial columns of the daily press — with a series of remarkable calls on the stock market and a showman's flair for publicizing those bull's-eye predictions.

The apotheosis of Joe Granville began, it now is clear in retrospect, in April 1980. Stocks were falling as the prime rate climbed to 20%. On April 21, the Dow Jones Industrials slumped to a two-year low of 759.13.

That was the day that a flamboyant technical analyst named Joseph Ensign Granville — a newsletter writer who had been pitching his investment advice in Barnum-like spectacles replete with costumes, balloons and bikini-clad women — sent out a buy signal.

The next day, April 22, the Dow soared over 30 points, its fifth largest gain in history. By mid-July, the average had topped 900, on its way to a three-year high of just over 1000.

For Granville, it was the start of something big.

Those who subscribed to his early-warning service got his next major market call in January 1981, many of them in the dead of night. On Jan. 6, the market had closed at 1004. That evening, 30 staffers at Granville's Florida headquarters in Holly Hill worked until nearly 3 a.m. to deliver a brief, ominous message: "This is a Granville early warning. Sell everything. Market top has been reached. Go short on stocks having sharpest advances since April."

The waves of selling hit Europe first, as prices of American stocks nose-dived in London, Zurich and Paris. The news spread like brushfire through Wall Street long before the New York market opened. Sell orders swamped the New York Stock Exchange. The ticker tape couldn't keep up. The Dow was off as much as 31 points — comparable to a 100-point drop today — and closed at 980, down almost 24 points. The volume that session, nearly 93 millions shares, was the heaviest in the 188-year history of the New York Stock Exchange. It easily topped the previous record, set on the day after Ronald Reagan's landslide Presidential victory.

"One Forecaster Spurs Hysteria," declared *The Washington Post*: "Markets Sink in Panic Selling." That day the picture of Joe Granville was on the front page of *The New York Times*. Suddenly, the once-obscure newsletter writer was a household word across America. "A hole-in-one, an ace," is how he described his performance. When it came to moving markets, he crowed to *Newsweek*, "Many have said I have four times the power of the Federal Reserve."

Grumbling investors immediately called on the Securities and Exchange Commission to rein in this man who, singlehandedly, could cause such destruction. But the agency replied that it found no overt regulatory violations. "I wish they would call on me," Granville told *The Wall Street Journal*. "They'd have to explain to everyone what I'm doing that they don't like. That's what's going to win me the Nobel Prize. I have solved the 100-year enigma, calling every market top and bottom.

Crowds at his "investment seminars" swelled to over-flowing and the performances grew increasingly antic. It wasn't enough to dress as Moses and deliver the "Ten Commandments" of investing. Or to drop his tuxedo trousers and read out the stock quotations printed on his boxer shorts. (The punchline of this routine, of questionable taste but vintage Granville, was to point to the front of his shorts and announce, "and here's Hughes Tool.")

Granville began predicting earthquakes.

Before a capacity crowd of 1,800 in a Vancouver ballroom — 500 people had to be turned away at the door — he forecast that a major earthquake would strike 23 miles east of Los Angeles at precisely 5:31 a.m. on April 10. He claimed to have refined his technical indicators so he would "never make another major mistake." And he updated followers about the Nobel Prize, he would win it, he forecast, "by next year at the latest."

April 10 came and went, with nary a tremor. Yet Granville's reputation as a stock-market prophet grew, even though it wasn't clear that his Jan. 6 sell signal was any better than his seismic forecast. In fact, the market didn't peak until nearly four months after his call. Subscribers who had sold short, expecting a "straight down" decline, as he had forecast, might well have been badly bloodied in subsequent rallies. Even as late as June, the Dow was bouncing above 1000. The real drop didn't get underway until July. But when it did, by September, it had slashed 150 points off the index.

So, in truth, Granville's call was months premature. That said, the actual top, on April 27 at 1024, was only 20 points higher than on the day he said "Sell everything."

The delay between prognostication and event was no idle period for Granville. He performed non-stop. In May, he was hauled on stage in Atlantic City in a coffin filled with ticker tape, screaming, "I'm rising from the dead."

He had "quaffed a number of vodka tonics" beforehand, he later conceded, and, at one point, had to be helped from the stage. (He wasn't drunk, he insisted. The vodka was a "standard procedure." He believed he had been slipped "a Mickey Finn.") More warmly received was his debut at Carnegie Hall on June 25, where, between other acts, he clowned around on the Steinway concert grand, and, as he recalled it later, was brought back "for three curtain calls amid a wild standing ovation."

By mid-September, with the Dow around 850, Granville took his show on the road — or, more accurately, across the sea — to Europe.

On September 23, he told a radio interviewer in London that prices of the London Stock Exchange were headed for a fall. That day the London market suffered its second sharpest sell-off in its history. His message was simple: All major world markets would decline. Five days later in Tokyo, he set off what one press report called "a trading frenzy," as the Nikkei Index collapsed in its biggest one-day plunge on record.

The shock was felt around the world. Stocks declined in Brussels, Paris, Milan, Frankfurt — even in Sydney. The plunge in Zurich and Basel was the largest in over half a decade. The Hang Seng Index in Hong Kong suffered its biggest drop in eight years.

While Granville strutted across the investment stage, the market pretty much followed his bearish script. And it would be almost a year before the Dow Industrials finally bottomed, in the summer of 1982.

But that bottom, on Aug. 12 at 776.92 for the Dow, did come. And the market roared back with a vengeance. Over the next six sessions, on huge volume, it gained more than 90 points.

That week, Granville told *Barron's* that the move would be "very brief, like an explosion." While other investment professionals interviewed by this magazine forecast the beginning of a new bull market, he scoffed at the idea. "No bull market in history ever begins with institutional buying," he railed. "Where were all those institutions at the top? They were buyers. Now if they couldn't recognize the top, what makes them so expert at recognizing the bottom?"

In fact, the institutions had recognized the bottom. The train was roaring out of the station. And Granville wasn't on board.

Nothing daunted, he remained relentlessly bearish as the Dow easily broke through 1000 and closed over 1070 before the year was out. He predicted a drop in 1983 that would take the market to between 650 and 550 on the Dow, and he confidently told the *Barron's* Roundtable, "I think now the probability is heightened that you could go as low as 450."

But the stock market never looked back.

And it wasn't long before the crowds were gone. His subscribers defected in legions. In late 1982, broker friends told the press how Granville failed to return their phone calls and described him as withdrawn and reclusive.

It is, as noted, 10 years since Granville failed to recognize the greatest bull market ever, a failure that dramatically and profoundly reversed his fortunes. Oh, people still remember the name. And it's often the only one they can think of when asked to name an investment newsletter writer. But his errant call in 1982, and his stubborn persistence in that wrong-headed view, dealt him professionally a near-fatal blow, personally a crippling one.

When Mark Hulbert of *Hulbert's Financial Digest* recently compiled performance records for market-letter writers since 1980, the Granville Market Letter ranked dead last. It was down 93% over the 12 years. Granville complained to *The New York Times*, which published the results, that it was his mistake in 1982 that so cost him. "He keeps averaging that to make me look bad," he groused bitterly. "Why do I have to keep suffering every damn year because of Hulbert?"

Granville's errors, though, were hardly confined to 1982. He turned wildly bullish, for example, just before the 1987 Crash. But he is absolutely right in suggesting that if you pick a different time frame, his performance looks dramatically better. With his usual modesty, he describes his post-Crash record as perfect: "dead solid perfect."

Even Hulbert concedes that Granville did well post-Crash. From Nov. 1, 1987, through June 30, the Granville Market Letter was up 166.9%, compared with a gain of 92.6% in the Dow and 90% in the S&P 500. That performance ranked him fifth of 78 newsletters.

And if you lop off the last two months in 1987, Granville's showing is even better. From January 1988 to June 30, his letter was up 256.2%, compared with gains of 96.8% for the Dow and 92.4% for the S&P. Over those 4–1/2 years, Granville's letter ranks No. 2 on Hulbert's list.

Of course, to put a lot of weight on such numbers can be hazardous to your blood pressure, possibly your financial health. His basic investment style is to swing for the fences, relying heavily on options to translate his market predictions into strong comparative performance. Result: One quarter he's down 69%, to next he's up 97%. In a sense, it's a shrewd strategy. Put some good market calls back to back, recommend a slug of options, and suddenly you're No. 1, at least for a quarter, maybe even for a year.

And Granville desperately wants to be No. 1. He desperately wants once more to make Wall Street tremble, to move markets, to hog the limelight.

And what drives him, what fires his already blazing intensity and makes him persevere through ridicule, pinched circumstances and in the shadow of millions of unpaid taxes is that he has risen from the dust before. The "genius" strutting on the global investment scene in 1981 had so badly miscalled the 1973–74 bear market that he was forced to live in his office, too broke to fix his Volkswagen squareback and unable to get his letter out for five weeks because he couldn't pay the printer. Yet less than a decade later, he was the most prominent investment figure in the nation, a familiar name to millions who never owned a share of stock and the scourge of markets not only here but in Europe and Japan as well. He was the magical Comeback Kid and he's convinced he can do it again.

$

"Oh, our aching angst"
Forbes
September 14, 1992
by James W. Michaels

When you're my age you don't have to ask: Are Americans really materially better off than they were in the recent past? Those of us born in the 1920s and with vivid memories of the Depression simply know how much better things are today. The improvement is implicit in almost our every memory, every experience.

Even for comfortable middle-class people life was much more difficult and insecure in the 1920s than it is today. If he was fortunate enough to have central heating (less than one-third of the population in 1920 did), middle-class Dad had to pull himself from bed at 4 a.m. on cold winter mornings to unbank the furnace and shovel coal; if he over-slept, the pipes froze. But he usually didn't have to rake leaves or shovel snow. Not in the 1930s. That was done by shabby, humble men who knocked at the back door mornings, asking for a warm meal in return for doing chores.

In 1921, when this magazine was four years old, the typical American workweek was 60 hours, and many people worked longer. The most common American household appliance was a woman, who worked a lot more than 60 hours in her home. Leisure-time industries scarcely existed because few people had leisure. For more than half the population, the family toilet was a hole in the backyard with a shack built over it. In those shacks, Scott Paper products competed with difficulty against old Sears and Montgomery Ward catalogs; real toilet paper was a luxury.

Senior citizens? We called them old folks, and they were old in their 50s; if they were lucky, one of their kids had a spare room for them, maybe in the attic. Life expectancy was about 54 years, which was just as well because there were few pensions beyond what the gold watch might bring at a pawnshop.

I'm not talking about the 19th century. I'm describing the first three or four decades in our own century. Unless they blow their money and energy on booze or drugs, the American poor have more physical comforts today than the average American did when *Forbes* first appeared 75 years ago.

We've come a long way, and although the rate of improvement has slowed lately, our economy put on an amazing performance in this century. So amazing that almost every U.S. consulate has a waiting list for immigration visas.

Yet just last week on television I watched a sweating Bill Clinton harangue a midwestern audience. Work with me to change America, the candidate shouted, punching the air, Kennedy-like, with his fist. That cliche produced the expected cheers and waving of banners. Cut now to a local living room where a TV reporter interviews a well-dressed middle-aged woman. What did she think of the speech? "I liked it," she said. "God knows we need change in this country."

Change from what to what? The lady didn't say and the newscaster didn't even think to ask; everyone just assumes the country is in rotten shape. Where do they get their certainty? From the mass media that keep telling them that the economy is a mess, America is a mess.

$

INDEX